NER
press

# THE EAGLE &
# THE BIBLE

# THE EAGLE
# &
# THE BIBLE

## LESSONS IN
## LIBERTY FROM
## HOLY WRIT

### By
### Kenneth Hanson, Ph.D.

Published by New English Review Press
a subsidiary of World Encounter Institute
PO Box 158397
Nashville, Tennessee 37215


Cover Design by Kendra Adams


ISBN: 978-0-9854394-0-8


First Edition


NEW ENGLISH REVIEW PRESS
newenglishreview.org

*To my mother, who always believed in the American republic, and the eternal principles on which it has always rested.*

# CONTENTS

# INTRODUCTION

**W**hat do we think of when we think of the Bible? The "Good Book." A book of Faith. The Word of God. All very nice designations. But how often to we dare to think of the Bible[1] as a book of politics? Doesn't the Bible engender enough religious disputes without throwing politics into the mix? But what if the Bible actually weighs in on political issues and principles relevant to our own times? What if it teaches valuable political lessons that we can't afford to miss?

It's important to stress from the outset what this little tome is not. It's not a bombastic, "Thus saith the Lord" volume of sermons. It's not "sectarian" in any way, in the sense of embracing one religious perspective or another. While I have my own faith convictions, I'm not out to proselytize anyone. Rather, I'm looking at holy writ to find practical political advice at a point in our history when we are more divided as a nation than any time since the Civil War. I did not, moreover, set out deliberately to write this book. By contrast I came upon these insights from my experience as an educator, and soon realized that the Bible contains an amazing "backstory" that is aching to be told.

Much of what I write is the product of my own classroom instruction, as a professor of Jewish history and biblical literature. As a way of making the biblical narratives come to life, I found

---

1 The Modern King James Version of the Bible has been used throughout, unless otherwise noted, modified occasionally by the author.

that I couldn't help drawing comparisons between the Bible and the story of America. Ever since my undergraduate studies in American history, I was acutely aware of the tension that existed from the beginning of our republic, between a strong, centralized government, with occasionally heavy-handed authority, and the idea of a diffuse and decentralized loose federation of sovereign states. My most basic adage is this: "Conflict drives everything!"

How sad, as I told my students, that history is rarely taught so as to emphasize the very real disputes that shaped every decade of the American experience. Students are usually just given a set of facts to memorize and dutifully spit back on exams, like a pack of Pavlov's dogs. How boring! Many of my university students weren't even aware that there was a lively argument at the founding of the nation about the role government should play in the daily lives of the people. But argue the Founders did, almost coming to blows.

On one side were the Federalists, led by the likes of Alexander Hamilton and John Adams. They favored creating a strong, fiscally sound, central government, using Britain as a model. Their base consisted of urban folk and banking interests. "Big government" was for them more than an ideology; it was a "mantra." On the other side were the anti-Federalists, championed by Patrick Henry, Thomas Paine, Samuel Adams and Thomas Jefferson, who felt that government is tyrannical by nature and that it must be restrained in order to preserve the fundamental liberties of the individual. They favored a "strict construction" of the Constitution, in order to prevent tyranny and foster the primacy of the "yeoman farmer." It was their agitation that ultimately led to the Bill of Rights. Their "mantra": "Don't tread on me!" Jefferson bitterly opposed the Federalists, becoming convinced that Washington's successor, John Adams, was leading the country down a very dangerous path. Only his election, as America's third president, could, he believed, save the republic.

There wasn't any fence-sitting in those tumultuous days. You girded up your loins and jumped into the fray, because you knew what was at stake. The battle was ferocious, though few of today's students appreciate the many pivotal moments in the great debate. Think of the issues swirling about, that even the Revolution had left unresolved: What is the role of government? When is government good, and when is it oppressive? How much power can be safely vested in any one leader? The one thing the Founders concurred on to a man is that the power of the federal government must be strictly limited, lest it spiral out of control. The greatest power, they reasoned, should be entrusted to individual states and localities, which are, after all, the most closely connected with the people they represent.

Now, do we see in any of this a reflection of the tension going on in the biblical narratives, or is the Bible such a "holy book" that we never even notice? America's Founders certainly did notice, and were convinced, as the adage goes, that those who don't learn from the mistakes of the past are condemned to repeat them. Moreover, the fact that quite a number of them were in full rebellion against religious authority (many being Deists, Unitarians, and members of disparate sects – Quakers, Separatists and the like) enabled them to look at Scripture with a critical eye and glean from it valuable political lessons. That "rebellious" attitude is what got them over here to begin with, and it further informed their entire philosophy of government (hence the First Amendment).

As I stood in front of a full auditorium to teach a class on ancient Israel, I took notice as well. What do we have in the Bible but an ancient "Revolutionary War" in Egypt's New Kingdom, at which time a mass movement of oppressed Hebrews break free from a Pharaoh as tyrannical and more so than England's King George? But as America's Founders learned, it's one thing to win a revolution; it's quite another to figure out how to govern those liberated.

What resulted after forty years of wandering through the Sinai was a loose confederation of tribes, twelve in all, where power was diffuse and localized. Centralized power lay in the priests and of course in Moses – an ancient Washington – but after his passing, and after the dazzling career of his successor Joshua, Israel entered a chaotic time known as the period of the Judges. Central authority was almost entirely lacking, except when a charismatic leader was able to raise a militia. Does it sound perhaps like the first years after the Revolutionary War, when our loose confederation of sovereign states, thirteen in all, was governed by the Articles of Confederation?

As with the early American experience, there was broad agreement in ancient Israel that government needed to be stronger. But what kind of central authority should there be? The young American republic settled on a "chief executive," a "president person," to be indirectly elected by representatives from each of the thirteen states. In biblical days, the "chief executive" would be a king, reluctantly selected by a prophet named Samuel and "confirmed" by an assembly of leaders from all twelve tribes. But Samuel's acquiescence to the demand for a king came with some strong caveats, the prophet warning that the end result would be oppression and heavy taxation.

"If you insist on a monarch," said he to the people at large, "he will make soldiers of your sons, while others will plough his fields. He will take a tenth of your harvests and of your flocks, and you will all become his slaves."

Samuel it seems was an ancient "anti-Federalist." But never you mind; a strong central government would be the new reality, both for the Kingdom of Israel, and early America would follow suit. However, a constitution for the United States was no more able to assuage the clamoring for "states' rights" than Israel's first kings (Saul, David and Solomon) were able to put a lid on the demand for "tribes' rights." The demand for local as opposed to central government would continue to bubble underneath the surface of both societies. In Philadelphia, at the Constitutional Convention of 1787, the Founders attempted to solve the dilemma through adopting a brilliant idea of "checks and balances," that would ensure that no one branch of government was invested with too much power. The executive, legislative and judicial branches would "check" each other, the end result being a "balanced center" between tyranny on the one hand and anarchy on the other.

The distinguished framers were of course indebted to the likes of Montesquieu, Locke, Burke and others for their political theory. What we don't usually consider, though, is the degree they were looking to the Bible to escape the pitfalls of governing. Returning to Saul's warnings, didn't the Scriptures envision an early form of "checks and balances" to prevent one form of tyranny or another from gaining the upper hand? The king wasn't allowed to rule in an unfettered manner; he was to be "checked" by priests and prophets, whose job it was to hold him accountable to a higher authority, who could and frequently did put him in his royal place.

In the American experience, as, we know, all the tensions that were bubbling underneath, between the North and the South, between the big states and the little states, were never resolved. They were discreetly shoved under the carpet, but they were still there, destined to erupt later. The framers tried various compromise solutions, especially regarding slavery. They decided, notoriously, to count a slave as three-fifths of a person for purposes of allotting representation to the states. This of course was a temporary fix at best. The slavery problem came to be fused to the looming issue of states' rights, and historians to this day debate what it was that precipitated the great rift that culminated in the Civil War. Was it slavery, or was it in fact the question of how much autonomy can and should be granted to each individual state?

Perhaps slavery was only a pretext, the spark that ignited the conflict that was there from the beginning, between top-heavy central authority and the idea of a diffuse "confederacy" or "conglomerate" of sovereign state governments. In any case, the new reality after the Civil War was that the United States really was one nation rather than a "league" of states. The power of the federal government would grow steadily from then on, as would the expectation among the populace that it do more to benefit the lives of ordinary Americans. A few post-Civil War presidents would try to hold back the tide of bigger government, taking the position that the main role of the Chief Executive was to keep bad laws from being enacted. President Grover Cleveland famously quipped, "Though the people should support the government, the government should not support the people." But such sentiments only got him into trouble, politically. The nation and the vision of the Founders had fundamentally changed. Government was destined to become stronger and more centralized – huge, bloated and bureaucratic, scarcely resembling the "balanced center" of the Founders. Some call it a "soft tyranny."

What readers of the Bible scarcely if ever notice is that the same paradigm existed in ancient Israel, between those who favored a top-heavy central government, namely a monarchy, and those who wanted a diffuse "confederacy" of tribes – "tribes' rights." Just as in the United States, the issue could not be swept under the carpet or in any way resolved. The one biblical monarch who tried to preserve a balance was Israel's first king, Saul, who gets condemned, justly or unjustly, for "disobeying God."

The man who comes to power in his stead is the venerated David, about whom no one is to utter a negative word. Yet, it was David who clearly favored his own tribe of Judah over the other eleven Israelite tribes. Scholars point out that this was what precipitated the real troubles to come. It was a centralization of power in Jerusalem, the city that David chose. In centralizing authority there, the other tribes felt trampled, "tread on." The issue of tribes' rights actually came to the fore in the form of bloody civil war during David's reign, fostered by his wayward son, Absolom. Later, during the rule of King Solomon, things get even worse, as various regions under Israelite control chafe at the rule of Jerusalem. The only way Solomon can preserve his hegemony is through a tyrannical approach to governing. He puts a lid on rumbles of revolt, building an ever larger army.

It will all come to a head during the reign of Solomon's son, Rehoboam, when open civil war breaks out. It's the "War Between the Tribes," and it is never resolved. Unlike the American experience, where the South capitulates to the Union, in ancient Israel it's the North that breaks away; furthermore, the rebels win! The "Union" is never restored. A long time has passed since those days of yore; yet it seems that the issue of states' rights is back on the "front burner" again in American politics.

In these chapters I will not shy away from the passionate discourse that characterizes the political landscape today. Politicians love to appeal to the sacred text, but we can't allow them to make the Bible say whatever they want it to say. Bearing that in mind, there's one more issue we will deal with in this book. With the likes of the Reverend Jeremiah Wright on the scene, the concept of "liberation theology" has been catapulted into the public square. But whereas "liberation theology" has traditionally been the domain of the hard left (even the Marxist left), isn't it time we redefine the Bible's take on freedom in libertarian terms – in ways America's Founders would have agreed with, and appreciated? This little tome is designed to lend some timeless biblical perspective to such very pesky political problems.

# 1
# "GO YE!" – PATRIARCHS AND PIONEERS

*"Liberty, next to religion has been the motive of good deeds and the common pretext of crime... In every age its progress has been beset by its natural enemies, by ignorance and superstition, by lust of conquest and by love of ease, by the strong man's craving for power, and the poor man's craving for food."* – Lord Acton[1]

O pen the pages of the Bible. Pull it off the dusty shelf, and whom do you meet from the outset? The Patriarchs – biblical "pioneers" – rugged individualists in search of a new land. They were the ancestors of Israel's twelve tribes, just as America's Pilgrims and early colonists were the founders of the thirteen separate states that would one day comprise a federal union.

We're all familiar with the story of Abraham, the revered father of Judaism and progenitor of the people who came to be known as Israel. According to holy writ, he hailed from ancient Babylonia, today known somewhat ignominiously as the country of Iraq. He didn't, however, follow the advice that most people today would give a son: "Get an education. Become a professional, perhaps a doctor or a lawyer. Find a nice Jewish girl. Settle down. Raise a family. Put something away for retirement." Surprisingly enough, ancient Mesopotamia boasted such an advanced culture that young

---

1 *The History of Freedom in Antiquity*, 1877

Abram, as he was called before his famous name-change, could have done just that.

But this illustrious individualist chose a very different tack. He and his family uprooted themselves and left the city they had called home, known as Ur of the Chaldees. They followed the trade routes that took them far to the west, toward a land they knew not. We take the story for granted, as we do most well-trodden tales of biblical lore, but its particulars strain credulity. While already en-route, at a way-station in the vast deserts called Haran, a voice from the unknown addresses Abram's inner being and bids him: "Go ye!," or perhaps better translated, "Go! Go!" – or as we say in the South, "Git!" It's greatest imperative in religious history, as the voice continues: "Leave the land of your birth, your father's house, and go to the land that I will show you." The otherworldly command is delivered in the future tense, since this "land of promise" hasn't yet been revealed. Abram must take it on faith, along with the secondary declaration, that his descendants will be "as sands of the seashore."

The question prompted by this peculiar text is never addressed by sincerely religious readers: Is Abram out of his mind? Has he lost touch with reality? Why does a man who came of age in the "cradle of civilization," where humankind's earliest geniuses invented everything from writing to the wheel to giant ziggurats to barley beer, take to the roads as a wandering nomad? What might have troubled him so much about this splendid culture that he felt compelled to leave it? We can only take the Bible at face value when it suggests that Abram's erratic behavior had something to do with matters of faith.

We are of course told that Abraham was history's first monotheist, but a case can be made that there was something more going on here. The "bottom line" about Mesopotamian religion is that every one of its many gods and goddesses were integral parts of nature itself. They were aspects of the cosmos. To name a few, there was An, the sky god, Enlil, god of the atmosphere, Enki, god of the primordial waters, and Marduk, who slew the goddess Tiamat, creating the heavens with the top portion of her torso and the earth with her lower half. This ancient pantheon was of course immortal, and no single deity could die, lest an aspect of the cosmos itself die. But an unfortunate consequence of this was that the Mesopotamians felt a sense of helplessness before nature. Since the forces of nature are obviously fickle, "the gods themselves must be crazy!" Rains may water the land in just the right quantity to produce an abundant harvest, or too much rain may fall, and everyone may be carried away by a flood. The sun may shine down mercifully to warm the earth, or it may shine relentlessly, parching the ground, turning gardens into deserts and bringing inevitable famine.

Sure enough, when students of the literature of ancient Babylonia pour through the crumbling cuneiform tablets on which the texts are preserved, what they find is a profound sense of fatalism. "No one knows what tomorrow may bring; so eat, drink and be merry, and have another barley beer!" Perhaps Abram simply couldn't make peace with this fatalistic approach to life and existence. Things don't just "happen." There has to be an overarching sense of purpose and meaning, co-mingled with divine justice, as only a good and just God can bestow. So it was, that he saddled up his camels and left.

Whatever the reason that Abram left this storied land, there's a pattern to be discerned in his narrative that wasn't lost on the "patriarchs" of early America, who not only devoured the Bible, but were intent on making it part of their personal experience. We know them as the "Pilgrims," who sadly have been reduced to little more than caricatures in children's books.

These "Pilgrims," as we know them, were people of extraordinary faith. It's rather difficult in our own day to imagine that people might really be motivated to do extraordinary things by pure faith, but such were the Pilgrims. It was their powerful piety that led them to withdraw from the religious structure of their European land – the Church of England. Originally part of a larger movement known as the Separatists, they incurred the wrath of Britain's King James I, who expected strict obedience from his subjects and condemned them as fanatics. Their first move involved crossing the Channel to the Netherlands, taking refuge in Amsterdam and subsequently Leiden. Holland was their equivalent of the ancient city of Haran, Abram's midpoint on his long trek out of Mesopotamia.

Such parallels weren't lost on the likes of William Bradford, who later became governor of this rag-tag group and recorded their adventures in an illustrious memoir, *Of Plymouth Plantation*. Of their desperate crossing for the New World, undertook in September, 1620, he wrote: "They knew they were pilgrims, and looked not much on those pleasant things they were leaving, but lifted up their eyes to the heavens, their dearest country, and quieted their spirits."[2] Whereas Abram followed the desert trade routes of the ancient tribal nation called the Amorites, the Pilgrims navigated the sea routes of English colonists. Theirs was as much a voyage into the unknown as was that of the first biblical Patriarch, who knew nothing of his future "promised land."

## Politics and Pilgrims

Whether speaking of Abraham's clan or the Pilgrims, a case can be made that their creed was individualism, and that for them freedom meant deliverance from the intrusive power of empire (whether Mesopotamian or British) to tyrannize their lives by forced conformity. To be a bit adventuresome, we might imagine both Abraham and William Bradford's Pilgrims not only as people of religious fervor, but as distinguished political scientists. They well understood what Lord Acton would later famously articulate, "Power corrupts, and absolute power corrupts absolutely." Furthermore, hasn't it always been the nature of the state to stifle individuality and retard creativity? So it is, that history's most brilliant thinkers, from Socrates to Gandhi, have often found themselves at odds with it.

Literary theorists love to point out that the meaning of texts (such as the Bible) is in the eye of the beholder. They like to see them as a product of the dynamic interchange between author and reader. Self-proclaimed "progressives" naturally want to read the Bible as a testament to a caring and compassionate state, to the virtue of centralized authority. They choose to emphasize the concept of "covenant" in God's promise to Abraham, as well as the promise that his descendants will be as the sands of the seashore (Genesis 22:17). This, however, is more than a trifle at odds with religious individualists, who find in the stories of the patriarchs a bulwark against state intrusiveness.

Bearing this in mind, let's consider another possible rationale for Abraham's departure from the "cradle of civilization," that involves the political realities of that ancient day. History tells us that by 2334 B.C.E. a single king named Sargon comes to dominate Mesopotamia. Having built an Akkadian army, Sargon hastens to take

---

2 William Bradford, Edward Winslow, Robert Cushman, John Robinson, George Barrell Cheever, *The Journal of the Pilgrims at Plymouth: in New England in 1620*: reprint from the original volume (New York, J. Wiley, 1848) 182.

control of southern Mesopotamia. During a reign of fifty-six years, Sargon conquers northern Mesopotamia, Syria, and westward to the Mediterranean coast, even capturing southeast Asia Minor. He carves out for himself the world's first empire, encompassing people of assorted nationalities, religions and cultural traditions. Sargon's empire is unique in organization as well as scale. He is the first king who claims to possess a standing army – 5,400 men in arms – conscripted from all the cities in his domain. An army being a costly venture, Sargon initiates a new tactic by which to feed the troops – plunder. The soldiers simply raid and loot the cities and towns along the road of conquest, setting out on the warpath each spring. Some might call it history's first version of the income tax! For all its advances, the price of developing a complex civilization turns out to be oppression. In 2197 B.C.E. Sargon's empire collapses at the hands of raiders, who swoop in from the mountains, visiting the Akkadian warlords with a dose of karmic justice.

Chaos follows, during which time a nomadic people known as the Amorites rush in, only to settle down and become absorbed in the larger culture. In 1792 B.C.E. a new king arises – the illustrious Hammurabi. During the course of his long reign he decides to emulate Sargon, casting a covetous eye on cities with whom he had previously been allied. His military adventures are characterized by the increasingly popular practice of taking hostages, who are held for ransom. Specialized merchants ransom Babylonian soldiers from the enemy and then demand repayment with interest. War thus becomes an enterprise, as Hammurabi extends his domain from the Persian Gulf to Syria. While Hammurabi is best known for his renowned law code (resembling in many respects the laws of Moses), it's also true that even his legal ordinances reveal a striking inequity between various classes of citizens, the upper classes being treated quite differently than servants and slaves. Again, we find the state eminently capable of oppressing its own subjects.

It's difficult to know for certain in what century Abraham may have lived, and some question whether he is a historical figure at all. His wanderings, though, are consistent with those of the Amorites, and we may suspect that he possesses a healthy disdain for state-sponsored oppression, and the kind of rugged individualism that links him with America's early pioneers – the Pilgrims. His ultimate destination (revealed to him only after he had already set out on his way): the land of Canaan, a patchwork society that was diffuse and localized, conspicuously lacking anything that remotely resembled a strong central government. Its contrast with the empire of Babylonia's legendary kings, Sargon and Hammurabi, couldn't be more striking.

We may liken Abraham's journey to an ancient version of Pilgrim's Progress, John Bunyan's seventeenth-century classic that depicts the hero, Christian, setting out from the City of Destruction to the Celestial City, meeting many adversaries along the way. The story is an emblem of the kind of religious individualism that came to characterize Protestant theology in both England and America.[3] But let's cast Abraham instead as "Hebrew" and his destination much more "down-to-earth" in a Jewish sense than the notion of "going to heaven." Moreover, the lessons are not merely spiritual, but political as well, for individualism is what the "civil society" envisioned by America's Founding Fathers was all about.

Abraham's rugged individualism does not, however, override his sense of community, another lesson grasped by America's earliest settlers. Indeed, in the case of both patriarchs and Pilgrims, clan was everything. Nor does individualism undermine the need for a solemn pact by which to live. There is broad agreement that the most important word in the entire Hebrew Bible is "covenant" – *brit* – that may best be understood as a legal contract binding Israel to God and the subsequent tribes to each other.

*The Pilgrim Chronicles* makes deliberate allusion both to Abraham and the covenant, extrapolating the term to their own society:

> A covenant, or confederation, according to all the Congregational fathers, is what constitutes a church, and a person a member of it; it may be in writing, or verbal, implicit or explicit... A separation from the world into the fellowship of the gospel and covenant of Abraham, is a true church, truly gathered, though ever so weak.[4]

Their core principles were arguably even more radical, for the Pilgrims audaciously proclaimed that "every ... church is strictly

---

3 Bunyan's work has been described as "a study of an individualist sensibility." See Vincent Newey, *The Pilgrim's Progress: Critical and Historical Views* (Liverpool, England: Liverpool Univ. Press, 1980) 3, 19.

4 Nathaniel Morton, William Bradford, Thomas Prince, Edward Winslow, *New-England's Memorial* (Boston, Congregational Board of Publication, 1855), 423.

independent of all uninspired authority."[5] In other words, in a day when ecclesiastical and temporal authorities tended to be wedded at the hip and at the head, their greatest desire was to be completely free from the coercive power of the church-state. Freedom was thus understood as emancipation from coercion, from the arbitrary power of others. Moreover, at every juncture, the American pioneers chose to root this understanding in the biblical text.

### The Tension We Never Mention

All of this in time set up an inevitable tension (though glossed over by religious-minded readers of the Bible). Who, exactly, is Abraham, venerable forefather of Judaism and Christianity? And what does he represent? Is he (according to one socio-political model – "liberation theology") an individual, leading to a family, leading to a clan, leading to some sort of "national commune"? Or is he an individual, leading to a family of individuals, leading to a clan of individuals, leading to a nation of individuals – the "libertarian vision"? That's more in line with Adam Smith's *Wealth of Nations* and, arguably, the "American dream."

The famed existentialist philosopher, Soren Kierkegaard, loved Abraham for the individualism of his life-choices, dubbing him his "knight of faith."[6] He makes no apology for parts of the narrative that strain credulity, even praising the patriarch for the most controversial of his actions. Students of the Bible are well familiar with the disturbing story of how Abraham hears the divine voice yet again, being told to take his son, his only son, the one he loves, to the land called Moriah, and offer him there as a burnt offering on a makeshift altar. To the impartial reader this amounts to nothing less than child sacrifice, commanded by a barbarous deity. The story is called the *Akkedah*, or "binding" of Isaac, by Jewish sages and rabbis, who have engaged in multiple forms of mental gymnastics down through the centuries trying to defend it. True enough, Isaac is not sacrificed in the end, since Abraham's hand is stayed by an angel at the last minute, before he can perform the grizzly act. It was only a test, the commentators rationalize, to prove that Abraham was in fact prepared to follow the divine command, even at the cost of his son. But

---

5 Ibid., 422

6 Edward F. Mooney, *Knights of Faith and Resignation: Reading Kierkegaard's Fear and Trembling* (Albany, NY: State Univ. of New York Press, 1991), 33.

such justifications sound weak and strained to many.

There is perhaps another, more important message of the *Akke-dah*, namely, that if Abraham's promised son, Isaac, is to become the vanguard of an empire, then he is to be relinquished on the altar of vanity. Abraham's calling is not about creating a dynasty or a monarchy. He mustn't become an autocrat; that was for other build-ers of empire. His son and scion is to continue a legacy of faith, not raw power. His descendants, who will be as "sands of the seashore," are not a mob to be ruled; they are "we the people" – just "folks," comprising a new body politic in which all are "created equal." The politics of Abraham is revolutionary, especially for its time, when power comes through sword point and grows at the expense of in-dividual liberties.

True, Abraham and his clan understand the power of the sword and are not above acts of brutal brigandry. For example, he and his band of three hundred eighteen rescue his nephew Lot from an alliance of four Mesopotamian kings who had taken him prisoner when they attacked his city of domicile – Sodom. Military conquest, yes, but empire-building, hardly. The Mesopotamians are aware of the riches that pass across the land bridge known as Canaan, and they want their cut, taking it by force if necessary. Lot happens to be in the wrong place at the wrong time. The Mesopotamians are all about creating empire; Abraham's rag-tag force of fighters are all about thwarting it.

Some have identified Abraham as one of a number of tribal brigands known as *Habiru*, a word that sounds curiously similar to "Hebrew."[7] They are semi-nomadic people described by ancient Egyptian sources as "wanderers" or "outcasts." They are shep-herds, agriculturalists, stone-cutters, and soldiers. They should be understood as "guerilla warriors" – a kind of ancient militia who rose up as needed. America's Pilgrims understood that they likewise were wanderers and outcasts. Hardly pacifists, they also brandished weapons as needed, for survival in a sometimes inhospitable land. While their little outpost was initially organized as a colony of the British empire, the first American settlers were, like their biblical model heroes, fundamentally at odds with autocracy.

In another biblical episode, we are told that Abraham journeys down to Egypt during a famine, only to become fearful that he will

---

7 Robert Wolfe, *From Habra to Hebrews and Other Essays*, (Minneapolis: Mill City Press, 2011), 11ff..

be killed and his beautiful wife Sarah be taken into the Pharaoh's harem. He cowardly pretends that Sarah is only his sister and allows her to enter into the great Egyptian's household. As divine punishment, plagues are sent upon Pharaoh and his clan, and Sarah is sent back to her true husband. After receiving many gifts from Pharaoh, lavished upon him in order to placate patriarch's incensed deity, Abraham heads for the desert of Canaan once more, resuming his nomadic ways. However, in focusing on Abraham's moral deficit, we forget another issue regarding his choice of residence. Why doesn't he simply opt to join the venerable civilization of the Nile? After all, if you're not going to live in the splendor of Mesopotamia, with its temples, palaces and ziggurats, isn't Egypt, with its equally grandiose temples, obelisks and pyramids, an acceptable second choice?

Well, not really, if individuality means anything. Abraham might have found security and relief from occasional famine in the land of the Nile, but he still prefers his nomadic existence. What's so great about being a nomad, and having to cope on a daily basis with camel spit? Perhaps it has something to do with the simple fact that the Egyptians are history's first true bureaucrats. Being for the most part protected from marauders by deserts to the east and west, and by the Mediterranean Sea to the north, they are free to focus inward. The phenomenal growth of the empire of the Pharaohs also means the proliferation of unfettered bureaucracy. Egypt is in fact able to stretch its tentacles all the way up the Mediterranean coast, even taking on the Hittites in Asia Minor. Their overarching attitude: "You will be absorbed; resistance is futile!" When it comes to the ancient near east, the Egyptians are everywhere, and "omnipresent," but the Bible seems to be shouting at us, that Abraham wants no part of them, or their well-oiled bureaucracy. In spite of its obvious cultural superiority, Egypt traditionally symbolizes slavery and bitter servitude – the "house of bondage." And so, Father Abraham is content to sojourn down to Pharaoh's household when the need arises (taking advantage of Egypt's "famine protection plan"), but he's also more than happy to hit the dusty roads again after the scandalously embarrassing interlude with wife/ "sister."

By the end of his life, however, Abraham does in fact become "rooted," when he makes a point of not just settling, but actually buying the land in which he settles. Driving home the point is the fact that when it comes time for him to secure a proper burial place for Sarah, he goes to the trouble of purchasing the Cave of Machpelah in the fabled site of Hebron:

> And he spoke with them, saying, If it is your mind that I should bury my dead out of my sight, hear me, and ask for me of Ephron the son of Zohar, that he may give me the cave of Machpelah which he has, which is in the end of his field. For as much silver as it is worth he shall give it to me for a possession of a burying-place among you.[8]

On a political level we understand the precedent set by the great patriarch, given that private property rights are ensconced as "sacred" in the U.S. Constitution. The idea is that land held in one's own hands is less likely to fall prey to government control.[9]

It seems, then, that the Bible is no friend of "big government" and/or bureaucracy. Oh yes, the Israelites will develop their own bureaucratic system of government, wrapped in a chief executive depicted as a God-appointed monarch, but that will be a long time coming, and laden with dark controversy and sharp rebuke from Israel's great prophets. In the meantime, however, the "people's patriarchs" will continue to dwell in tents, water their feisty camels, cope with famine and scrounge for food. In the final analysis, wayfarers are wayfarers, and Abraham's clan and the passengers on the Mayflower are doubtless cut from the same pilgrim-cloth.

### Patriarchal "Capitalism"

He's the "child of promise," born supernaturally to a barren woman who happened to be ninety years old, or so the story goes. Isaac doesn't come off as the same kind of visionary we see in his father. He isn't a pilgrim, and he doesn't have to journey to any destination in particular. Whereas Abraham set forth from the land of his birth to an unknown country, Isaac stayed put for the most part. That doesn't however, mean that he ceased his migratory ways. On

---

8 Genesis 23:8-9.

9 Jay W. Richards, *Money, Greed, and God: Why Capitalism Is the Solution and Not the Problem* (New York: Harper Collins, 2009), 72-3. Richards compares Abraham's acquisition of permanent title to the land with the observation of Peruvian economist Hermando de Soto, that the key that unlocks the mystery of capital is a formal property system.

the contrary, when a famine grips the land, we're told that he follows in his father's itinerant footsteps, venturing to the land of the Philistines, on the Mediterranean coast, passing his wife off as his sister, just as Abraham had done. Far from being models of moral probity, as most religious folk would like to see them, the patriarchs make us mindful of John F. Kennedy Jr.'s famous quip, that his family consisted of "poster boys for bad behavior." But Isaac's ruse is discovered by King Abimelech (who might have taken Rebecca into his own tent) just in time, and the crisis passes.

Isaac is thereafter said to have "sowed in the land" (Genesis 26:12), which seems to indicate that he settled down, for a change. The nomad has become a planter, but still an eminent individualist. We might in fact go so far as to call him an ancient "capitalist." Abraham, after the disgraceful episode in which he passed off Sarah as his "sister," became "very wealthy in livestock and in silver and gold" (Gen. 13:12). In Isaac's case we are told that in the same year "he reaped a hundredfold." Why? Because God "blessed him." Of course it could also be a case of God helping those who help themselves. The text recounts that he not only prospered but that "his wealth continued to grow until he became very wealthy" (Gen. 26:13). The Hebrew word here is *gadal*, which means "great," but the clear intention of the narrative is to tell us that he was flat-out "rich." In spite of the oft-repeated biblical notion of the "collective," what we have here is a supreme expression of individualism. Isaac has become a quintessential biblical "fat-cat." Where in the text do we find any condemnation of such "selfishness"? Why is there no call for him to "spread the wealth around"? We can only observe that in the textual silence there is consent. This is individualism wrapped up in what America's founders saw as the fundamental right of property, and, vice-versa, private property as the supreme expression of individualism. The Founding Fathers were no strangers to such biblical paradigms; nor was Abraham Lincoln, who eloquently stated:

> Property is the fruit of labor...property is desirable...is a positive good in the world. That some should be rich shows that others may become rich, and hence is just encouragement to industry and enterprise. Let not him who is houseless pull down the house of another; but let him labor diligently and build one for himself, thus by

example assuring that his own shall be safe from violence when built. I take it that it is the best for all to leave each man free to acquire property as fast as he can. Some will get wealthy.[10]

In another speech Lincoln commented:

I don't believe in a law to prevent a man from getting rich. It would do more harm than good.[11]

The coercive redistribution of wealth was no more in Lincoln's mind than in that of the biblical writers. One of the most seminal volumes of economic and political theory ever penned was Adam Smith's *Wealth of Nations*, that laid out a blueprint for the modern "capitalist" free market economy. Thomas Jefferson commented: "In political economy I think Smith's Wealth of Nations the best book extant."[12] Nonetheless, as some see it, Adam Smith's message for Main Street was later embodied by Wall Street: "Greed works." Those who read the Bible, however, will notice Smith's emphasis on the idea of an "invisible hand" that promotes the good of all through interest in the self. He famously wrote:

It is not from the benevolence of the butcher, the brewer or the baker that we expect our dinner, but from their regard to their own self-interest... [Every individual] intends only his own security, only his own gain. And he is in this led by an invisible hand to promote an end which was no part of his intention. By pursuing his own interest, he frequently promotes that of society more effectually than when he really intends to promote it.[13]

Such observations are denigrated to scorn in most contempo-

---

10 Roy P. Basler, ed., *The Collected Works of Abraham Lincoln*, Vol. VII, "Reply to New York Workingmen's Democratic Republican Association," (New Brunswick: Rutgers University Press, 1953–1955), 259-260.

11 J. G. Nicolay and J. Hay *Abraham Lincoln*, I. (New York: Cosimo Classics, 2009), 615-616.

12 Letter to Thomas Mann Randolph, May 30, 1790.

13 *An Inquiry into the Nature and Causes of the Wealth of Nations*, Chap. 2: Of the Principle which Gives Occasion to the Division of Labour.

rary classrooms and presented by university professors as a hopeless relic of greedy capitalist imperialism. Let's face it; in modern citadels of education, you won't even be exposed to the *Wealth of Nations*. Karl Marx yes; Adam Smith no![14]

When it comes to the stories of Abraham and Isaac, it isn't their charity that strikes us as much as their self-interest. Isaac, as a tiller of the ground, was one from whom we might expect our dinner. Yet, the Bible's "invisible hand" indicates that he was "blessed." The Bible, like Adam Smith, doesn't seem bothered by self-centeredness at all; but don't tell modern "statists," who seem convinced that only governmental institutions can promote the greater good.

The Bible – as politics – is telling us that in spite of their personal foibles, Abraham and Isaac relentlessly pursued their self-interest, and in so doing promoted not only their own families, but the larger units of tribe and ultimately the nation that came to be called "Israel."

### Jacob the Entrepreneur

We can see in Isaac's cultivation of the fields a prophetic prefiguring of a settled nation, which the seed of Abraham would one day become; but the vagabond lifestyle of the patriarchs by no means vanishes, and might even be seen as the biblical "ideal." Rebecca, we are told, is carrying two sons in her womb. One, to be called Esau, is destined to be a "hairy" fellow, a hunter, a man of the open fields, while the other, known to us as Jacob, is an "indoor" type, a "momma's boy." Esau comes out of the womb before his twin brother, thereby securing his father's birthright, as firstborn.

Jacob, however, is not satisfied with an inferior status and connives with his mother to "steal" Esau's birthright. He dons sheepskin and deceives the aged and near-blind Isaac into thinking that he is in fact his "hairy" brother, Esau. Sure enough, Isaac mistakenly conveys his blessing and his inheritance to Jacob, who now fears for his life from Esau. Before his enraged twin can slay him, Jacob decides to abandon his secure "homebody" lifestyle and take to the roads, like earlier generations of patriarchs.

His ultimate destination is Mesopotamia, where his grandfa-

---

14 Adam Smith is generally ignored as a trade theorist in textbooks of international economics. See Kibritçioğlu, Aykut (1994): *On Adam Smith's Contributions to the International Trade Theory*. Published in: Uluslararası (Makro)İktisat (1996): 31-38.

ther had originated. He has extended family there, specifically an uncle named Laban, to whose household he will join himself. He will fall desperately in love with a beautiful damsel named Rachel, for whose matrimonial sake he will do anything, including the perpetration of foolhardy "business" deals. His uncle Laban will agree to give his daughter to Jacob, but only on condition that the grandson of Abraham become his "indentured servant."

Laban is certainly motivated by self-interest and "capitalism," but so is Jacob. Having tended Laban's flocks for seven years, in order to acquire Rachel as his bride, he agrees to work an additional seven years, since Laban has decreed that his older daughter Leah must be married first. Only by agreeing to work a total of fourteen years can Jacob take to wife both Leah and his beloved Rachel. At first blush Jacob doesn't seem to be a very astute businessman, but he is not to be outdone.

After the requisite number of years go by, the two capitalists strike a bargain, by which Jacob will stay on with Laban and receive, as "wages" for his labor, the black lambs and spotted and speckled goats from among the flocks. Laban, perhaps recognizing Jacob's conniving character, does a little conniving of his own. He removes from the flock the male striped or spotted goats, the female specked or spotted goats, and all the black sheep, creating a separate flock for himself. He nonetheless underestimates his nephew, who now devises a scheme to produce speckled and spotted goats from among the flocks in his charge. He does it by using what appears to be a measure of "conjuration," by having the animals mate in front of branches into which he has cut stripes. Some magical power apparently emanates from the stripes, causing the newborn of the flock to bear stripes as well. How exactly this works is anyone's guess, but the bottom line is that Jacob emerges as the one with the most animals in his charge, beating his uncle in the game of one-upmanship.

Shouldn't there be some scorn heaped on Jacob from the pages of the Bible? Doesn't he know that it's better to give than to receive? Instead, what he does seem to know is that in the rough-and-tumble world of business, it's dog-eat-dog. That's capitalism. It's *The Art of War,* and the one who "builds a better mousetrap" ultimately wins. In fact, modern businessmen who seek inspiration from the east's famous tome on military tactics ought perhaps to read the Bible in tandem with Sun Tzu. Both agree that success isn't about planning, in the sense of working through an agreed-to "list" of "dos" and "don'ts," but rather embodies sharp and suitable responses to changing situations.[15] Jacob understands his own changing situation and instinctively decides to exit Laban's household at the opportune moment. He saddles up his camels with his wives and children and drives his flocks in front of him, taking with him all he had acquired during his tenure with Laban. Rachel even makes off with her father's household idols. Ten days later, Laban catches up with the fleeing band, but no retribution is meted out. Instead, the two businessmen pile up a mound of stones to commemorate a rapprochement of sorts between them.

But there is yet more insight to be gained here, for the story is as much about private property rights as it is about tactics and strategy in the game of life. The right to property and its improvement by personal labor was to be enshrined in American political theory as something akin to sacrosanct, and political theorists from John Locke to Thomas Jefferson were keenly aware of biblical commentary on the same. Locke observed in 1690:

> Every man has a property in his own person. This nobody has any right to but himself. The labor of his body and the work of his hands are properly his.[16]

Jefferson added (1801):

> A wise and frugal government ... shall leave [men] free to regulate their own pursuits of industry and improvement, and shall not take from the mouth of labor the bread it has earned.[17]

Jacob bears out these adages by his years of labor, that results in the improvement of his dubious fortunes. Fortunately for him, there is no unwise or un-frugal government back in Mesopotamia to confiscate (or tax) his earnings. Throughout his story, he proves

---

15 Sun Tzu, *The Art of War* (eBookEden.com, 2009), 3; Gerald A. Michaelson, Steven Michaelson, *Sun Tzu - The Art of War for Managers: 50 Strategic Rules Updated for Today's Business* (Avon, MA: Adams Media, 2010), 171.

16 Micheline Ishay, ed., *The Human Rights Reader: Major Political Essays, Speeches, and Documents from Ancient Times to the Present* (New York: Routledge, 2007), 117.

17 Jedediah Purdy, "Languages of Politics in America," in James Boyd White, Jefferson Powell, eds., *Law and Democracy in the Empire of Force* (Univ. of Michigan Press, 2009), 14.

to be a schemer and a conniver, as so many capitalists generally are. This is precisely why they get such a "bum wrap." Yet, it is precisely Jacob's character as a "supplanter" that finds him in a climactic encounter with the Almighty, in the form of an angel. It's while he's en-route back to Canaan, after so many long years of indentured servitude to his wily uncle that he meets someone along the road, who engages him in a wrestling match. The stranger struggles with Jacob all night, but by daybreak is still unable to overpower him. That's when Jacob's mysterious adversary resorts to a little "magic," touching his hip joint and wrenching it from its socket. He finally adjures Jacob to let him go, but the son of Isaac will not relent until he receives the man's "blessing." The stranger asks Jacob his name and subsequently declares that he will henceforth be known as "Israel," denoting one who "wrestles with God." We identify with the story because we know viscerally that there has never been a successful entrepreneur who hasn't done his or her share of wrestling. Jacob's road is our road, full of risk and reward, peril and blessing.

After the strange encounter, Jacob does some "naming" himself, dubbing that precise locale "Peniel," meaning "the face of God." Apparently, Jacob gets the idea that he had not just met a stranger, or even an angel, but the living God, who had appeared to him in fleshly manifestation – what theologians call a "theophany." Jacob/ "Israel" will walk with a limp thereafter as a memento of the occasion – testimony to the fact that it's a fearsome thing to wrestle with the Almighty. But the episode also hints that the Divine must be rather pleased with Jacob's hutzpah, with his unwillingness to settle for second-class status. Hidden in the word "Israel" is another Hebraic term – *Sar-El* – meaning "prince of God." What we may have here is a play on words, telling us that it's not through blind obedience, but by wrestling with the Divine that one becomes God's prince. It's a supreme reward to the patriarch who isn't satisfied with his lot in life, who pulls himself up by his own proverbial sandal straps. After all, isn't that what capitalists do?

### Joseph the Bureaucrat

Jacob, who is now officially "Israel," has twelve sons, who become the progenitors of twelve tribes. The trouble starts, however, when one of his sons, a precocious and ingenuous lad named Yosef (whom westerners call Joseph), has some dreams, depicting him as the greatest of the bunch, and his brothers as subservient. This, understandably, doesn't strike his eleven siblings well, and they plot to be rid of Joseph and his arrogance. They seize him, throw him into a pit, grab his cloak (an exquisite garment bestowed on him by Jacob, who favored him over the others) smear it with goat's blood, and subsequently return it to his grief-stricken father, explaining that Joseph was killed by a wild animal.

Joseph, however, hasn't really died; he has been sold to some nomadic Ishmaelites as a miserable slave and in turn taken down to the Nile Delta, being resold to a prominent Egyptian named Potiphar. Entrepreneurial like his father, Joseph soon rises to become chief of Potiphar's entire household. As we might expect from this particular family line, everything in his care – meaning the property of the great Egyptian – prospers. We're not told exactly what Joseph does to grow the fortune of his master and benefactor, but he had to have been the consummate businessman. He makes use of his wits to bring enrichment to his boss, and is rewarded in kind. There's no sense that Joseph is envious of Potiphar's wealth or position. What an attitude! He doesn't ask what his benefits are, or how many paid vacation days he acquires per month. He's happy to serve, and we respect him for that. Like his father, he's a model capitalist. Furthermore, Egypt must not have had anything like a "progressive income tax" that effectively redistributed wealth. And the Bible does not complain. It only lauds Joseph for his acumen.

Unfortunately, Joseph's good fortunes are destined to plummet, as he runs afoul of Potiphar's adulterous wife. According to the classic narrative, Joseph is accosted by the lusty lady, who makes advances on our hero only to be ignominiously refused. As the righteous Hebrew flees from her, she pulls off his cloak, which she next presents to Potiphar himself, claiming that Joseph had tried to rape her. The enraged Egyptian has Joseph thrown into prison, where he languishes in an even worse kind of bondage. But once again he rises to the top, impressing his jailer so much that he is put in charge of all the other inmates. Dreamer that he is, he successfully interprets the dreams of the other prisoners and is finally called upon to interpret the dream of the great potentate of all the land, the pharaoh himself. All of the other magicians and soothsayers were quite clueless as to the meaning of Pharaoh's dream, involving seven skinny cows who devoured seven fat cows and seven scorched and dry heads of grain that swallowed seven full and healthy heads of grain.

But when, through a quirk of fate, Joseph is summoned, he is by supernatural agency shown the exact meaning the dream is intended to convey. Egypt is soon to experience seven years plenty, including bountiful harvests and abundance for all. These good years, however, will be followed by seven more years of terrible famine that will bring ruination to the whole land. The great pharaoh, on hearing this lucid interpretation, is, to say the least, impressed. Ingenuous and unassuming as he is, Joseph doesn't display self-congratulation; he simply suggests that the mighty potentate find "someone" in the land capable of putting Egypt in "hoarding" mode for seven years, so that when the famine inevitably arrives, there will be enough gain in the storehouses to last for all seven years of scarcity. Who could such a man be?

"Joseph," says the pharaoh, "You are the man!" In an incredible reversal of fortunes the lowly slave turned even lowlier prisoner becomes the second most powerful person in the world's greatest civilization. His new job description: "Chief Bureaucrat." Sure enough, he becomes a pretty good manager of the new bureaucracy that he now creates.[18] The silos burst with grain during the years of plenty, and we wonder what kind of commentary the Bible is bringing. Isn't this the quintessential ancient expression of "big government"? Isn't it the very thing our third president warned about?:

> If we were directed from Washington when to sow and when to reap, we would soon want for bread. – Thomas Jefferson[19]

One wonders whether Mr. Jefferson might have been reflecting on the story of Joseph when he wrote this quip. But thanks to Joseph, Egypt doesn't lack bread. "Does God love bureaucrats?" we might justifiably ask. Is bureaucracy and big government perhaps a better way than greedy capitalism, with its cycles of boom and bust? Isn't the story of Joseph the world's best example of what an efficient regulation regime can accomplish? Of course calling it "regulation" understates the case. It's "centralized planning," Soviet-style! But before we get carried away calling Joseph a Communist, we should

---

18 David W. Tandy, *Warriors Into Traders: The Power of the Market in Early Greece* (Berkeley: Univ. of California Press, 1997), 103-4.

19 Warren L. McFerran, *Political Sovereignty: The Supreme Authority in the United States* (Sanford, FL: Southern Liberty Press, 2005), 123.

reflect that bureaucracies can indeed accomplish impressive ends, as long as they are well-administered. What's wrong with that? For his part, the pharaoh was untroubled by the idea that government was becoming too big, and Joseph was equally untroubled.

What a flattering picture the narrative paints! As the good years turn to ruin, our hero opens the storehouses, first to the Egyptians, then to foreigners, who begin flooding into Egypt for relief. Through it all, there are some lessons to be learned, politically, from how Joseph administers Egypt. For one thing, our hero seems well aware of an important political adage: "Never let a crisis go to waste!" Fortunately for Egypt, Josephs knows nothing about deficit spending. What he does know is that he is sitting on a vast treasure in the form of grain, and he capitalizes on that fact in the capitalistic tradition of his forebears. He sells the produce of the storehouses, not only to the foreigners who come knocking at his gates, but to the Egyptians themselves. We can only imagine the level of wealth that must have come flooding into the land of the Nile. But rather than enriching the populace, it seems to have enriched only the pharaoh's coffers. Nonetheless, what we have here does resemble an ancient form of "welfare," for which Joseph is highly credited, as "Bureaucrat-in-Chief." Over time Joseph will purchase all the land in Egypt on behalf of the pharaoh, and the increasingly hungry Egyptians will be all too happy to sell.

### "Big Government," Slavery, and Indentured Servitude

Does the Bible, then, give a "thumbs up" on "big government"? Should we hail Joseph as an ancient Marxist, who effectuates the complete nationalization of property and the means of production? After all, in addition to saving the Egyptians, Joseph ends up saving his wayward brothers, who end up in Egypt themselves, in search of food. Of course they don't recognize their brother and don't know that the pharaoh's great administrator is in fact the sibling they had betrayed and sold into slavery. This enables Joseph to turn tables on them all and, through a clever ruse, force them to admit their wrongdoing, only to be reconciled through their sincere repentance in an emotionally climactic scene. Joseph's entire family comes down to join him in Egypt, settling in the rich and fertile land of Goshen, and all ends well … or appears to.

At first blush it looks as though Egypt's great bureaucracy, created and administered by Joseph, is not just a "good thing"; it is genuine "salvation" for the seed of Abraham. Joseph announces to his wayward siblings that what they intended for evil God has turned to good:

> And now do not be grieved, nor angry with yourselves that you sold me here. For God sent me before you to preserve life.[20]

Nonetheless, what begins as Joseph's grand ambition to save his people from famine will end up enslaving them, over time, to an intrusive and totalitarian state. It will become nothing less than a four-century sojourn into slavery for all the children of Israel.[21] We don't know the exact circumstances by which the Hebrews go from being Joseph's honored guests – who live in the land of Goshen and become rich (Gen. 47:27) – to "slaves," but one intriguing theory links them with the semi-nomadic Habiru, a group including farmers, merchants, construction workers, and warriors. While the Bible suggests that Jacob's descendants peacefully coexist with the Egyptians for two of those four centuries, if the Habiru theory is correct, they would actually have been employed as an integral component in the defense of Egypt, protecting it from the Canaanite menace to the north. This is why the Bible takes pains to point out that they settle in the northern Nile Delta area – the land of Goshen.

Some speculate that this mercenary army is only about a thousand strong, but they are significant enough to trouble "a pharaoh ... who did not know about Joseph."[22] The reference might conceivably be to Seti I (c. 1294-1279 BCE), who becomes concerned about the growing power of this Habiru horde, declaring:

> Let us deal wisely with them, lest they multiply, and it will be when there comes a war, they join also to our enemies, and fight against us, and get out of the land.[23]

---

20 Genesis 45:5.

21 Geoffrey P. Miller, *The Ways of a King: Legal and Political Ideas in the Bible* (Gottingen: Vandenhoeck & Ruprecht, 2011), 103. As Miller comments, the author of Genesis fails to recognize that a centralized bureaucracy can be an agent of oppression as well as a vehicle for stability.

22 Exodus 1:8.

23 Exodus 1:10.

He decides that the best course is to set them to work, building fortifications and city walls. The tradition persists at every Passover meal celebrated to this day: "Once we were slaves in Egypt..." In point of fact, we're not really sure what this "slavery" amounted to. The traditional idea that vast throngs of Hebrews wearing shackles labor under the cruel whips of their taskmasters is undoubtedly a stretch. By contrast, while standard English translations tell us they are "slaves," the actual Hebrew word is avadim, meaning "laborers," perhaps "corvée laborers," or "day laborers."[24] Such work is generally without compensation, being imposed by aristocrats or nobles on people of lower-class standing. The Hebrews, according to this theory, aren't "owned" in the way we imagine slaves in bondage; rather their servitude consists only in the dispensation of their labor.

If we translate this into political/economic theory, it means that a direct result of trusting Joseph and the Egyptians he serves, they go from being "capitalists" (as was the tradition of the earliest patriarchs) to something akin to "indentured servants." But isn't this what often happens when government – in this instance, the great bureaucracy of Egypt – owns the means of production? Of course their basic needs are now provided for, and it's difficult to overestimate the value of such security. The pharaoh's laborers are certainly free from the nagging fears that plague so many of the ancient world's populace, who can never be sure what the future would hold, whether the next harvest will be bounteous or scant, whether they might be invaded and ravaged by enemies, and in the final analysis whether they will live or die.

Nevertheless, trusting in "Big Brother," even when doing so yields tangible security, has an ironic downside; for owing one's livelihood to the state involves significant tradeoffs – most often the loss of "self-determination." We can even draw a parallel with the tendency of certain twentieth century European societies to surrender to collaborationist regimes during the Second World War. These included governments headed by fascists like Mussert in Holland, and others, which over time evolved into full-fledged Nazi regimes under the likes of Seyes Inquart. How many people in the modern world would indeed be more than happy to trade in their freedoms for "indentured servitude" to the state? Isn't a government job more secure, "cushier," and even better paying than working in the private

---

24 Richard Gabriel, *The Military History of Ancient Israel* (Westport, CT: Praeger Publishers, 2003), 61ff.

sector? The comparison is hardly a stretch, for scholars have noted that ancient Egypt's bureaucracy persisted for many centuries and seemed to run quite efficiently. And while debates rage about the nature of Israel's sojourn in Egypt, their servitude in the land of the pharaohs must certainly have been a function of the region's entrenched bureaucratic structure.

Hindsight being twenty-twenty, it must have seemed to the editors of the Bible that entering into the pharaoh's employ, however it came about, was a grievous form of bondage. If the Bible is indeed political, then it is not-so-subtly preaching: "Don't rely on any pharaoh's government to be your salvation!" After all, who would not argue that it might have been better for the children of Abraham to suffer the ravages of famine in the land of Canaan than to enter the "safety" of servitude in Egypt? But enter they do, and in the end they will require nothing less than a revolution. They will need an "exodus."

# 2

# "GIVE ME LIBERTY!" MOSES MEETS "BRUTUS"

*"The fault, dear Brutus, is not in our stars, But in ourselves, that we are underlings. Brutus and Caesar: what should be in that "Caesar"? Why should that name be sounded more than yours?"* (Cassius, in Shakespeare's *Julius Caesar*)

From almost the beginning of the American experiment, there have been voices who issued stern warnings against creating a federal government with too much centralized authority. That, they reasoned, would smack of the very thing the Revolution struggled against – a monarchy. A series of essays published in the New York Journal between October 1787 and April 1788 were penned anonymously by one "Brutus," in deference to the assassin of Julius Caesar, who in turn perpetrated his grizzly deed to "save" the Roman Republic. The real author was most likely a New York judge by the name of Robert Yates, a delegate to the Constitutional Convention and a noted anti-federalist. His admonitions about the potential abuses of power by an overly strong executive branch served as a serious counter-balance to the arguments of pro-federalist Alexander Hamilton. They also remind us of certain warnings found in the Bible regarding the excesses of power that were destined to produce, not a federation of twelve tribes under God, but

37

an absolute monarchy.

In Brutus no. 17, we read the following of the proposed U.S. Constitution, that would one day become the supreme law of the land:

> This [new] government is to possess *absolute and uncontrollable powers*, legislative, executive and judicial, with respect to every object to which it extends... It is declared, "that this Constitution, and the laws of the United States ... shall be the supreme law of the land; and the judges in every State shall be bound thereby, any thing in the Constitution or law of any State to the contrary notwithstanding." It appears from these articles, that ... *the Constitution and laws of every State are nullified and declared void*, so far as they are or shall be inconsistent with this Constitution... The government, then, so far as it extends, *is a complete one, and not a confederation.* It is as much one complete government as that of New York or Massachusetts; has as absolute and perfect powers to make and execute all laws, to appoint officers, institute courts, declare offenses, and annex penalties, with respect to every object to which it extends, as any other in the world. So far, therefore, as its powers reach, *all ideas of confederation are given up and lost... All that is reserved for the individual States must very soon be annihilated...* The powers of the general legislature extend to every case that is of the least importance-there is nothing valuable to human nature, nothing dear to freemen, but what is within its power. It has the authority to make laws which will affect the lives, the liberty, and property of every man in the United States; nor can the Constitution or laws of any State, in any way prevent or impede the full and complete execution of every power given. The legislative power is competent to lay taxes, duties, imposts, and excises;-*there is no limitation to this power...*[1]

The lack of limitation on the power of the central government was the central defect, in Yates' mind, of the seminal document of

---

1 *Debates and Proceedings in the Convention of the Commonwealth of Massachusetts, Held in the year 1788, and Which Finally Ratified the Constitution of the United States* (Boston: W. White, 1856), 368-9.

the new nation.[2] It echoes a much larger debate – one that has been going on almost since the dawn of civilization – over what should be considered good government, and what should be recognized as tyranny. As we will see, the debate also comes into focus in the pages of the Bible. Following that line of inquiry, we ought to at least consider the suggestion of modern critical scholarship of the sacred text, that the Bible engages, not merely in occasional literary "swipes" at "authoritarian" rule, but contains a number of "subtexts" sandwiched into the larger narrative, that are rabidly opposed to the very idea of a king.[3] Never mind the storied legacies of King David and King Solomon; the "Brutus" movement was alive and well in the holy land!

## Moses the Autocrat, and Echoes of Dissent

We see this in evidence as early as the account of Israel's great Lawgiver, Moses. More than a literary character, he is a marble figure, a Michelangelo sculpture with rays of divine light emanating from his furrowed brow. He is an emblem of freedom and emancipation. He is the great lawgiver. As a religious symbol he has inspired untold millions, and he is beyond reproach. But make no mistake; he was as fallible as anyone. Moreover, as a leader we have to evaluate him for what all leaders are at one point or another in their careers – politicians. First, of course, a leader must establish him or herself. In Moses' case, that meant leading what amounted to a revolution. It's a classic story of a people suffering under the harshest of overlords, namely, Egypt's tyrannical pharaoh, identified by most scholars as the son of Seti, Ramses the Great (1279-1213 BCE).

For the descendants of Jacob (Israel) it's been quite a descent, from a "protected" class of honored guests of Pharoah's "Number

---

2 See Robert Yates, John Lansing, Luther Martin, *Secret Proceedings and Debates of the Convention Assembled at Philadelphia, in the Year 1787* (Ithaca, NY: Cornell Univ. Library, 2009).

3 Some have argued that the anti-monarchy source was perhaps added by a textual editor of the exile, presenting a commentary on the unsavory character of Israel's kings. Eichrodt, Spicer, Anderson and others delineate the ambivalent attitude of Israel toward monarchy and trace it back to its origins. See John A. Wood, *Perspectives on War in the Bible* (Macon, GA: Mercer Univ. Press, 1998), 29. See also Barry Bandstra, *Reading the Old Testament* (Belmont, CA: Wadsworth Publishing, 2008), 249, 258; Joseph P. Schultz, *Judaism and the Gentile Faiths: Comparative Studies in Religion* (East Brunswick, NJ: Associated University Presses, 1981), 150.

Two," Joseph, to the degradation of servitude. Perhaps it was the very trust they placed in Joseph, and by extension the ruling house of the Egypt, that has reduced them by degrees to slavery. Perhaps, as we have suggested, they amount to "corvée," or "day laborers," dutifully employed building defensive walls and fortifications for Egypt's great potentate. Nevertheless, even day laborers can be mistreated, and the Hebrews are not exempt from the whip. How often, we wonder, do bureaucracies turn into "thugocracies"?

What they need now is someone to rescue them, an ancient George Washington, and Moses will prove to be their man. From the beginning, however, we see a violent streak in the redeemer. The baby boy, set adrift in a reed basket on the Nile, discovered by pharaoh's daughter and raised in the opulence of the royal court, has grown into a man with a considerable chip on his shoulder. He observes a fellow Hebrew who is being beaten by an Egyptian. Thomas Jefferson once quipped, "All tyranny needs to gain a foothold is for people of good conscience to remain silent." Moses by no means holds his peace, but he does a great deal more than just speak up. He impetuously strikes out and kills the cruel taskmaster. For this act of violence he becomes a marked man, who must flee into the desert. It is in fact argued that this proclivity toward violent retribution will later manifest itself in his dealings with his own people, and spark open revolt against him. But for now, he must spend forty years in the Sinai.

He is ultimately commissioned by God in the famous "burning bush" incident to return to Egypt and confront the pharaoh. On his way back, however, we find a curious story sandwiched into the larger narrative. Seemingly out of nowhere, we're told that God encounters Moses as he overnights by the roadside and attempts to kill him. It's his wife Zipporah who comes to the rescue, armed with a knife. But she doesn't fend off God with the weapon; rather, she severs her son's foreskin. (The biblical account is vague at this point, since we're told that she "cast it at his feet" but doesn't tell us at whose feet "his" refers to – Moses' or perhaps God's.) Apparently, the prior command that Abraham circumcise his descendants has been neglected, and this is Zipporah's attempt to rectify the oversight. God seems to be placated, for the text relates, "So he let him alone." Zipporah, however, slings an accusation against her husband: "A bridegroom of blood you are to me!"[4]

---

4 Exodus 4:24-26.

Researchers have long noticed that the story interrupts the flow of the narrative, as though someone has interjected it into the account. It also seems more than a little odd that God would seek to kill the very man he has groomed as the great deliverer, a man who has served him faithfully for a full forty years. Some believe that the story may be transposed from a later period in Moses' career and that the Bible may be hinting at the existence of an "anti-Moses tradition" that is perennially distrustful of power figures who are a trifle too big for their sandals. In other words, God in the narrative may be a surrogate for the multitude of complainers and dissenters who later surface to challenge Moses' authority. Somehow, according to this theory, the barely audible grumblings of this ragtag group of opponents escapes the censorship of those who later edit the Bible; but the story is "scrubbed" by turning God, not the multitude, into Moses' divine opponent.[5] This is quite possibly an example of the consistent "anti-tyranny" subtext that surfaces repeatedly in Bible, that we might well label the "B" (for "Brutus") current.[6] It represents the kind of government spoken of by America's Founders (Thomas Paine and others), perennially distrustful of centralized authority, even at the hands of a deliverer of Moses' stature.

Bear in mind, such theories are relatively recent. Our purpose here isn't to prove or disprove the Bible or the accuracy of any of its stories, but to suggest that there's a tone in these narratives that is profoundly distrustful of authority and authority figures, even Moses. Nonetheless, we know in fact that America's Founders were looking hard at Moses, and it's equally clear that the place of Israel's lawgiver in American history is hard to minimize. Thomas Jefferson, John Adams, and Benjamin Franklin and went so far as to suggest that Moses be depicted on the Great Seal of the new nation. We can easily think of multiple parallels between Moses and George Washington. They were both, after all, deliverers, who fomented revolution. Both fought "statist" regimes, bloated governments that tyrannized their subjects, one staring down the pharaoh,

---

5 See Jonathan Kirsch, *The Harlot by the Side of the Road* (New York: Random House, 1998), 156; Trent C. Butler, "An Anti-Moses Tradition," *Journal for the Study of the Old Testament* 12 12 (May 1979): 9, 11.

6 I am not suggesting that there is an independent "source" that might be called "Brutus." There are, it is theorized, multiple independent sources comprising the Torah, J,E,P and D, among others. Rather, I am referring to a "theme" developed across various passages and attested repeatedly in these sources.

the other defying King George. Both were strong leaders who were essential to their people's survival. While some researchers are audacious enough to question Moses' very existence; others rightly point out that if there had been no Moses we would have to invent him. The reason is that great national movements are never born from ether; they require the kind of leaders who inspire discipline, self-sacrifice, and dedication to a cause larger than their own self-interest. In Washington's case it has been argued persuasively that his stature and leadership qualities were such that the young American republic literally wouldn't have survived without him.

Then, there's the military angle. No one denies that General Washington was a phenomenal tactician. Everyone agrees that Washington's greatest military exploit was his daring crossing of the Delaware River on Christmas Eve, 1776, to surprise the British at Trenton. We all thrill to the idea of a relatively weak and diminutive force triumphing over a nefarious and powerful tyranny. Moses' "revolution" finds yet another commonality with Washington at this point. Indeed, we cheer the thought of Moses and his troupe of Hebrews gaining the upper hand over the mighty charioteers of the pharaoh, who pursue them through the Red Sea, only to be drowned as the parted waters return again and swallow them up.

However, military historians notice a few things of interest that escape those who read the story only on the level of a religious tractate. The famous pillar of smoke by day and fire at night, for example, can be likened to an ancient command and control device, a kind of signal flare/ brazier. At night the brazier would burn brightly to signal the army's encampment, while in the morning it would be half covered, producing smoke that would signal the army to move out. But in this case the Bible relates that when night approaches, the pillar of fire stations itself between the Israelites and the Egyptians, meaning at the rear of the Israelite column. To the Egyptians, who assume that the fire marks the head of the troupe, it would appear as though Moses is lost and leading his people back into Egypt – directly at the pharaoh's army. Moses, however, is not lost; he appears to have turned his column around deliberately, leaving the fire to his rear. The Egyptians are both deceived and blinded, their "night vision" having been compromised by the bright light. They are unable to focus their vision on the fleeing Hebrews, who take this occasion to cross over the Red Sea (or "Sea of Reeds," as it appears in the text).

### Institutionalizers and Radicals

Make no mistake; the story of the Exodus from Egypt is as much an account of a "Revolutionary War," commensurate with the founding of a new nation, as it is book of pure faith. Nor were the parallels with the American experience lost on the revolutionary generation. In January, 1776, Thomas Paine anonymously published his classic pamphlet, *Common Sense*, in which he compared England's King George with Egypt's pharaoh.[7] Not all revolutions, however, produce rosy results. Those who have studied revolutions down through the ages have noticed that after virtually any revolution takes place, its course can proceed in one of two directions. It can either stabilize and become "institutionalized," or it can radicalize. Invariably, there comes to be a tension within each revolution between the "institutionalizers" and those who want to keep the revolutionary spirit alive. The latter sometimes manifest as true "radicals," who ironically become tyrants themselves. There's no better example of this conflict than what we find after the American Revolution. In those days, some were so fearful of a new tyranny developing that they opined loudly of the need to keep the spirit of the revolution alive. Thomas Jefferson famously declared, "Every generation needs a new revolution." Said he: "The tree of liberty must be refreshed from time to time with the blood of patriots and tyrants. It is its natural manure."[8] Our third president sounds like quite the radical.

By contrast there were the Alexander Hamiltons of early America, whose goal was to settle things down. As George Washington's Secretary of the Treasury, Hamilton was responsible, more than any other, not only for the implementation of the new Constitution, but for institutionalizing its connection with the economy of the private sector. Very much a monarchist, he, along with the powerful "Federalist" faction of the new republic, constantly stressed the importance of checking what Hamilton called "the amazing violence and turbulence of the democratic spirit."[9] Ultimately, while America resisted anything resembling a monarchy, it definitely took

---

7 For additional background on the parallels between Moses, the Exodus and the American experience, see Bruce Feiler, *America's Prophet: Moses and the American Story* (San Francisco, Harper Collins, 2009).

8 Letter to William S. Smith, Nov. 13, 1787.

9 Wilfred E. Binkley, *American Political Parties* (New York: Alfred A. Knopf, 1943), 40.

the route of institutionalization.

A very different course was adopted in the aftermath of another revolution, this one in Europe and almost simultaneous with the American Revolution. It was the French Revolution of 1789. In France another Moses-like character came to the fore, one Maximilian Robespierre, who was so "pure" in his revolutionary spirit as to be called the "Incorruptible." His countrymen actually looked at him as a kind of "redeemer;" yet he, along with the new leadership of the French Republic, became increasingly radicalized. They indeed decided to keep the French Revolution churning, splashing their own tree of liberty with the blood of countless thousands of martyrs. The sacrificial blade would be that of the guillotine, nicknamed the "National Razor," which let loose streams of blood in the streets of Paris.

History teaches that the French Revolution was hardly an anomaly. What do we find but the same pattern in almost every revolution we study? The Russian Revolution, that birthed the Soviet Union, is a case study in the same kind of tension. There were "purists," or "maximalists" such as Leon Trotsky, who wanted a "permanent revolution," only to find himself outmaneuvered and ultimately assassinated by Joseph Stalin. Italian political theorist Antonio Gramsci summed it up well in 1917, when he wrote:

> The maximalists ... were the active agents needed to ensure that events should not stagnate, that the drive to the future should not come to a halt and allow a final settlement – a bourgeois settlement – to be reached. But now these maximalists have seized power and established their dictatorship, and are creating the socialist framework within which the revolution will have to settle down...[10]

And settle down it did, Stalin producing a more-or-less permanent tyranny of a small elite.

Then, we might consider the Communist revolution in China of 1949, after which the victorious and notorious Mao Zedong became increasingly fearful that his grand design was becoming institutionalized via a new quasi-capitalism. His response: an even more repressive "institutional" dictatorship, combined with the Cultural

---

10 Stephen Eric Bronner, *Twentieth Century Political Theory: A Reader* (New York: Routledge, 1996), 170.

Revolution of 1966, that killed hundreds of thousands, perhaps millions of people in order to keep revolutionary fires burning. The Red Guard were dispatched across the countryside, unleashing their machetes against all connected with the "liberal bourgeoise."[11] The bloodletting would not subside for a full decade, with Mao's death in 1976.

We can make the case that the reason the American Revolution turned out so well is that the Framers of the Constitution deliberately sought a "balanced center," between tyranny on the one hand and anarchy on the other. As we have argued, they must have been inspired, at least in part, by lessons learned from the Bible.

Let's therefore go back in time and consider the revolution at the hands of Moses. The Bible paints a very strong picture that this revolution is "incomplete," even following the great Exodus from Egypt and the crossing of the Red Sea. This isn't just a rescue out of tyranny, but a redemption that looks toward something. There is a destination that lay ahead, namely, Mt. Sinai, and the giving of the Law. Moses goes up the mountain, disappears into the cloud of the Divine Presence, comes down forty days later carrying the tablets of the Ten Commandments. The whole Torah, or Pentateuch, revealed there to Moses, will be their "Constitution" and will provide structure and form. It will prevent the kind of chaos that revolutions often engender. In tradition the giving of the Law at Sinai occurs exactly fifty days after Passover (when the Israelites left Egypt), and is commemorated to this day by a springtime feast called Shavuot, or Pentecost in Greek.

Here we have the biblical model to which the Framers of the Constitution looked. The new Israelite nation is given structure and form from On High, and that's what prevents any potential breakdown into anarchy. We can think of it as the biblical version of a "balanced center," between too much government (Egypt) and no government. Yet, there seems still to have been a fear among the newly freed Hebrews that Moses's revolution just might tilt toward tyranny. It's a curious paradigm, that the "outs," once they become "ins," often become just as corrupt and tyrannical as the people they were fighting against to begin with. (That was certainly the case with Robespierre.) Here are the Hebrews, breaking out of the pharaoh's chains under a brutal tyranny, and the fear is that they just might

11 Christine Loh, *Underground Front: The Chinese Communist Party in Hong Kong* (Hong Kong: Hong Kong Univ. Press, 2010), 100ff.

have replaced it with another tyranny, now under Moses.

### Moses and the "Contras"

Again, we're not supposed to say anything "contra-Moses," who's about as unassailable as God Almighty. But shouldn't it raise an eyebrow for discerning readers of Holy Writ, that there is so much "grumbling and complaining" against God's deliverer from the get-go, and that it never seems to dissipate? Yes, the grumblers are put in their place, not once but repeatedly. Edward G. Robinson, cast as the despicable Dathan, opposite Charlton Heston's Moses, asks in his gangster-twang, "Were there not enough graves in Egypt that you brought us out into the desert to die?" Of course, we know whose side we're on. Could it be, however, that such a long, forty-year litany of complaint against the "deliverer" might actually mean that the complainers have a point? Might the Bible be "covering" for possibility that Moses is a tyrant in his own right?

Bear in mind, the Exodus was by anyone's estimation a revolution, and Moses was a revolutionary leader. Sometimes, when revolutions go too far, they produce counter-revolutionaries – "Contras." That at least was the term used to describe a number of rebel groups who opposed the radical Sandanista junta in Nicaragua, who had overthrown a prior dictatorship in 1979. The Contra groups were able to unify in 1987 as the Nicaraguan Resistance movement. They most often called themselves "commandos," while sympathizers among Nicaragua's peasants dubbed them los primos – "the cousins." These "cousins," with significant covert aid from the United States (via a somewhat renegade colonel by the name of Oliver North), kept up enough pressure on the dictatorship of Daniel Ortega that in 1990 an opposition candidate (Violeta Chamorro) was elected, and the Sandanista domination of Nicaragua came to an end.[12]

Consider, then, the situation with Moses' revolution, which is followed by such an endless litany of complaint that not a few biblical scholars are convinced that there must have been a considerable "anti-Moses" current among the early Israelites – ancient "Contras." – perhaps representing a continuation of the "Brutus current." They charge that these "complainers" might well be cloaking the

---

12 Robert S. Eliken, *Why Nicaragua Vanished: A Story of Reporters and Revolutionaries* (Latham, MD: Rowman & Littlefield, 2003).

larger tension between the authority of a single leader and the individualism of the "Twelve Tribes," who wanted to preserve their own character and self-determination in the face of the all-powerful Moses. We hear their voices of protest at the bitter waters of Marah, where the people decry the lack of fresh water. Moses miraculously purifies the waters by hurling a log into the brackish pool. We hear them complain again, that they are without food, and Moses tells them that their accusations against him are really against God, since he and his brother Aaron are in fact agents of the Divine.

Does this sound just a trifle authoritarian? Moses essentially tells his newly liberated people that any complaint against him is a complaint against the Deity. And his authority is demonstrated again, as he announces that quails will fly into their camp by night and that "manna" will fall with the dew in the morning. Many researchers have speculated about what the "manna" may have been – perhaps resin from the tamarisk tree, or the crystalized honeydew of certain scale insects, or the shoots of specific lichens, or even some kind of mushrooms. But focusing on the trivia of what the manna may have amounted to skirts the real message looming under the surface of the text. Moses, by demonstrating that he has harnessed the divine energy to meet the want of his flock of desert fugitives, has effectively shut down all dissent.

Yet, the complaining continues. As the troupe leaves the desert of Sin and camps at Rephidim, the people again demand fresh water. "Why did you bring us out of Egypt?" they ask. "To kill us with thirst?" Moses must be more than a little shaken, for he declares to God, "They are almost ready to stone me!" Stone him? Oh really? Has he become that much of a tyrant? Are there really those who want him dead? It's a possibility we will revisit as the story continues. In the meantime, Moses is instructed to strike the rock that stands at the foot of Sinai, whereupon a stream of water miraculously gushes forth. Another magic trick has confirmed his uncontested power.[13] For some, however, Moses has become the new "pharaoh."

How interesting, that the next part of the story depicts Moses wearing himself out settling disputes among the people. So it is,

---

13 On Moses' "uncompromising authority," see Walter Brueggemann, *Theology of the Old Testament: Testimony, Dispute, Advocacy* (Minneapolis, MN: Augsburg Fortress, 2005), 579. On the relative role of Moses in the Sinai narrative, see Thomas B. Dozeman, *God on the Mountain: A Study of Redaction, Theology, and Canon in Exodus 19-24* (Atlanta: Scholars Press, 1989).

that his father-in-law, Jethro, makes the timely suggestion that he appoint "some capable men" as co-leaders of the people: leaders of thousands, hundreds, fifties and tens. They are to serve as judges on an ongoing basis. Only the most difficult cases should be brought to Moses personally. What's going on here? Perhaps this is more than just the end result of the outbreak of so many childish squabbles in the camp. Perhaps it's the camouflaged reflection of a demand for a distribution of power among what the American Founders would later call "We the people."

Elsewhere the Bible depicts Moses asking God for permission to distribute his authority (as if he needed such permission):

> I am not able to bear all this people alone, because it is too heavy for me. And if You are going to part this way with me, I beg You to kill me at once, if I have found favor in Your sight, and let me not see my misery. And the LORD said to Moses, Gather to Me seventy men of the elders of Israel, whom you know to be the elders of the people, and the officers over them. And bring them to the tabernacle of the congregation so that they may stand there with you. And I will come down and talk with you there. And I will take of the spirit on you, and will put it on them, and they shall bear the burden of the people with you so that you do not bear it yourself alone.[14]

Could it be, however, that Moses "request" merely masks what he well knows is increasing unrest within the Israelite camp over his growing "tyranny"? Could it be that the Hebrew refugees had had enough of their "divine dictator"? Perhaps Moses realized that coming up with some way to share his power with what amounted to a "body politic" was the only way he could survive as their leader. In that case we might be looking at history's earliest formulation of the concept of "checks and balances."

By way of analogy, we might think of the early twentieth century example of Russia's Czar Nicholas II, who was essentially forced to give up the autocratic principle and share power with a representative council – a duma – to which he reluctantly gave his consent. But the czar's acquiescence proved only to be a stopgap measure in the inevitable march toward the violent overthrow of the

---

14 Numbers 11:14-17.

regime, involving the murder of Nicholas' entire family and the rise of a new and different kind of autocrat, Vladimir Lenin.[15] Is it possible that something similar was Moses' fate, but that the holy text is too embarrassed to tell us? It is a possibility we can't afford to ignore.

Returning to the American experience the revered Framers, as they gathered at the Constitutional Convention of 1787, had to have been mindful of the lessons of power sandwiched in the narrative accounts of the Exodus and the wilderness wanderings. The "distribution of powers" became a stirring refrain in their deliberations, seeing to it that a judiciary be established independent of the legislative and executive branches. James Madison, quoting Montesquieu, wrote in Federalist Paper # 47:

> Were the power of judging joined with the legislative, the life and liberty of the subject would be exposed to arbitrary control, for the judge would then be the legislator. Were it joined to the executive power, the judge might behave with all the violence of an oppressor.[16]

Moses, to his credit, gives ground to the impetus, wherever it came from, toward decentralization. Perhaps he's well aware of the "Brutus movement" among the people and hopes that this kind of power sharing will placate the malcontents. Whether he knew it or not, he had just established history's first precedent for an independent judiciary. But would these measures be enough to keep everyone in line behind his unquestioned leadership, especially as his next act will involve a forty-day absence from the camp? During this period he will make his hallowed trek up the mountain, to receive the Ten Commandments and a plethora of other laws covering everything from Sabbath and festival observance, to the construction of the Tabernacle, to rules regarding the kind of foods that may be consumed. Can kosher delis be far behind?

## The Constitution of the "United Tribes"

---

15 Robert K. Massie, *Nicholas and Alexandra* (New York: Random House, 2011); Berle Wein, *Triumph of Survival: The Story of the Jews in the Modern Era, 1650-190* (New York: Mesorah Publications, 1990), 176ff.

16 James Madison, *The Federalist No. 47*, "The Particular Structure of the New Government and the Distribution of Power Among Its Different Parts," New York Packet, January 30, 1788.

Most readers of the text simply gloss over the multitude of legal strictures that occupy page after "boring" page. Nonetheless, something very important and politically vital is going on here. Moses is settling his revolution down, taking the path of "institutionalization." He is providing needed structure for his band of refugees, giving them a "constitution" of sorts. It's a simple formula: freedom without chaos, because there is form. In time, this set of laws, this "Torah," would do for the Israelites what the United States Constitution did for the new American nation. It would provide a framework for orderly rule, a "social contract" between the governors and the governed. America's Founders understood these biblical principles as conveying an "ordered liberty," maintained by a "civil society."

Looking back across the millennia, today's scholars argue about how much of the Torah actually originated with Moses and how much may have been composed later, even centuries later, and simply transposed back upon the great lawgiver. But even if Moses brought nothing more down Mt. Sinai but the Ten Commandments, their impact can hardly be overstated, for a nation was being born, as surely as the nation the Founders "brought forth upon this continent." The standard image is of two stone tablets, with five commandments engraved on one and five on the other. But why couldn't all ten have been inscribed on a single tablet? Because God couldn't write very small? More likely, these were two identical copies of the commandments, all ten on each tablet – a legal "contract" between Israel and God, requiring each party to the agreement having its own copy.[17] A disjointed horde from Egypt are now glued to God and to each other, as the "United Tribes." Like that later generation of Americans, engaged in forging their own biblically modeled nation, they ought to have declared:

> With a firm reliance on the protection of Divine Providence, we mutually pledge to each other our Lives, our Fortunes, and our sacred Honor.

Unfortunately, however, their minds are elsewhere, and so are their morals. After all, the lawgiver has remained enveloped in Sinai's thick darkness for forty days, and there isn't much to keep a rambunctious horde preoccupied. We are told they erect an infa-

---

17 Peter C. Craigie, *The Book of Deuteronomy* (Grand Rapids, MI: Eerdmans, 1976), 134.

mous golden calf and fall into idolatry, coupled with some raunchy, orgiastic festivities. Party-time in the desert! The common assumption, in the midst of all the debauchery, is that the golden calf was a substitute for God, but this isn't quite accurate. We should more properly see the golden calf as a substitute for Moses, on whom they had grown dependent as an intermediary between themselves and God. On a political level, the Bible seems to be telling us that reliance on a single leader (the very kind of unquestioned authority Moses cultivated) isn't a sign of maturity, but of immaturity. It is a regression to infantility. The political ideal of the Bible is not "blind obedience" to authoritarian leaders, but a direct compact with the Divine, without recourse to intermediaries. Ironically, once the "anti-Moses" faction (the "Contras") in the camp is quashed, the door to dependency on Moses – and the golden calf when he vanished atop Sinai – is flung open.

Moses, coming down the mountain, is not pleased. God warns him that his people have corrupted themselves and offers to destroy them and make a new nation from his progeny. However, Moses intercedes with his God, pleading on behalf of his wayward flock. Hearing the sounds of revelry in the camp, the lawgiver hurls the two tablets of the law to the ground, shattering them in pieces, which he grinds up and forces the people to drink. The nation is to be spared, but the transgression must be punished, and justice must be done, relentlessly. The covenant has been broken even before it could be ratified. Moses issues a ringing interrogatory, coupled with call to action:

Who is on the LORD's side? let him come to me![18]

### The Praetorian Guard

Who should respond but Moses' own tribe, the one known as Levi? As the Levites gather around the lawgiver, they receive his horrific instructions. They are to go through the camp, swords in hand, slaughtering all who had participated in the idolatrous behavior, including their neighbors, their friends, even their own brothers, even their own sons. It is to be a ruthless bloodletting comparable to anything unleashed by their despotic Egyptian overlords. By the time it is over the ground will be soaked in blood and entrails of

---

18 Exodus 32:26.

some three thousand fellow Israelites. The violence is on such a grand scale that it is difficult to imagine that it could be sanctioned in the Bible, and just as difficult to come to grips with the directive having been issued by Moses, the great lawgiver, and, as he is elsewhere described, "more humble than anyone else on earth."[19]

It's common to make excuses for Moses. These are, after all, difficult times that demand the utmost of the new nation. The Israelites must become a single great army, who, like America's early Colonial Army, require discipline, obedience, and strong leaders whose orders must be obeyed. In military terms, the golden calf episode is worse than idolatry; it is treason. And the penalty for treason is death. It's as though three thousand Benedict Arnolds are getting their just desserts. Still, Moses' commendation of the Levites for becoming the nation's executioners is troublesome to those who have any sense of compassion at all. He announces that by these acts they have consecrated themselves as priests in God's service.[20]

Priests? This is what renders people worthy in the eyes of Divine Providence? Such are the prerequisites for godly service? These aren't priests; they're butchers! Yet, from now on the Levites will be the priestly tribe, the ones who will perform sacrifice and tend God's altar. For this they are well-known in religious history. They are not so well-known for their *political* role, as Moses' personal "Praetorian Guard," just as brutal as Caesar's military cohort, ready and eager to slay without hesitation the "Brutuses" of the regime.[21] Moses remains, however, unimpeachable, even as he goes back up the mountain and returns bearing a second set of stone tablets. He is almost divine in his depiction, with rays of light literally beaming from his head. The people have finally learned their lesson ... or have they? By this point Moses' rule has, in the eyes of some modern critics, reinvented itself as a reign of terror. The desire for freedom has collapsed into a new "thugocracy."

Moses' regime, in any case, will not go unchallenged. What about the other eleven tribes? Why couldn't they have a "tribal confederation," an egalitarian form of government in which all the tribes are on equal footing? Why does one tribe have to be privileged above all the others? What about "Tribes' Rights"? There's no need

---

19 Numbers 12:3.

20 Exodus 32:29.

21 Richard Gabriel, op. cit., 99

here to give Moses a particularly hard time. After all, the Bible itself gives Moses a hard time, the next challenge, oddly enough, arising from the ranks of the Levites themselves. A member of a particular Levite clan named Korakh is joined by three members of the tribe of Reuben – Dathan, Abiram, and On. Approaching Moses and Aaron, they declare:

> You have gone too far! All the members of the camp are holy, each and every one, and God is with them all. Why, then, Moses, do you elevate yourself above the rest of the community?[22]

It seems the "anti-Moses tradition" in the biblical text has reared its head again. Whichever editorial hand was responsible for the final version of the Torah that has come down to us today (traditionalists insist it was Moses himself; most modern scholarship that it was a long process, over centuries), it was deemed fit not to suppress the many stories about opposition to the great lawgiver. They may, across the centuries, be seen as a warning about the limits of power, one taken to heart by the Framers of the U.S. Constitution. But the narrative is written in such a way that Moses is affirmed in the eyes of all Israel, for all time.

As the story continues, Moses issues a challenge: Korakh and his friends are to appear on the morrow, bearing fire and incense in their censers. God will then determine who is deemed worthy to approach the altar. Presumably, the Deity will smite the unworthy in divine judgment. Not wanting to take the chance that they will be the "smitten" ones, the troublemakers respond:

> We will not come up. Is it a small thing that you have brought us up out of a land that flows with milk and honey, to kill us in the wilderness, but must you also seize dominion over us?[23]

The accusation is nothing short of calling Moses a "divine dictator." In the end Korakh summons the whole community to a mighty confrontation, face-to-face with the supreme lawgiver. It's the whole congregation that stands with Korakh, not just a few ne'er-

---

22 Numbers 16: 3-4, author's paraphrase

23 Numbers 16: 12-13.

do-wells, all of which leads scholars to believe that dissatisfaction with Moses' dictatorial ways must have run very deep. But we're not allowed to ponder this angle of the story, since God now threatens to wipe out the entire camp and raise up a new nation from Moses. The lawgiver intercedes on behalf of his wayward flock, putting their interests above his own in some very effective ancient "PR." God chooses in the end not to annihilate the whole people, but only Korakh and his compatriots. In one of the most vivid depictions in the entire biblical canon, the ground itself opens up and swallows the entire cadre of rebels. Once again Moses' "divine dictatorship" has been confirmed.[24]

### Whiskey Rebels and Whoremongers

As we have already noted, George Washington surely stands out among various American heroes who have been compared with Moses. Such was his stature that had he ever been offered kingship, he would have been universally hailed as America's "King George." As we know the general had no such inclination; but on second thought, if Washington had really wanted to be Moses-like, perhaps he should have grabbed for a crown.

In any case, the uncanny parallels between the biblical Exodus and the American revolutionary experience continued in the tradition of rebels who rose up after the revolution succeeded, only to claim that a new tyranny had been imposed. It all had to do with a federal excise tax on Whiskey, tension over which came to a head in Washington's second term. The farmers of Pennsylvania (like Korakh and his cohorts) decided in 1794 that they had had quite enough tyranny from the British and that they didn't need any more from their own new republic. The outrage was even worse inasmuch as drinking was pandemic in early America, so much so that historians have dubbed it the "Alcoholic States of America." Dusting off an old slogan that had served the revolutionary generation quite well, the farmers cried, "No taxation without representation!" For them "big government" was not an option. Washington's position, however,

---

24 Some (e.g. Lincoln Steffens and Thomas Mann) go as far as to view the Moses narrative from the perspective of the hard left, highlighting the "necessity" of violence in revolutions in general. This, it is argued, is why the Bible appears to endorse dictatorship. See Brian M. Britt, *Rewriting Moses: The Narrative Eclipse of the Text* (London: T&T Clark, 2004), 27.

proved just as inflexible as Moses' when faced with such a challenge to the authority of the new federal government. He pointed out that in 1776 the American patriots had rebelled against tax laws passed by King George and his parliament in far-away London. These taxes by contrast had been passed by the Americans themselves in Philadelphia; as the law of the land, they must be payed.

For his part Washington, facing his own incarnation of Korakh's rebellion, assumed his role as commander-in-chief and personally recruited a force of twelve thousand troops, who marched on Pennsylvania. As in the days of Moses, this demonstration of power was sufficient to end the rebellion. In this early clash of federal authority versus "states' rights," it was abundantly clear that central government would reign supreme over local autonomy.[25] Was Washington a tyrant? The whiskey rebels doubtless thought so, even though hardly anyone today would agree with them. But the incident does underscore the tension in every revolution between keeping its spirit alive and "institutionalizing" it. The verdict of history is that both Moses and George Washington were great institutionalizers. Neither Moses nor Washington would take the mantle of royalty, but they were definitely prepared to show everyone who was the boss.

In the case of Israel's "wilderness generation," however, the people still harbor resentment against Moses' "tyranny." The book of Numbers tells us that they complain yet again: "You have killed some of God's people!"[26] Given what they have just witnessed, this is remarkable audacity, indeed hutzpah, and suggests to some critics that the anti-Moses ("Brutus") sentiment was strong enough to propel the dissenters to risk life and limb. On account of this "treason," we are told that a devastating plague breaks out, that would have destroyed the whole camp had not Aaron intervened by standing in their midst with his sanctified fire pan. The plague is halted, but at the cost of some fourteen thousand seven hundred souls.

On the heels of this catastrophe, that leaves the camp littered with corpses, the heads of all the tribes are instructed to bring their wooden staffs of authority to the entrance of the Tabernacle, whereupon a wondrous sign is witnessed. Aaron's rod miraculously

---

25 William Hogeland, *The Whiskey Rebellion: George Washington, Alexander Hamilton, and the Frontier Rebels Who Challenged America's Newfound Sovereignty* (New York: Simon & Schuster: 2006).

26 Numbers 16:41.

sprouts, blossoms, and produces ripe almonds. It is a dire warning, for the entire camp is put on notice that unless they submit to the authority of Aaron, representing a single tribe – Levi – they will all die. Moses' "Praetorian Guard" has once more received the divine endorsement. There will be no "checks and balances," only, in the minds of the dissenters, unbridled autocracy. "Tribes' rights" will be squelched, opposition silenced. It almost sounds like a bad science fiction script: "Resistance is futile!" Of course, this is still the Bible, and we like not to go hard on it. Nonetheless, the political lessons are there, if we care to find them.

Again, Moses is revealed in bloody brutality, whose only excuse is that God is really behind all the violence. We start to wonder when enough is enough, especially as we find yet more internal purgation on the way. It all comes about when the Hebrews are camped in the land of Moab, en-route to Canaan, and they begin to cohabit with the Moabite women. The book of Numbers (chap. 25) accuses them of committing "harlotry" with these foreigners, who also invite them to bow down to their gods. Yet another plague is visited upon the camp, causing multiple thousands more to perish. Moses' response is characteristically heinous. He orders all the Israelite leaders who had participated in the idolatry to be impaled facing the sun, in order to assuage God's wrath. The whole community is reduced to mourning and bitter wailing, when, under their eyes, a young Israelite approaches with a Moabite woman in tow, intending to join her to his family.

The grandson of Aaron, named Pinkhas, apparently schooled in the brutality that runs in the family, follows the Israelite and his female friend into the family tent. Catching them in a moment of intimacy, he grabs a spear and runs them through, completely piercing the Israelite, into the woman's abdomen. Only then is this latest plague lifted, having felled a total of twenty-four thousand. Pinkhas for his part is commended for having deflected the divine anger. We are told that upon him is bestowed God's "Covenant of Peace." Peace? After such grotesque slaughter?[27] Of course, one way to achieve peace is simply to eliminate all one's "enemies." To most readers, Moses remains unimpeachably Moses, but to others he sounds more like "Mr. Mafia." Which leads at least a few research-

---

27 For a discussion of the troublesome attempts to justify such behavior, see George Robinson, *Essential Torah: A Complete Guide to the Five Books of Moses* (New York: Random House, 2006), 481ff.

ers to a daring, unorthodox trifle of speculation, revolving around the end of the lawgiver's life.

## Moses "Snuffed"?

Again, we have to consider the possibility of a "Brutus" tradition hidden away, or perhaps deliberately plastered-over, in the text. As we read about the end of Moses' life, something rather odd strikes us. The great deliverer isn't allowed to enter the Promised Land. In one of the most poignant of biblical passages, Moses, who had spent his career pleading on behalf of his people, beseeches God on his own account and relates to the congregation the divine response:

> And I begged the LORD at that time saying, O, LORD God, You have begun to show Your servant Your greatness, and Your mighty hand. For what God is there in heaven or in earth who can do according to Your works, and according to Your might? I pray you, let me go over and see the good land beyond Jordan, this good hill-country and Lebanon. But the LORD was angry with me because of you and would not hear me.

Notice that he blames the people for his own failings – a serious indication that something isn't "kosher" in Moses' relations with his fellow Israelites. He goes on:

> And the LORD said to me, Enough from you! (author's translation). Speak no more to Me of this matter. Go up into the top of Pisgah and lift up your eyes westward and northward and southward and eastward, and behold it with your eyes. For you shall not go over this Jordan.[28]

The passage seems a trifle peculiar, since the actual reason for Moses being denied the chance to enter the Land of Promise is never specified. We are left to surmise from other places in the narrative that it was due to specific disobedience on Moses' part. We wonder, couldn't God be a little trifle lenient toward his hero, given the tough times through which he had led his flock? Apparently not. The heav-

---

28 Deuteronomy 3:23-27

ens are brass, the verdict unwavering.

Moses goes up to the mountain top, he looks over, and he sees the other side. It's a passage immortalized by Dr. Martin Luther King the night before he was assassinated, as he declared to the world, "I may not get there with you, but we as a people will get to the Promised Land." There he dies, atop Mt. Pisgah, at the very ripe age of one hundred twenty, having led his people through the desert for forty long years, through trial, tribulation and unrelenting hardship. Isn't it unbelievable, that the great lawgiver, the most upright of God's prophets, whose authority was confirmed time and again, by divine intervention, never makes it to the final destination, toward which they had all been traveling? What was the terrible transgression he must have committed that disqualified him from finally setting foot in Canaan and partaking of its bounty, its milk and honey? The generation of the faithless were destined to die in the wilderness, but surely not Moses, the inspired leader, God's "right-hand man."

The one and only reason given by the Bible on which account Moses is sentenced to die is that when the people had earlier complained of thirst, and when God directed the lawgiver to speak to a rock, whereupon water would miraculously gush out, Moses instead struck the rock with his staff. And yes, water gushed forth. That was it? That was the unforgivable sin, the horrible transgression that barred Moses from entering Canaan? Most readers at this point look up from the biblical narrative and mutter to the Almighty, "You've got to be kidding!" But that's the reasoning the Bible gives us. Given the incredibility of the whole story, there are at least a few daring researches who have come up with an audacious theory. It is suggested that the anti-Moses faction never abated, but in fact intensified in the face of the lawgiver's unrelenting autocracy. Moreover, the people had experienced not only triumphs during the course of their forty-year sojourn, but perilous times as well, from merciless exterminatory campaigns against surrounding peoples (Midianites, Ammonites, Amalekites and others), to humiliating attacks on their own ranks by Moses' "Praetorian Guard," the Levites. Could it be, as certain commentators (Freud included) speculate, that at some point the same people who had long chafed under Moses' autocratic rule finally rose up and struck him down?[29]

---

29 Enamuel Rice, Freud and Moses: *The Long Journey Home* (Albany, NY: State Univ. Of New York Press, 1990), 144; Jonathan Kirsch, *Moses: A Life* (New York: Ballantine,

People understandably recoil at the very thought that Moses, ancient paragon of righteousness, may have been killed by his own people, and that the Bible may be "covering" for him. The very thought seems ...sacrilegious. We do in fact have to be careful before glibly assenting to this theory, since even those who advance it admit that there is not a shred of hard evidence to back up the supposition. This is the kind of sleuthing we might expect from Sherlock Holmes, not serious researchers, but when the rather peculiar circumstances of Moses' death are examined with a discerning eye, the murder theory might not be as spectacular as it might be regarded at first blush. Holmes might exclaim, "Elementary!" Moses may have cried, "Et tu, Brute?"

1999), 329ff.

# 3
# "HERE COME THE JUDGES!" - THE FIRST "LIBERTARIANS"

*"The ultimate aim of government is not to rule, or restrain, by fear, nor to exact obedience, but contrariwise, to free every man from fear, that he may live in all possible security; in other words, to strengthen his natural right to exist and work without injury to himself or others... In fact, the true aim of government is liberty."* – Baruch Spinoza[1]

**F**or the young American nation the revolution lasted a few tumultuous years, from 1775 to 1783, and then it was over ... but not really. From the beginning there was an understanding that gaining independence from Britain was only the "first act" in an ongoing play, to determine what the boundaries of the new nation would be. Like the Israelites of old, this was a growing republic, expanding inexorably westward, according to "divine providence." Israel would cross the Jordan River to the west; the Americans would in time cross the Mississippi. In both cases, "providence" turned out to be a long and bloody process.

In 1751 the Pennsylvania Assembly had ordered the casting of

---

1 *Theological-Political Treatise*, 1670

a great bell to commemorate the fiftieth anniversary of the state's first constitution. Bearing the inscription from Leviticus 25:10, "Proclaim Liberty throughout all the land unto all the inhabitants thereof," it was pressed into service of the revolutionary cause on July 8, 1776. When it rang that day, it was literally the chime heard round the world. The Liberty Bell represents more than the simple tradition of appealing to biblical/ religious language in the public square. It tells us that rank and file Americans indeed thought of the new nation in terms of biblical Israel. It tells us that the American revolution was indeed conceived as a modern "exodus" from the bondage of Egypt. But it also tells us that revolution was only the beginning of a process that would culminate in the conquest of "the Promised Land." When Moses passes his mantle of leadership to Joshua, a new story will begin – the conquest of the land of Canaan. When General Washington passed his own mantle – the presidency – to a cadre of successors, John Adams, Thomas Jefferson, James Madison, et al, he was also passing the new republic to generations of pioneers, who would expand the country across the plains and prairies, west of the Appalachians, and one day on the the Pacific. For better or for worse, the early American citizenry grasped the parallels with Joshua and the ancient conquerors of Canaan, as they pressed their claims on boundless new territories.

### The Would-Be Joshua's of 1600 Pennsylvania Avenue

In 1803 Jefferson bought from the French the entire land mass stretching from the Gulf of Mexico to Canada – the Louisiana Purchase. In 1830 President Andrew Jackson sensed the need to establish total hegemony over the eastern half of the continent, in the expectation of moving west, and issued the Indian Removal Act. This enabled the Chief Executive to forcibly uproot the five Indian nations who inhabited the land east of the Mississippi River. The Choctaw, Chickasaw, Creek, Seminole, and Cherokee tribes were directly impacted by the edict. One of these tribes, the Cherokee, who at the time resided in Georgia, decided on a surprising course of action. Rather than going on the warpath, as their ancestors would surely have done, their strategy was to file a lawsuit against the State of Georgia. Battling their cause all the way to the Supreme Court of the United States, they were surprised when they discovered that they had in fact won their case. Andrew Jackson, however, didn't quite see things in the same light as the Chief Justice, declaring with harsh invective, "John Marshall has made his decision, now let him enforce it!"[2] In the end, the five native American nations were compelled at gunpoint to begin their melancholy "Trail of Tears," evacuating their tribal lands on a forced march westward. Of the Cherokees alone, we know that one out of every four perished along the way.

The decision represents one of the most tragic moments in American history and definitely tainted Andrew Jackson's career and his presidential legacy. But never mind that; a catchy phrase, "manifest destiny," would be employed by those who called for the annexation of Texas, a seemingly inevitable part of the nation's great expansion.[3] The term first appeared in print in 1839, and, thanks to journalist John L. O'Sullivan, found its way into the New York press in 1845, the same year that James K. Polk, a consummate American expansionist, entered the White House. Polk was the president who, more than any, was cut from Andrew Jackson's cloth, described by one historian as being wedded with Jackson at the hip and at the head.[4] As such, he favored the supremacy of the executive branch over Congress, and that made him a "big government guy." His party, the Democrats, were accused by the opposition Whigs as being nothing less than autocrats.

Though seldom considered today among the pantheon of "great" presidents, Polk was in many ways America's Joshua. He accepted implicitly the quasi-religious doctrine of "manifest destiny," which he personally embodied and considered his presidential mandate. Specifically, he threatened war with Britain over the issue of the Oregon territory, stirring up the western pioneers, who in turn adopted the slogan, "Fifty-four forty (the desired northern parallel for the border) or fight!" Polk has been credited for his flexibility in the matter, as he ultimately settled on the forty-ninth parallel, thereby avoiding further conflict with America's old nemesis across the "pond."

Polk did not flinch at all, however, when it came to the southwest, which he greatly coveted in that nation's push to the Pacific.

---

2 Charles Warren, *The Supreme Court in United States History: Volume Two, 1821-1855* (Washington, D.C.: Beard Books, 1999), 219.

3 Richard A. Harris, Daniel J. Tichenor, eds., *History of the United States Political System: Ideas, Interests, and Institutions* (Santa Barbara, CA: ABC-CLIO, LLC, 2010), 52ff.

4 See John Seigenthaler, *James K. Polk* (New York: Times Books, 2004).

His declaration of war on the government of Mexico in 1846 was roundly criticized by such notables as Unitarian minister Henry David Thoreau, but he didn't care. God was on his side, or so he thought. This land was his land. The result of America's lopsided victory of 1848 would be the acquisition of Texas and California. During Polk's tenure as president, he extended the country's borders all the way from the Mississippi River to the continent's western shores. He made the United States a truly continental nation, "from sea to shining sea." Joshua of old could hardly have done better.

### Joshua: General or Jihadist?

Polk of course was only a president. Looking back on biblical days, we can think of Joshua as real "general," a military commander of unsurpassed acumen, the Douglas MacArthur of his day. He wasn't a Moses, and there's no indication that he wanted to be. Was he an "autocrat," a "divine dictator" in the tradition of Moses? Oddly enough, there's no sense of backbiting against him, no "anti-Joshua" tradition that we can discern in the narrative. What we do see in Joshua is a leader capable of the wholesale slaughter of his enemies, the Canaanites who are occupying the land promised to Abraham, but at the same time keeping the tribal league of Israelites intact as a loose confederation, owing allegiance to no man, only to God. We go as a far as to say that politically speaking, Joshua is notable not for what he was but for what he wasn't, namely a king.

The worst we can call Joshua is a "jihadist," for mounting a brutal campaign of extermination against the Canaanite population that some liken to "genocide." But we can't get away with calling him a political tyrant. There's no mention of Joshua slaying his own people, as Moses had ordered the Levites to do. He does seem to have established the first set of "republican" laws for the new nation. No one knows exactly which laws these early Israelites are able to put into practice, but the Bible prominently mentions a "Mayflower Compact" of sorts, set forth by Joshua. No one knows with certainty exactly which laws are in force during this early "league" of Israelite tribes, but we are told:

And Joshua made a covenant with the people that day, and set them a statute and an ordinance in Shechem. And

Joshua wrote these words in the book of the law of God.[5]

Which words, exactly, did he write? Hadn't Moses already delivered reams of laws in the Torah itself? What kind of government does Israel's greatest general have in mind? It must have been "diffuse" and decentralized, yet cemented together by a "covenant" – a "compact" that demanded loyalty, not to a Moses-like leader with total authority, but God alone, via a series of ethical precepts. Scholars speculate that Joshua's "statute" may have consisted of nothing less than a stand-alone set of laws, as found in the book of Exodus, known as the so-called "Covenant Code":[6]

> And these are the judgments which you shall set before them. If you buy a Hebrew servant, he shall serve six years. And in the seventh he shall go out free for nothing... And if the servant shall plainly say, I love my master, my wife, and my sons. I do not want to go out free his master shall bring him to the judges. He shall also bring him to the door or to the door-post. And his master shall bore his ear through with an awl, and he shall serve him forever... He that strikes a man, so that he dies, shall be surely put to death. And if a man does not lie in wait, but God delivers him into his hand, then I will appoint you a place where he shall flee. But if a man comes presumptuously upon his neighbor to slay him with guile, you shall take him from My altar, so that he may die. And he that strikes his father or his mother shall surely be put to death... And if a man strikes his servant, or his maidservant, with a rod, and he dies under his hand, he shall surely be punished... If men strive and strike a pregnant woman, so that her child comes out, and there is no injury, he shall surely be punished, according as the woman's husband will lay upon him. And he shall pay as the judges say...[7]

---

5 Joshua 24:25-26.

6 The passage contains what appear to be "echoes" of the specific language of the book of Deuteronomy. See Mar E. Mills, *Joshua to Kings: History, Story, Theology* (London: T&T Clark, 2006), 123.

7 Exodus 21:1-20.

While rudimentary in many ways and definitely "severe" by most modern standards, these simple statutes nonetheless express a remarkable concept for an ancient society – that specific rights are to be allotted in equal measure to all people, not on the basis of social class or societal standing, imposed by some rigid hierarchy. Moreover, these rights extend to society's most vulnerable members, even to servants, even to the unborn. Such notions are not to be taken for granted, down to our own day, when, for example, a Supreme Court nominee finds it difficult, during confirmation hearings, to embrace the constitutional language, that people are endowed by their Creator with certain inalienable rights.[8] The Constitution is of course based on the ideas of "natural law," which in turn can be traced back to the Hebrew Bible; but in the twenty-first century "natural law" is out, relativistic ethics "in."

Joshua, by contrast, has no difficulty recognizing the divine source of law or his own mandate for applying the law fairly, as God's "agent." Scholars point out that these laws from the Torah seem to fit the needs of a simple society of shepherds and farmers.[9] They don't reflect a hierarchical society of monarchs and serfs. In fact, the first thing we notice is that under this code (while it allows slavery, as did almost all ancient societies), slaves are allowed to go free after serving six years. But the slave might also "love" the master to the extent of wanting to remain a slave in perpetuity. How odd, that even slaves are to be treated as valuable members of the ancient household. Beyond this statute, there is provision for capital punishment, but also provision for a place where one might flee, so as to avoid the death penalty. Other statutes, covering, for example, an assault on one's parents, or on a servant, or an assault on a pregnant woman resulting in a miscarriage, fall into the category known to-

---

8 *The Washington Post*, TRANSCRIPT: The Elena Kagan Hearings - June 28, 29 and 30, 2010.
COBURN: So -- so you wouldn't embrace what the Declaration of Independence says, that we have certain God-given, inalienable rights that aren't given in the Constitution, that they're ours, ours alone, and that the government doesn't give those to us?
KAGAN: Senator Coburn, I believe that the Constitution is an extraordinary document, and I'm not saying I do not believe that there are rights pre-existing the Constitution and the laws, but my job as a justice is to enforce the Constitution and the laws.

9 In an agrarian society, for example, land was the primary means of production, and the legal statutes of the Torah are designed to make sure that the Israelite peasant may retain this important asset. See Joshua Berman, *Created Equal: How the Bible Broke with Ancient Political Thought* (New York: Oxford Univ. Press, 2008).

day as "tort law." The guiding principle is that punishment must be appropriate and proportional. The "revolution" of the exodus from Egypt is evolving into an ordered society. As the Israelites abandon their nomadic ways and settle down, it is being "institutionalized."

So, is Joshua a "jihadist"? Hardly a palatable designation for a true biblical hero. In his defense, we can say: certainly not from the look of these early statutes governing a rudimentary, agrarian society. Moreover, archaeologists have for decades been turning over their spades all over modern Israel, looking for evidence of the jihad itself, without much to show for their efforts. Even the fabled city of Jericho, whose walls "came tumblin' down," doesn't show evidence of massive destruction during the period in question. In fact, the majority of scholars are of the opinion that it wasn't even inhabited at the time Joshua would have invaded (around 1200 BCE). And if it had been inhabited, it most likely would have been a small, unwalled village.[10] By the same token, archaeology seems to indicate that someone invaded the land of Canaan in the Late Bronze Age, the most telling example being the fortress city of northern Galilee, Hazor. The remains of this city are impressive, and show hard evidence of having been burned and pillaged. There are even remains of pagan idols, that appear to have been systematically decapitated. "If Joshua did not conquer this city," asks Israeli archaeologist Amnon Ben-Tor, "who did, people from outer space?"[11] There is, however, no evidence of blitzkreig, no wholesale destruction of the entire land, no genocidal slaughter of the inhabitants of Canaan.

Some have advanced the idea that Joshua's conquest of Canaan may have been more of a peaceful infiltration of semi-nomads, turned "yeoman farmers," the latter of course being Thomas Jefferson's ultimate ideal. As the term evolved in England, and later in colonial America, it denoted those who cultivated their own land, not "serfs," but maintaining genuine political rights. These were free individuals, destined to be made or broken by their own diligent labor. Historically, yeoman farmers gained a solid reputation for their industriousness. Little wonder that Jefferson appealed directly to biblical Israel when he declared: "Those who labor in the earth

---

10 Amon Ben-Tor, R. Greenberg, *The Archaeology of Ancient Israel* (New Haven, CT: Yale Univ. Press, 1994), 131; Carolyn Pressler, *Joshua, Judges, and Ruth* (Louisville, KY: Westminster John Knox Press, 2002), 45.

11 Amnon Ben-Tor, R. Greenberg, op. cit., 284; see also "Digging for the Truth: Archaeology and the Bible," History Channel production, 2001.

are the chosen people of God, if ever He had a chosen people."[12] He held that the closer the bond between the people and the land, the more free they would be to live in a manner that is more "natural." This in turn would lead to a more complete expression of their "inalienable rights," and a closer connection to God, as the supreme source of those rights.

Law today has in fact been described as having variable content, where sociological good, as determined by the consensus of society, is king.[13] The ideas of the Founders, predicated on the biblical model, are seen as curiously antiquated if not hopelessly out-of-date. The weakness of the modern approach, however, is that law ultimately becomes whatever the justices say it is. And more often than not, the judges are influenced by whatever a majority of the population at any given time want it to be. As noted, if we're looking for "genocide" in the Bible, we'll be hard pressed to find it, based on historical/ archaeological evidence. But the genocidal legacy of the last century – the extermination of millions by Hitler and millions more by Stalin, among others – are ample testimony of what happens when law becomes the fickle product of a 51% majority.

### Enter, the Spinmeisters

At the end of the great general's life, the Bible declares:

Now Joshua was old, going on in days. And the LORD said to him, You are old, far along in days, and there remains yet very much land to be possessed.[14]

Instead of jihad and genocide, we find that a great deal of the Promised Land has yet to be conquered by the Israelites. We actually start to wonder how good a general Joshua is after all. In the final analysis, the picture that begins to emerge from the biblical account is a gradual, two-century long process of "conquest" that encompasses the books of Joshua and Judges together, as one on-

---

12 Thomas Jefferson, Notes on the State of Virginia, Query XIX. See Jed Rubenfeld, *Freedom and Time: A Theory of Constitutional Self-Government* (New Haven, CT: Yale Univ. Press, 2001), 20.

13 Francis A. Schaeffer, *How Should We Then Live?: The Rise and Decline of Western Thought and Culture* (New York: Fleming H. Revell, 1976), 218.

14 Joshua 13:1.

going narrative of migration, settling down, and occasional battles and skirmishes with the local Canaanites.[15] The "real" history of the period doesn't make as compelling a story as the glorified hero-stories of biblical lore, but it tells us a lot about the struggles, not only of ancient Israelites, but of early Americans, to form "a more perfect union."

But there's yet something more going on in the account of Joshua-Judges than an homage to Israel's conquering heroes. In fact the best way to understand the book of Judges, right from the out-set, is to look at how it ends. There, in the last chapter, the very last verse, we read:

> In those days there was no king in Israel. Every one did the right in his own eyes.[16]

The words sound pious and well-intentioned. What an indict-ment of the people's apostasy, of their self-centeredness, their lack of trust in the Almighty. Surely, the two-hundred year period from the exodus from Egypt to Israel's first kings – Saul and David – must have been very dark indeed. It must have been chaos epitomized, lawless and brutal, an ancient version of the "Wild Wild West." This, however, might amount to "somebody else's" version of his-tory, perhaps the work of an editorial hand, centuries removed from the events being described.[17] The key piece of evidence, that any Sherlockian sleuth would point to, lies in the implicit comment that the period of the judges is so bad because Israel had no king. What? Can we believe our spiritual eyes and ears? In other words, the brave band of refugees from Egypt's tyrannical pharaoh, whose only goal is "freedom," are helplessly doomed to chaos and apostasy unless they have a king? How should we view this: truth or spin?

But who would spin holy narrative, and why? The answer is again, as Holmes would put it, "elementary." Who but a royal scribe, living some two hundred years later, in the direct employ of the Jerusalem monarchy, whose principal task is to write a history that will justify the House of King David? The main rule in produc-

---

15 William G. Dever, *Who Were the Early Israelites and Where Did They Come From?* (Grand Rapids: Eerdmans, 2003), 228

16 Judges 21:25.

17 Robert H. O'Connell, *The Rhetoric of the Book of Judges* (Leiden: E.J. Brill, 1996), 230.

ing this history is simple. Whatever the period of the Judges may have been like, however noble the principles of the early Israelite confederation, it must be presented as an age that is out of control, pregnantly waiting the imposition of the Davidic monarchy.

The reality, however, is that after the days of Joshua but before the people begin clamoring for a king, there is what may best be described as a "confederacy" of tribes. They may not know it, but they are taking part in a grand experiment in political theory that will one day serve as a model for the United States of America. Both ancient Israel and the American republic are founded on a single principle, namely, of avoiding tyranny, the rule of any single individual over the many. Their ideal is a conglomerate of self-governing units – Israelite tribes or American states.

Thomas Paine, in his classic *Common Sense*, draws the analogy in the clearest of terms:

> Near three thousand years passed away, from the Mosaic account of the creation, till the Jews under a national delusion requested a king. Till then their form of government (except in extraordinary cases where the Almighty interposed) was a kind of Republic, administered by a judge and the elders of the tribes. Kings they had none, and it was held sinful to acknowledge any being under that title but the Lord of Hosts. And when a man seriously reflects on the idolatrous homage which is paid to the persons of kings, he need not wonder that the Almighty, ever jealous of his honour, should disapprove a form of government which so impiously invades the prerogative of Heaven.[18]

Preserving the values that Thomas Paine and his comrades struggled for was the aim of the new nation's earliest government. They insisted, as did ancient Israel, that "we have no king but God!" It is no accident that in Hebrew liturgy, down to the present day, God is referred to as "exalted King." This isn't just an elitist, sexist way of identifying the Divine; it's a bold statement that we, down here, don't have, nor will we accept any human potentate. We let God fill that role. That was the model the Founders looked to, which is why

---

18 Thomas Paine, *Common Sense* (Alexandria, VA: TheCapitol.Net, 2009), 13.

the Second Continental Congress selected a committee to formulate a series of "Articles" ... of Confederation. Drafted during the revolution, they were sent to the states and finally ratified in 1781.

Thirteen semi-independent, sovereign states, joined together by a loose "covenant" of sorts, twelve semi-independent, sovereign tribes, plus a "universal" priestly tribe of Levites, joined together by Moses' commandments and Joshua's statutes. Under the Articles, there was no executive branch of government, no president, and a very limited judiciary. The federal government had no power to wage war, raise armies, collect taxes, control trade, or pass any number of laws that might interfere with the powers of the local state governments. After all, power and authority were what took natural rights away, which is why they must be curbed.

And curbed they were during the Israelite "confederacy." Gone is the Levitical "Praetorian Guard" of "hit men," such as existed under Moses. Instead the Levites seem to be in their proper place, acting as, of all things, priests! The semi-nomads of the previous generation become true "yeoman farmers," adopting the Jeffersonian ideal before ever there was a Jefferson. We might think of them as the Bible's "Libertarians." Each tribe takes care of its own affairs, within more-or-less defined borders established by Joshua, from Judah and Simeon in the south to Asher and Naphtali in northern Galilee. All authority, all power, is local, deriving from the extended family units comprising the tribes. Each tribe of course has "elders," tribal "chiefs" who coordinate among themselves and act as representatives in negotiating with other tribes, as the need arises.

The society itself is remarkably "egalitarian" for the ancient world, with no sense of rigid hierarchy, as we find in other monarchical states such as Egypt.[19] A prime example is the book of Ruth, set in the period of the Judges and giving us a "slice of life" in those days. It's been described as "a woman's story in a man's world," telling the tale of two brave heroines, Naomi and Ruth. The women journey back to Naomi's ancestral home in Bethlehem of Judah, after a famine had brought her now-deceased husband eastward to Moab. Ruth, a Moabitess who had married Naomi's son (also now-deceased), meets a Bethlehemite "man of means" named Boaz, who ends up marrying her. As Providence has it, Ruth becomes the

---

19 Joshua Berman, op. cit. Berman demonstrates that in contrast to other ancient societies, all Israelites are equal citizens because all were liberated from Egyptian bondage; all stood at Mount Sinai to receive the law, and all entered into a covenant with God.

grandmother of Israel's greatest hero, David. The age described by the book has been described by commentators as largely peaceful and marked by mutuality and cooperative endeavor among families and tribes.[20]

When trouble comes in the form of hostile invaders, what's the answer? Since there is no standing army – something George Washington railed against in his Farewell Address – their only recourse is to mobilize a militia. They are Israel's version of the "minute men," who can spring into action at a moment's notice.

## The Man Who Would Not, and the Man Who Would Be King

Take the case of one of Israel's most famous judges, Gideon, who does battle against a horde of Midianite and Amalekite invaders and occupiers. They had crossed the Jordan River, westward, setting up camp in the Jezreel Valley. A member of the tribe of Manasseh, Gideon sets out to gather a militia, by dispatching messengers to the neighboring tribes of Asher, Zebulun, and Naphtali. There is always question as to whether numbers raised will be sufficient to drive out the enemy, an obvious weakness of the "militia system."

We should contrast the period of the Judges with other ancient nations, that did maintain standing armies. In Babylon, the great emperor Sargon "invented" the standing army. From every city in his empire he conscripted an enormous force of five thousand four hundred men. Expensive as this army was to maintain, Sargon devised the perfect means to support them. He set them loose to fend for themselves – by pillage and plunder. At the beginning of every harvest season the campaigns were set to go, and what followed was a bona-fide "age of terror" beyond our worst imagination.

Israel, however, is designed to be different. Like early America, it will field "citizen soldiers," not conscripts or mercenaries. They fight when the need arises, going back to their farms and businesses when they are no longer needed. Gideon gathers his troops, but is surprised when God delivers a message: he has raised too large an army. "Oy vey!" he must surely be thinking. He has to pare them down. He is divinely instructed to bring his men down to the water and observe how they drink. Those who lap the water like dogs are sent home; those who cup it in their hands are "hired." The total

---

20 Peter H.W. Lau, *Identity and Ethics in the Book of Ruth: A Social Identity Approach* (Berlin, New York: Walter de Gruyter GmbH & Co., 2011), 48.

number: 300. But never mind; size doesn't always matter. Furthermore, Gideon is a master tactician.

He leads his little flock to the edge of the Midianite camp and instructs them to conceal torches inside clay pitchers, which they will break in unison at the sound of the ram's horn. Then they will commence blowing their own ram's horns, conveying the impression that a huge army has gathered against them. The plan works. When the pitchers are broken, the enemy behold a sea of torches surrounding them, and, as the Israelites jointly shout, "A sword for the Lord and for Gideon!", they flee in panic, striking each other down in confusion. It's an utter rout. Needless to say, the tribes are pleased with their "judge."

But what they do next is a definite "precedent breaker" for the young Israelite "republic." In a moment of seeming madness, they beseech Gideon:

> Rule over us, both you and your son, and your son's son also. For you have delivered us from the hand of Midian.[21]

What? The previous generation having endured the tyranny of Egypt, they nonetheless want a k...k...k...king? Fortunately for all their sakes, Gideon is not amused, and retorts:

> I will not rule over you, neither shall my son rule over you. The LORD shall rule over you.[22]

When it comes to the basic principles of the Israelite nation, Gideon "gets it." As long as God is acknowledged as King, no human being can fill that role. Nor can there be any "dynastic succession" of judges, but leaders will arise as needed.

Thomas Paine "got it" too. On this precise biblical narrative he comments:

> The children of Israel being oppressed by the Midianites, Gideon marched against them with a small army, and victory thro' the divine interposition decided in his favour.

---

21 Judges 8:22.
22 Judges 8:23.

The Jews, elate with success, and attributing it to the generalship of Gideon, proposed making him a king, saying, "Rule thou over us, thou and thy son, and thy son's son." Here was temptation in its fullest extent; not a kingdom only, but an hereditary one; but Gideon in the piety of his soul replied, "I will not rule over you, neither shall my son rule over you. THE LORD SHALL RULE OVER YOU." Words need not be more explicit: Gideon doth not decline the honour, but denieth their right to give it; neither doth he compliment them with invented declarations of his thanks, but in the positive style of a prophet charges them with disaffection to their proper Sovereign, the King of Heaven.[23]

George Washington also "got it." He harbored a lifelong abhorrence of monarchy and would never have entertained the notion of becoming a king himself. The story has been circulated that he was once offered a crown by his own troops, only to turn it down. The account is probably apocryphal, but if anyone had an ability to grab for a royal title at the dawn of the new nation, it would without question have been G.W. One writer labelled him a "virtuoso of resignations," since he surrendered power not once but twice.[24] First, he resigned his commission at the close of the Revolutionary War, returning to Mount Vernon. Later, he walked away from the presidency at the end of a second term, in spite of appeals that he stay on.

Unfortunately, however, one of Gideon's many sons, with a curious name to match, is destined to make a bold power-grab after his father leaves the scene. He is called Abimelech (not to be confused with the Philistine king of the same name whom Abraham encountered). It ironically translates as "my father, the king," and seems to indicate that he felt an inherited right to power, notwithstanding that he was only the son of Gideon's concubine. His objective: to establish his personal, authoritarian rule over the tribe of Ephraim.

He starts by approaching his relatives on his mother's side, noting that his father (very much the virile fellow) had left some seventy offspring in his mighty wake. Fairly good with persuasion, his rea-

---

23 *The People Shall Judge*, Vol. 1, Part 1 (Chicago: Univ. of Chicago Press, 1976 ), 186.

24 See Gary Wills, *Cincinnatus: George Washington and the Enlightenment* (Garden City, NY: Doubleday, 1984), 3

soning is as follows:

> Which is better for you, either that all the sons of [Gide-
> on], seventy persons, reign over you, or that one reign
> over you?[25]

Isn't that how tyrants gain power? By convincing the gullible
that rule by one person is a lot less "messy" than rule by the many?
How many times in history has the liberty purchased by the blood
of true liberators has been squandered, often within a single generation, for some kind of imposed order? As the story proceeds,
the dastardly Abimelech rounds up his brothers – all seventy – and
puts them to the sword on a single rock. The only survivor is young
Jotham, the most junior of the troop, who goes up to the mountain,
takes up a woeful lament, and recounts a fearsome parable to the
assembled tribal elders:

> The trees went forth to anoint a king over them. And they
> said to the olive tree, Reign over us. But the olive tree
> said to them, Should I leave my fatness … and go to be
> promoted over the trees? And the trees said to the fig tree,
> You come and reign over us. But the fig tree said to them,
> Should I forsake my sweetness and my good fruit, and
> go to be promoted over the trees? Then the trees said to
> the vine, You come and reign over us. And the vine said
> to them, Should I leave my wine, which cheers God and
> man, and go to be promoted over the trees? Then all the
> trees said to the bramble-bush, You come and reign over
> us. And the bramble-bush said to the trees, If you truly
> anoint me king over you, come put your trust in my shad-
> ow. And if not, let fire come out of the bramble and burn
> up the cedars of Lebanon.[26]

The book of Judges is shouting a lesson at us, that the price
of liberty is eternal vigilance. And to many scholars it looks like
the anti-monarchy source (the "Brutus" source) is again interject-
ing itself into the narrative.[27] Abimelech for his part proceeds with

---

25 Judges 9:2.
26 Judges 9:8-15.
27 Geoffrey P. Miller, *The Ways of a King: Legal and Political Ideas in the Bible* (Gotten:

his royal ambitions, setting himself up as king in the Israelite city of Shechem. But the city's inhabitants resist. "Who is this Abimelech?" asks Gaal son of Ebed, a "troublemaker" with ambitions of his own. "Are we to be his slaves? If the people were to transfer their allegiance to me, I would oust him!" On receiving word that a rebel has come to the city to incite revolt, Abimelech adopts a new *modus operandi*: "If you can't convince 'em, slaughter 'em!" As if to fulfill the fearsome prophecy, Abimelech "the bramble" sets fire to the city, burns it to the ground and sows it with salt, using the massacre as an example to all others who might resist his authoritarian rule.

Fortunately for the Israelite tribal alliance, Abimelech's bold gambit ends in disgrace, but not without a touch of ironic humor. The man who would be king next lays siege to the city of Thebez, but just as it looks as though he might prevail, a heavy stone is tossed down from the top of the outer defensive wall, and it just so happens to land squarely on Abimelech's head, crushing his skull. And who is the stone-tosser but a woman - a tidbit that ancient audiences, patriarchal and sexist as they were, would have found more than a little amusing. We don't even know her name, but she isn't the only woman to feature prominently in the book. (Others include Deborah, Yael the prophetess, and the notorious Delilah.) Some researchers, having donned their detective beanies and following the trail of deductive reasoning, have gone as far as to speculate that the anonymous author of the book of Judges may in fact have been a woman - a ancient proto-feminist of no small literary acumen. But the writer, whoever he or she was, displays a keen sensitivity for the republican principles of that unique historical moment in early Israel. The text is virtually shouting its message: "Listen, Abimelech, you dummy! That government which governs LEAST governs best!" Tyranny, the rule of the few over the many (or in this case of the one over the many) is destined to fail. God will see to it that tyrants fall, sometimes by the agency of the most overlooked people in our midst. A lucky stone will find it's mark (transmuted in this story into a powerful symbol of liberation) - a stone tossed by a woman.

### Beating Up Benjamin

The book of Judges concludes with a hideous account of an

---

Vandenhoeck & Ruprecht, 2011), 240ff.

internecine conflict that nearly obliterates the tribe of Benjamin. It all begins when a Levite from the hill country of Ephraim acquires a concubine from Bethlehem, in the southern tribe of Judah. She takes leave of him, however, and returns to her home, provoking the Levite to seek her out. On arriving at her home in Bethlehem, the concubine's father insists that he stay with them. After remaining there several nights, the Levite takes his concubine and heads on his way. While in Gibeah, in the land of Benjamin, an old man offers them lodging. As they enjoy a repast together, a mob from the town begin pounding on the door, demanding sexual relations with the Levite. In order to satisfy them, the old man offers his own virgin daughter and the Levite's concubine. The Levite himself, we are told, casts his concubine to the mob, who rape and abuse her all night, leaving her dead at the door. The Levite takes her body home, where, in his rage, he carves it into twelve pieces, dispatching a piece to each tribe, in order to rally them against the tribe of Benjamin.

The result is internecine war. The tribal leaders assemble at Bethel inquire of God, "Who should be the first to attack the Benjamites?" God's answer is: "Let Judah go up first." Some scholars detect in this a later scribal hand, writing in such a way as to justify the kingly line of David, who hailed from Bethlehem, of the tribe of Judah. The whole story comes from the perspective of the pro-monarchy source, whose editorial task is to prove that Israel desperately needed a king, and that this king must be David.[28] The previous age of a loose tribal confederacy was unacceptable and chaotic. Judah, then, gets the "honor" of commencing the slaughter! It was all foreordained, and the fact that Judah does the grizzly work of leading the charge is even "prophetic" of the glorious Davidic dynasty that is destined to rise to power. And they do it pretty well, for the narrative tells us that over 25,000 Benjamite swordsmen die in battle. That, however, isn't enough. All the towns of Benjamin are put to the sword, including the livestock and everything else that draws breath. Thereafter, everything is burned to the ground.

Unlike the other stories in the book of Judges, there is no deliverance to be found here, no symbols of liberation. The weapons wielded do not bring about freedom; they are used against each other. This tale of woe is the "lead-up" to the final declaration of the book of Judges, that everyone did what was right in his own

---

28 Barry Bandstra, *Reading the Old Testament: An Introduction to the Hebrew Bible* (Stamford, CT: Wadsworth, Cengage Learning, 2004), 231f.

eyes, presumably because there was no king in Israel. But something doesn't quite seem right here, chronologically speaking. The tribe of Benjamin is decimated and depopulated at the end of the story; yet when we encounter them again in the very next book of the Bible – 1 Samuel – they are depicted as a vital and healthy tribe. Even if the Benjamites were veritable rabbits, they couldn't have spawned so many descendants so quickly. At this point, biblical scholars weigh in with a bit more textual sleuthing.

Could it be, that the devastating war against Benjamin actually transpired earlier, much earlier, than its last-place location among the stories of the judges? Might the internecine conflict have taken place more toward the beginning of the two hundred year period covered by the book? In that case it wouldn't be surprising to find a repopulated tribe at the beginning of 1 Samuel. Why would the editors of holy writ switch the order of the stories? They have plenty of motive, in wanting to show that the Israelites really do need a king to keep them from butchering each other. It is the best way to justify the very institution that had always been anathema both to Israel and to God.[29] And who are these editors with a political angle?

### Brutus in the Bible

A traditional interpretation of the book of Judges is to assert that "the land was not yet ready for a king," but do we have enough hutzpah to declare that no land is ever "ready" for a king? Part of the allure of the biblical monarchy is that it anticipates the line of King David, who at this point in history is still "waiting in the wings." It is David who will bring true greatness to the Israelite nation, who will turn Israel into an ancient version of Lyndon Johnson's "Great Society." That of course means emphasizing not so much the individual as the "collective" – not a bad idea in theory and as near to the Jewish psyche as lochs and bagels are to the Jewish palate. It is the collective, not the image of the "Lone Ranger," that has been central to Jewish culture down through the ages and into the present.

Collectivism, however, is exactly the idea used by many modern political theorists to justify "big government," and this may help explain why Jews have historically tilted to the left, politically. Indeed, it is the left, especially the socialist left, who have always

---

29 Miller, op. cit., 236ff.

hailed the virtue of the collective. After all, in Hillary Clinton's words, "It takes a village!" Karl Marx was certainly big on the collective, as was Comrade Lenin. Now, no one is trying to argue that the collective wasn't important in biblical Israel. But we also need to recognize that ancient Israel and kindred societies were made up of much smaller collectives within the larger community. This was a very different reality than the bloated "big government" we see today in many western capitals. On the contrary, it was much closer to the Founders' idea of "federalism." Never mind, however; later editors of the biblical text – the "spinmeisters" – would besmirch the period of the Judges, just as modern American history books generally denigrate the Articles of Confederation and the period prior to the Constitution of 1787. In both ancient Israel and modern America, "big government" decidedly wins the day. One thing is clear: *history is written by the victors.*

Of course there is considerable reason for "beating up" on the Articles of Confederation, due to their conspicuous absence of any provision for a strong central government. We shouldn't be surprised that this is exactly the line fed to us in school, in our earliest childhood civics classes. Nonetheless, while there were unquestioned weaknesses with the Articles, "Brutus" (Robert Yates) and others continued to sound the alarm about the perils of top-heavy, central government. In the book of Judges, the judiciary (like the authority of the individual tribes) is local. Individual judges preside over what amounts to a "people's court." All of that will be quashed when Israel's first monarchs arise, and the lesson will be appropriated by Yates' biting commentary on the proposed Constitution (*Brutus*, no. 11):

> The real effect of this system of government, will therefore be brought home to the feelings of the people, through the medium of the judicial power. It is, moreover, of great importance, to examine with care *the nature and extent of the judicial power*, because those who are to be vested with it, are to be placed in a situation altogether unprecedented in a free country. They are to be rendered totally independent, both of the people and the legislature, both with respect to their offices and salaries. *No errors they may commit can be corrected by any power above them*, if any such power there be, nor can they be removed from office for

making ever so many erroneous adjudications... This part of the plan is so modelled, as to authorise the courts ... [to] give the sense of every article of the constitution, that may from time to time come before them. And in their decisions they will not confine themselves to any fixed or established rules, but will determine, according to what appears to them, the reason and spirit of the constitution. The opinions of the supreme court, whatever they may be, will have the force of law; because *there is no power provided in the constitution, that can correct their errors*, or control their adjudications. From this court there is no appeal.[30]

To this he adds (*Brutus*, no. 15):

Perhaps nothing could have been better conceived to facilitate the abolition of the state governments than the constitution of the judicial. *They will be able to extend the limits of the general government gradually*, and by insensible degrees, and to accommodate themselves to the temper of the people.[31]

One day in Israel, the "wise King Solomon" will rise, in David's mighty wake. His authority as sovereign will be absolute, and his role as supreme judge unchallenged. When two women approach him, each one claiming to be mother of a baby boy, the wise judge-king orders that the child be cut in two, giving half to each claimant. Of course, the real mother instantly relinquishes her claim, to spare her son's life; and all know by this to whom the child belongs. Fortunately, the result of this case is just, and proves Solomon's judicial prowess. But where are the local judges, the magistrates of the individual tribes, who might have handled the dispute on their own? They are nowhere to be found. An "imperial judiciary" has by this time developed in Israel, from which "there is no appeal." The genteel days of the Judges would never return again.

We might ask, where is contemporary America on this downward slide toward state tyranny? Are the genteel days of the early

---

30 David Wootton, *The Essential Federalist and Anti-Federalist Papers* (Indianapolis, IN: Hackett Publishing, 2003), 81.
31 Ibid., 95.

American republic gone for good? Have individual state governments and state courts become as irrelevant as ancient Israel's tribes and judges? Have we all become "serfs" of the judicial tyranny of the centralized government? Perhaps. But one thing is certain; history's Brutuses are not easily dissuaded.

# 4
# SAUL, DAVID, STATISM &
# COUNTER-REVOLUTION

*"Freedom is never more than one generation away from extinction. We didn't pass it to our children in the bloodstream. It must be fought for, protected, and handed on for them to do the same."*
– Ronald Reagan[1]

H e had tried to stop them, as perhaps the last true leader of the "Brutus current." But who would listen to the old prophet Samuel? The inexorable decline of the tribal federation, toward what moderns would call "statism" and ultimately "state tyranny," has by now been underway for decades. The "Promised Land" has been plagued by a combination of false promises and true miseries, even as enemies from beyond their borders have threatened to overrun them. There in the "gap" is Samuel, standing athwart history, as it were, and shouting "Stop!"

The high priest in those days, Eli, has reared two scoundrel sons, Hophni and Phinehas (*Pinkhas* in Hebrew), whose moral wantonness has included cavorting with the women serving at the entrance to the Tabernacle.[2] Worse still, their eternal nemesis the Philistines, have gathered an army against them, which the Israel-

---

1 Address to the annual meeting of the Phoenix Chamber of Commerce, March, 1961.
2 See 1 Samuel 2:12 and Josephus, *Antiquities* 3.354.

ites feel compelled to engage in battle. As the situation pans out, the "invincible" Israelite forces (ever-victorious because they carried the famed Ark of the Covenant into battle with them), are not only routed, but the Ark itself is captured by the pagan Philistines. This is beyond national humiliation; it is religious and spiritual disgrace, a horrible abomination. The aged Eli, on hearing the news, literally falls backwards and dies.

### Where Is Cincinnatus?

There seems to be a pattern throughout history, that democracies never last, and republics are ultimately doomed to fail. However many "Brutuses" are on hand to defend them, they are destined to collapse of their own weight. When it comes to the American experience, it has been said that the "two greatest hours" in the history of the republic came after the revolution was over. It seems that the Continental Army, now triumphant over the British, had not been paid for many months, save in horribly inflated continental currency that was almost valueless. Angry officers, furious over such indignities, were talking openly of seizing power from the new government – a *coup d'état*.

Filled with righteous indignation and an incipient revolutionary sentiment, they were prepared to march on Philadelphia and force Congress to live up to its promises. George Washington was in a position to singularly determine which direction the young nation would take. Would he follow the path of the French revolutionaries, who responded to the growing chaos with an imposed order, finding themselves governed, first by Maximilian Robespierre and later by Napoleon Bonaparte? Would he become America's "King George I," or would he hold out for the dream of a government of laws, not men? In what was perhaps the single greatest act of a statesmen in American history, Washington rejected the path of tyranny and sat down with his officers in New York's now-famous landmark, Fraunces Tavern, to plead the republic's case.

He argued that we hadn't fought our war of liberation to substitute one tyranny with another – a monarchy for a military dictatorship. From the dawn of time, going back to Greece and Rome, and beyond, republics had invariably fallen to authoritarian rule. Julius Caesar took power and dismissed the senate, extinguishing the Roman republic. Was this pattern to repeat itself? Still trying to persuade his cadre of officers, Washington donned his spectacles to read an address to them. His audience was stunned, having never before seen the great general, whose strapping six foot five inch frame made him the most prodigiously athletic leader of his time, in eyeglasses. Declaring that he had lost his vision in the service of his country, his men were moved to the point of tears. Taking to heart every word the beloved general uttered, the disgruntled officers picked themselves up and quietly went home. The new nation had been saved once again.

Based on that historic meeting, Washington subsequently set up what came to be known as the Cincinnatus Society of the officers of the revolutionary army, later to be called the Sons of the American Revolution. It was named after the ancient Roman general, who, unlike Julius Caesar, returned to the fields and his plough after being victorious in the Punic Wars. Washington insisted that the model for the American experiment should be Cincinnatus, not Caesar. Leaders, like government itself, should be strictly limited.[3]

This, however, was not to be the model for the early Hebrew tribes. In a dramatic ironic twist, the fiercely independent Israelites began to clamor for some kind of imposed order. "Let's centralize power and authority." "Let's look to a strongman to deliver us." In due course representatives from the twelve tribes approach their revered prophet, the incorruptible Samuel, and ask for the unthinkable, a king. The reason? They want to be like "all other nations." But isn't the whole point of the Bible that Israel is not to be like other nations? That it is to be an "exceptional" nation?

This is the point at which the prophet holds forth his scurrilous diatribe, warning of the dire consequences of choosing a king. A monarch will conscript your children into military service, seize your property (or at least a tenth of it), and generally enslave you. "But wait a second!" we might interject. "Isn't a tenth basically what we call a 'tithe'? Isn't it good to give a tenth of our material wealth? Why does the prophet rail against such a practice?" The obvious answer is that tithing has always been voluntary; when a government commandeers even a tenth of the material wealth of its citizens, it tramples private property rights and reduces its own citizens to slavery. America's founders knew this and surely agreed with the prophet Samuel. They decided that while financial transactions could be taxed, personal income could not. It took a constitutional

---

3 See Gary Willis, *op. cit.*, Chap. 1.

amendment (the 16th) to allow a tax on income. The Revenue Act of 1861, which gave us the income tax, arguably violated, not just the spirit and letter of the Constitution, but the Bible as well.[4] Say hello to the IRS!

If, as Samuel himself declares, turning the land into a monarchy is completely against the divine will, why does he acquiesce? Why doesn't he stand firm and "just say no"? Why doesn't he declare, "No, I will not do this!"? Perhaps the mob would have selected a king anyway, but there would be no question as to the "mind of God" in the matter. Had the prophet refused to lend his blessing to the endeavor, might it have been that a monarchy would never have taken root in Israel? But Samuel is by now aged, and he lacks the mettle to hold his ground. Isn't this exactly how "creeping tyranny" is seen by many to be taking root in our own day? Legions of bureaucrats keep marching forward, while independent-minded folk acquiesce. There are larger lessons to be gleaned here.

Historians point out that almost every time a revolution occurs in history, away from tyranny and toward individual liberty, there follows some kind of "push-back" – a counter-revolutionary movement that tries to reassert authoritarian power.[5] We can think of the biblical exodus out of Egypt as a genuine revolution, toward a confederation of tribes, moving in the direction of their Promised Land. The establishment of the Israelite monarchy we can characterize as a "counter-revolution," leading them back to tyranny. Sure enough, as the biblical narrative progresses, liberty and tyranny will be engaged in combat with each other over generations to come.

### "That's Saul, Folks!"

In the meantime, Samuel seems to go out of his way to choose someone who would not be likely to abuse the privilege of power. He happens upon a young man named Saul, wandering through the hills, in search of his father's lost asses. An ass-hunter? It must have seemed to the old prophet to be a sufficiently humble occupation. We're told, however, that it is God who directs their paths to cross

---

4 See Alvin S. Felzenberg, *The Leaders We Deserved (and a Few We Didn't): Rethinking the Presidential Rating Game* (New York: Basic Books, 2008), 190-1.

5 See Dan Slater, *Ordering Power: Contentious Politics and Authoritarian Leviathans* (Cambridge University Press, 2010); Randall Baker, ed., *Transitions from Authoritarianism: The Role of Bureaucracy* (Westport, CT, Praeger Publishers, 2002).

and God who commands Samuel to anoint him king. Moreover, being exceedingly handsome and a head taller than any among the Israelites doesn't harm Saul's public persona. Nor does the fact that he quickly rises to the challenge, raises an army, and trounces the Ammonites, who had besieged the Israelite city of Jabesh-Gilead and threatened to force its inhabitants into slavery.

In this single act, Saul behaves like one of the Judges of bygone days, but the people are no longer satisfied with deliverers who rise up as needed, in ad-hoc fashion. They gather together at Gilgal and acclaim him king. The biblical text appears somewhat conflicted about how it should refer to Saul. While in places it unabashedly refers to him as "king" (*melekh* in Hebrew) there are numerous other places where it simply calls him "commander" or "leader" (*nagid*). It's the biblical way of saying, not "Hail to the king," but "Hail to the chief" – a designation far more amenable to America's Founders, who were always looking for biblical precedent.

Some critics of the biblical text have also concluded that these two approaches to Saul's rise to leadership represent two independent sources, woven together by a later editor.[6] According to one, he is anointed king by the prophet Samuel, with all due ceremony, while the other depicts him going out to battle as if he were a judge, then being hailed by the people for delivering them from the hand of the enemy. Let's concede that we probably do have two different "Saul-sources," struggling for a voice in the sacred text. One is a "monarchistic source," that sees kingship as "the way to go" for the Israelite nation. But if we're looking for a continuation of the "Brutus current," we need look no further than the "alternate account," that presents Saul rising up as a judge. That's the biblical "ideal" for leadership! If therefore the people demand a king, and even if the prophet Samuel acquiesces in their demand, the king they end up with acts more or less like a judge.

As we read on in the story of Saul, the text's "schizophrenic" treatment of Israel's first king becomes so pronounced that we have to ask ourselves how we're supposed to regard him: humble and benevolent? Vicious and cruel? Weak in character? Fatally flawed? After battling with the Philistines, Saul is next instructed by Samuel (who is still mentoring the situation from the sidelines) to slay all of the Amalekites, who had also made it to the top of Israel's "enemies

---

6 Paul Borgman, *David, Saul, and God, Rediscovering an Ancient Story* (New York: Oxford University Press, 2008), 14ff.

list." The young king goes out and routs them royally, slaughtering men, women and children, including infants – behavior grotesque enough for modern sensibilities – but he doesn't go far enough. He's supposed to kill every living thing; yet he does not slay the Amalekite king, and he leaves alive the best of the cattle.

This does not exactly make the aged Saul happy. He roundly condemns the very man he had chosen and anointed, declaring that God himself regrets having selected him. What? Does it seems a trifle odd that Saul should essentially be de-selected as king because failed to kill every last living soul? Because he failed to make the "genocide" of the Amalekites complete? Saul grabs Samuel by the cloak, as the latter is leaving, as if to say, "Give me a break!" He succeeds only in ripping off a corner of it, provoking from the prophet a fierce prophecy about what the future will hold: Saul's kingdom will be torn away from him and given to someone else. The prophet takes a sword and promptly hacks the captive Amalekite monarch to pieces.

We need to recognize here that not a few modern scholars have considerable sympathy for Saul, feeling that a later textual editor (with a pro-David slant) has given him a very bum rap.[7] Even famed Holocaust survivor, Elie Wiesel, has questioned why Saul should essentially be dethroned, not because he killed too much, but because he did not kill enough.[8] Isn't it odd, that in today's world, when someone kills in the name of God (or Allah), we call him a terrorist (or at the very least a jihadist); when it comes to the Bible, however, such a person is "excused." In any case, it's fair to speculate that the libertarian "Brutus current" of the narrative paints Saul as another judge, called upon in a time of national crisis. But the dominant voice in the text is "authoritarian" and pro-monarchy, and this is why "poor Saul" is treated with such disdain. As we have said, "History is written by the victors."

It's at this point precisely that we're introduced to one of the greatest, if not the greatest, hero of biblical lore. Samuel, we're told,

---

7 It is argued that the Bible contains a pro-Saul bias in "Saul traditions" and anti-David perspectives in "Davidic material." See Lester L. Grabbe, *Israel in Transition 2: From Late Bronze II to Iron IIA* (New York: T & T Clark, 2010), 109.

8 Wiesel notes, "Saul did not aspire to be king; they forced it upon him, and he ended up a suicide. A victim of God in a sense. I find myself drawn to him in a very profound way." See Francois Miitterand, *Elie Wiesel, Memoir in Two Voices* (New York: Arcade Publishing, 1995).

has been commanded by God to find a new king from among the sons of a man from Bethlehem, in the tribe of Judah, by the name of Jesse. The prophet goes to offer sacrifice in the vicinity, bidding Jesse to fetch his sons. One by one they come to Samuel, and all are rejected, until the youngest (handsome and ruddy, with "beautiful eyes") is brought in from tending sheep. His name reverberates across the centuries: David. Linguistically, the name is related to the word meaning "beloved" (*dod* in Hebrew), that well describes how he's treated, in the Bible and through all time. David is just about everyone's hero, for his candor, his transparency, and of course his spirituality. Nor should we downplay any of that. If, however, we evaluate him on a purely political level, we may reach some startlingly different conclusions about this "man after God's own heart."

Samuel instantly knows that this is God's man, fills the horn of a ram with oil, and pours it on David's head, symbolically "anointing" him king of Israel. What this means, of course, is that there are now officially two kings in the land – not a good sign. Whoever is writing this text doesn't just respect David, but adores him. The very word "anoint," we should point out, is in Hebrew *mashakh*, which, as a noun, becomes *mashiakh* ("Messiah") – "the anointed one." Indeed, David is a prototype of the Messiah to come, "a man after God's own heart."[9] Whatever the identity of the future Messiah, we understand that he is to sit on the throne that David is to establish, and linked to the town that spawned him – Bethlehem.

### Saul v. David; Taft v. Teddy

For now, however, the young Bethlehemite is depicted as the essence of humility, whereas Saul is painted as one who is slowly becoming "unhinged." Is this David really an unimpeachable "good guy"? Or is he a schemer, a conniver, and perhaps a cross between Machiavelli and Richard Nixon? This is the moment when my students generally start pitching fits: "Woa! You can't attack David! He's my Israelite idol!" All right, then. Let's take a step back and think of the tension between Saul and David as a classic personality conflict. With a little imagination we can draw a comparison between Saul and David, as dueling power figures in ancient Israel, and two American chief executives – William Howard Taft and his

---

9 1 Samuel 13:14.

friend-turned-arch-nemesis, Theodore Roosevelt.[10] Taft as an American president is generally eclipsed by the larger-than-life T.R., just as Saul pales by comparison to David (the difference being that Roosevelt was Taft's predecessor, David was Saul's successor). Taft, like Saul, never particularly sought the presidency, and wasn't much of a politician to begin with. It was in fact his wife (his version of the prophet Samuel) who egged him into taking on the job.

Trained as a lawyer, Taft's highest ambition had always been to serve as a supreme court justice, not at the helm of the ship of state. He once said that a good judge is the highest human type, and our model of what God is like. (Similarly, I have argued that the ideal biblical leader is a judge, not a king.) Taft, who succeeded T.R. to the presidency, could not have been more unlike his predecessor (just as Saul and David are cast as polar opposites). Taft's approach was narrow and legal, Roosevelt was a precedent-setter. T.R., like David, was famously athletic; Taft was so rotund of figure that he once had to be pried out of the White House bathtub. Once elected, Taft's jovial, outgoing demeanor began to turn dark, since he could not abide the endless knit-picking to which presidents are necessarily subjected.

We're again reminded of Saul, who, after becoming king, finds himself tormented by dark spirits. He summons, thanks to a servant's recommendation, a young harpist – David – to sooth him with music. Saul ultimately descends into madness. Taft's gloom and general irascibility manifested itself only at the dinner table, making him history's portliest president. He frequently procrastinated and fretted over decisions. He may not have had much affection for the nation's highest office, but (like King Saul) he no intention of being bullied out of it. The bully in this case turned out to be Theodore Roosevelt, who, after taking four years off from the presidency, decided to challenge his old friend for the Republican nomination in 1912. Taft for his part probably would not have run for a second term, had it not been for T.R.'s increasingly personal attacks.[11]

---

10 James Chace, *1912: Wilson, Roosevelt, Taft & Debs – The Election that Changed the Country* (New York: Simon & Schuster). See Chap. 3, "The Heirs of Hamilton and Jefferson."

11 It has been duly noted that "Julius Caesar could not get along with Mark Antony, nor Saul with David, nor Paul with Barnabas, nor Napoleon with his brothers, nor Theodore Roosevelt with William Howard Taft." See David Rhys Williams, *World Religions and the Hope for Peace* (Boston: Beacon Press, 1951).

The Bible of course can't depict David as openly challenging his king. No, David's challenge must be quiet and subversive, so that the reader doesn't even realize what's going on. Opportunity knocks again on David's door when a new threat comes from the hostile Philistines. Their great bully Goliath issues a challenge. He will take on any warrior among the Israelites – *mano y mano* – the caveat being that the losing side will serve the victors. Who should accept this duel to the death but young David? We all know the story of David's victory, with his trusty slingshot, and we all cheer. But for whom are we cheering? A golden-eyed hero, or a tyrant-in-waiting? Is this how republics (in the case the Israelite confederacy) end, not with a bang but a whimper? In scouring the details of this narrative, discerning scholars and critics recognize what very quickly dawns on King Saul – that in David we have a man who is out to foment a bloodless coup. This he accomplishes largely by relying on the natural course of events, aided by his personal charisma and the knowledge that the bulk of the people adore their handsome new hero.

When, in the wake of David's victory over the Philistine brute, King Saul hears crowds shouting in the streets, "Saul has slain his thousands, David his tens of thousands,"[12] when he realizes the degree to which the young Israelite has ingratiated public opinion to himself, he snaps. He attempts to run David through with a spear, not once, but twice. No one is defending Saul in this behavior, but perhaps there is a touch of genius in his madness. Perhaps he instinctively realizes that David covets the seat of power for himself. Saul next puts him in command of a thousand men, sending him off to battle, likely hoping that he won't return. But the young hero returns victorious. Again, modern critics find considerable sympathy for Saul, who, like most ancient monarchs, seems prepared simply to kill his young rival, but is remarkably conflicted and on other occasions being unwilling or unable to "neutralize" the man who will take his throne.

Saul's next move is to make David an offer he can't refuse, namely his daughter Michal's hand in marriage. If David really seeks power the way Saul thinks he does, he will jump at the bait and seek to marry into the royal house. The bride price, however, will be one hundred Philistine foreskins – requiring enough bloody engagements in battle to get the young suitor killed. Again, David surprises everyone, for he and his comrades proceed to slay twice the required

---

12 1 Samuel 18:7.

number of Philistines, bringing home two hundred foreskins. Sympathetic readers of course cheer David, who (as Saul had promised), gives him his prize, Michal. But who cannot notice the young hero's proclivity to violence, his eagerness to kill? Whereas Saul is always conflicted about killing, David slays without compunction.

Israel's new hero also knows that to finesse his way to power, he's going to need strong alliances in high places. At every turn David appears to be the consummate politician – a master of the art of "networking." All of this serves him well, for when Saul makes known his intentions to put an end to David, Jonathan (the king's son and David's good friend) approaches his father and reminds him of all the good deeds his perceived rival has done. Saul, typically conflicted, agrees that he will never harm David. The king nonetheless vacillates, evidently deciding that Israel's hero represents an existential threat. (Modern critics think he's probably right!) Saul grabs a spear and, while David is asleep in his bed, attempts to run him through. Luckily for David, he has been warned of the danger by Jonathan, and has already fled, leaving the king to stab an empty bunk.

### David Derangement Syndrome

Who doesn't admire David for his shrewd escape? His subsequent exile, as he flees from Saul, is the stuff of legend. Nonetheless, it's not uncommon for "troublemakers," including some of history's most sordid revolutionary types, to "check out" when the going gets rough, usually to organize a resistance-in-exile. It seems to be a pattern across the centuries that tyrants begin their careers as "outs," until they overthrow the previous regime to become the new "ins." That's when things start to go south. Hello, tyranny!

Today's hard-left, including advocates of "liberation theology," are likely to find parallel between David and the likes of Che Guevara, whose "revolutionary life" represents their highest ideal. At least Che had a motorcycle on his long trek across Latin America, where he discovered the "excesses" of capitalism and the "oppression" of colonialism. In his day, David (also hailed for his empathy with the "poor folk") would have been lucky to avail himself of a mule, as he wandered across Israel's "outback." Then, of course, there's the publicity angle. Today we know that any successful politician has to write a book to catapult himself to fame. Che managed to establish himself early on as an author, writing *The Motorcycle Diaries*, and becoming a champion of the poor and downtrodden.[13] David, though he lacked a prominent publishing house, immortalized himself with an assortment of poetic ramblings, many of which tradition later included in the book of Psalms.

We have, among others, Psalm 3, a "prayer for help" ("I have so many enemies ... who turn against me"); Psalm 17, a "cry for justice" ("Hide me in the shadow of your wings"); Psalm 22, a "cry of anguish" ("My God, why have you forsaken me?"); Psalm 25, a "prayer for guidance and protection" ("Save me from the shame of defeat"); Psalms 42 and 43, "prayers of a man in exile" ("As a deer longs for a stream of cool water, so I long for You"/ "O God, declare me innocent, and defend my cause against the ungodly; deliver me from lying and evil men"). Ever and always, David plays the role of the humble, upright man, committed to the ideals and values of the Israelite nation. In another Psalm , he declares, "Your people did not conquer the land with their swords; they did not win it by their own power; it was by your power and your strength, by the assurance of your presence, which showed that you loved them" (44:3). But discerning critics aren't buying the notion that this was David's true character. He sang a nice Psalm, played a mean harp, and was a PR master. Underneath it all, though, even as he wandered in exile, in full flight from King Saul, David played the role of outcast like he played his famed lyre, like a virtuoso.

Let's not forget another outcast in modern history, Fidel (*"Viva la Revolución!"*) Castro, who like young David, rose to power on a wave of "populist" sentiment.[14] After serving two years in prison for a failed attack on a Cuban army barracks, he subsequently fled to Mexico, where he gained support from "brother" Che Guevarra. The revolutionaries, upon their return to Cuba, fled to the mountains, garnering support from the local peasants. At the end of the day, Cuban strongman Fulgencio Batista was deposed, and the temporary rebel-outcast became the new permanent supreme leader – hardly the Cincinnatus model.

Or, we might look to Russia, and consider the legacy of Vladimir Ilyich Ulyanov, under his *nom de guerre*, Lenin. As a young ag-

---

13 Jon Lee Anderson, *Che Guevara: A Revolutionary Life* (New York: Grove Press, 1997).

14 Thomas M. Leonard, *Fidel Castro: A Biography* (Westport, CT: Greenwood Press, 2004).

itator for "social justice," in stern opposition to the authoritarian czarist regime of Russia, Lenin (whose brother had been executed for his role in the attempted assassination of Czar Alexander III), found himself in exile, in Siberia. After his release he headed west, to London and Geneva respectively. As we have seen for revolutionaries, exile can be an ideal arrangement, in this case affording Lenin the opportunity to write (revolutionary tractates rather than Psalms) and to coordinate with other revolutionaries. After nearly twenty years of exile, he returned to Russia, to fan the flames of the October revolution of 1917, which would in turn fall to a Communist coup. And who would emerge as supreme dictator? Vladimir (the very "un-Cincinnatus") Lenin.[15]

Few there be, who dare to cast the venerable David as a cross between Che, Fidel, and Comrade Lenin, but if one is at all attentive to the continuing "Brutus current" in the biblical text, it's hard to escape the conclusion that he had in him at least a modicum of downright subversion.

Where does he head next? The young David (some would call him a "tyrant-in-waiting"), sets off on his journey of exile. He travels first to a city in Israel's "outback" called Nob, where the local high priest (Ahimelech) shelters him, gives him consecrated "shewbread" from the local shrine (which ought to be a "no-no" for anyone but a fellow priest), Somewhere along the way David has picked up a troupe of followers, perhaps fellow outcasts. Are these David's version of the "merry men" of Sherwood Forest? David of course insists on their ritual purity, but more cynically-minded interpreters wonder if they might be more akin to Al Capone's "mob." In any case, we're told that they too eat of the consecrated bread. After all, they're hungry! To top it all off, Ahimelech gives him the sword of Goliath the Philistine. What a coincidence that this priest just happens to have had it handy! One thing of which we're certain is that David the "outcast" is politically savvy enough to make valuable alliances.

Next, our man on the lam with Goliath's sword approaches the Philistine city of Gath – not a particularly good choice for the young Israelite who had slain their hero. He is of course spotted by the servants of King Achish, who ask, "Isn't this David, the king of his country?" Do these Philistines know something that the rest of

---

15 Robert Service, *Lenin: A Biography* (New York: Macmillan, 2000).

us don't and that David himself has hidden quite well? That he does in fact have designs on the crown, and that as far as he is concerned, he is already the king in his own eyes? David, suddenly in terror, is brought before the king, whereupon he quickly decides that the best way to prove he's not a threat is to convince the Philistines that he's lost his mind. Acting like a maniac and literally foaming at the mouth, the bewildered king decides simply to let him go. We might wonder, however, why he was ever in the company of the Philistines to begin with. Had he really lost his way, as well as his mind? Had he conveniently forgotten that these were Israel's mortal enemies? Or in realizing that these people were actively engaged in a campaign to conquer Saul and his army, did he perhaps decide that "the enemy of my enemy is my friend," at least until his identity as the Goliath-slayer was compromised?

Whatever his motives for this "detour," David heads for a cave in another little hamlet called Adullam, where his brothers and extended "clan" joins his insurgency, along with other malcontents/ "merry men," swelling his ranks to some four hundred. We might think of Washington's fabled encampment at Valley Forge, Pennsylvania, where the Continental Army quartered in late 1777 and into 1778 – a true "exile" of sorts. Ill-equipped, ill-fed, and generally ill-prepared for the winter's wrath, Valley Forge represented the crucible of the Revolution, where a true army was shaped out of deprivation. After six months of struggle, they emerged intact, strengthened and well-trained for the ultimate victory to come.[16] But is this really an apt parallel with David and his troupe of subversives?

Whereas Washington was all about self-sacrifice, we can at least make a case that David was all about self-preservation, as the young Israelite hero next sends his parents off to live with the Moabites. Weren't they, like the Philistines, also counted among the enemies of Saul's kingdom? Such a "patriot"! There they were to remain, in a similar exile, until David's destiny becomes clear. His destiny? Unlike G.W., it looks as though a crown really is on his mind.

Word suddenly reaches Saul that there has been a David-sighting, along with his "mob." Saul becomes increasingly desperate – in fact "unhinged" – ordering the murder of the high priest Achimelech, who had given "aid and comfort to the enemy." Saul is invariably spun as the "mad emperor," in spite of the fact that he

---

16 Frank Hamilton Taylor, *Valley Forge: A Chronicle of American Heroism* (Philadelphia: Valley Forge Park Commission, 1920).

epitomized the ideal of the king who really behaved like a "judge" – a small government leader for a loose confederation of tribes. And we're left wondering how many of the sordid details of his David Derangement Syndrome might be the product of the scribes who later redacted the narrative, of course in the employ of the subsequent David monarchy.

### "Brokeback" David?

David, after a dustup with the Philistines (who had advanced on the city of Keilah), flees again before the rampaging Saul, to the land of the Ziphites, where he makes a covenant with Jonathan, who by now is more intent on helping his friend than his father. We forgive him for that, since Saul is, after all, suffering from David Derangement Syndrome. But the discerning reader will notice that David has succeeded, first, in taking the hand of the king's daughter (Michal), and now, is cementing a firm alliance with the person next-in-line for the throne. Politics is all about the art of alliances. Unlike modern "religious" notions of what "covenant" entails, we should think in terms of a legal/ political "contract" with binding force. In this case it means that in any struggle over the throne, there is no doubt on whose side Jonathan will be.

We should probably mention that some modern commentators question just what kind of covenant this is, and what kind of relationship David and Jonathan are engaged in. The intrigue is heightened by the fact that the Bible records David as calling Jonathan's love for him "...wonderful, passing the love of women."[17] Serious wincing begins among my students when I explain (duty-bound as I am) the theory that David and Jonathan may have experienced more than some polite male-bonding.[18] Has "Brokeback Mountain" come to Judea, long before it was fashionable to celebrate secretly gay relationships? Whatever the relationship between the king's son and his father's arch-nemesis, it is curious that Jonathan has such apparently little regard for his own position as successor to the throne, and every regard for the progenitor of an entirely new and differ-

---

17 2 Samuel 1:26.

18 George E. Haggerty, *Gay Histories and Cultures: An Encyclopedia* (New York: Taylor & Francis, 2007), 243; Boswell, John. *Same-sex Unions in Premodern Europe* (New York: Vintage, 1994), 135-137; Halperin, David M. *One Hundred Years of Homosexuality* (New York: Routledge, 1990), 83.

ent dynasty – one that will ultimately transform the Israelite nation from a "small-government" confederacy of tribes to a "Leviathan" state of absolute power in the hands of a single man and his court.

But for the time being more self-preservation is in order, as the Bethlehemite who would be king now heads for the ultimate refuge in Israel. If you happen to know the lay of the land, there's one obvious hiding place for anyone "on the lam." Stand atop the Mount of Olives, look due east, and you'll see the barren Wilderness of Judea stretching out to the horizon, with a faint band of blue in the distance – the Dead Sea. At its lowest place, the Judean Desert is in fact the lowest spot on earth, more than twelve hundred feet below the level of the Mediterranean Sea. It's a veritable moonscape. It rains but a handful of times in any given year, leaving it utterly parched, barren and desolate. Very little lives along the shores of the Dead Sea, just a few lonely flocks of sheep and goats, who feed on the sparse vegetation, as well as those who herd them, pitching their tents, as they were inclined to do, across the vast stretches of the ancient Near East. Those "in the know" are also aware of quite a number of desert caves that pock-mark the chalky marl cliffs.

It's the perfect hideout for a man with keen political instincts and a strong sense of survival, especially someone with a "mob" of four hundred as a personal entourage. Following the desert wadis east-southeast, David and crew ultimately find themselves in the surprisingly lush oasis of Ein-Gedi. It's the natural exit of the rains that water the Judean hill country in the winter months, seeping through the cracks in the limestone escarpments and inexorably exiting as natural springs that intermittently erupt among the cliffs – pockmarked with caves – in the Jordan Rift Valley. At Ein Gedi, this results in a palm-laden paradise, replete with swift-flowing waterfalls, pools to bathe in, and kilometers of nature trails, suitable for noblemen as well as vagabonds. David has to be thinking, "If you're going to be 'public enemy number one,' why not go in style?" We're told that David and his "gang of four hundred" hole up in a very deep cave (mighty close for comfort in any case), with Saul, as expected, in hot pursuit, along with three thousand of his own men.

It's easy to eviscerate Saul, standing him in the dock as it were, for attempted murder. Students of the biblical text have been doing it for millennia. But imagine the horror of a king who has to be aware of his realm being torn away from him by clever alliances and stealth, at the hands of a "usurper" anointed by the prophet/judge

Samuel and hailed by whole population. It's the last dying gasp of tribal "confederacy," and the dawn of what will one day become "absolutism" under a very different royal line. Those who so choose may see in Saul (in spite of his "David Derangement Syndrome") an emblem of "libertarianism," and in David a "messianic" representation of power and authority.[19] In the former we find the "Brutus current" in the text; in the latter, the hand of the royal editor, sewing the stories (doubtless handed down by word-of-mouth), decades or even centuries later. The two literary streams are at war with each other, but there is no doubt which emerges victorious.

### The Joke's on Saul

The biblical text never misses a chance for levity, even at such a moment of high drama. Saul ends up searching for a place to relieve himself, and by sheer coincidence stumbles into the very cave where David was hiding. Being duly appraised of the situation by one of his gang, David has a perfect opportunity to slay the unsuspecting king on the spot. Ancient listeners to this story must have been rolling in side-splitting laughter, imagining such a humiliating way for hapless Saul to perish.

David, however, will not kill his king. He manages to sneak up on Saul, doubtless squatting in the cave's shadows (again the ancient audience cackles hysterically) without his knowing it, deftly severing a piece of the monarch's garment. How touching! Isn't the young Bethlehemite the very model of godly restraint? Isn't he the stuff of what true kings are made of? As Saul leaves the cave, David chases after him, prostrates himself, and shows him the piece of his robe, declaring that he might indeed have killed him, but could not. Saul at this moment breaks down in tears, openly acknowledging to David that he will in fact be king, supplanting Saul himself. The moody monarch has by now recognized that he is no match for the crafty and charismatic David, and he appears simply to give up. The latter swears that when this comes to pass, he will not harm Saul's descendants, whereupon the two part company and Saul returns home – at least for the time being.

---

19 Simcha Shalom Brooks, *Saul and the Monarchy: A New Look* (Hampshire, England: Ashgate Publishing, 2005), 46-47. As Brooks observes, Saul, at the beginning of his reign, behaved in a manner consistent with that of a "judge." It is only later that we find anti-Saul propaganda, as Saul became a symbol of the monarchy.

Of course it makes a great story, but discerning critics of the text still ask why David didn't simply grab Goliath's sword and sever the king's head with nary an afterthought. Again, however, we must think politically, and some would argue, much more cynically. This must be a bloodless coup. If it looks as though David has gained power through assassination, he will lose all legitimacy in the eyes of the people. It isn't necessarily David's godliness that prevents him from harming Saul; it's his keen political acumen.[20] No, Saul must not be touched. His demise must come some other way, and David must be content to bide his time.

In the interim the young Bethlehemite will be given yet another chance to spare Saul's life. This time Saul, who has had a sudden relapse of David Derangement Syndrome, learns that his adversary is hiding in the Wilderness of Maon. Having brought his three thousand men with him, the weary king makes camp and falls fast asleep. David, his nephew, and another, stealthily enter the camp and come upon the king, our hero absconding with his spear and a water flask. Ascending a nearby hill, David – on the moral high ground as well – calls out, arresting Saul's attention and proving, by display of the flask and spear, that he might have slain him yet again. Saul again acknowledges David's superior character. "I have been a fool!" Saul retorts, promising never again to harm the other and returning to his palace. Some wonder why certain biblical stories such as this one seem to be "reruns" of another episode. Might two different versions have came down and a later editor, unable to choose between them, decided to incorporate them both? In any case, the "doubling" of this episode underscores to the ancient audience that David in his rise to the throne was beyond guiltless – in fact "immaculate."

One final "divine joke" on the hapless Saul comes when, in his growing madness, he seeks out the notorious Witch of Endor (later immortalized in Shakespeare's Macbeth), through which he gains a supernatural audience with the now-deceased Samuel. And what does the great prophet now declare? That Saul is doomed, along with his kingdom, which has been given to David by divine fiat. The ancient audience is glibly to assume that this is the will, and the pro-

---

20 Ibid., 75. Brooks argues that any generosity of David on behalf of his "beloved" king derives from his simple reluctance to kill Saul openly, as 1 Samuel 26:10 suggests: "It must be the Lord himself who strikes him down, whether his time comes and he dies or he goes down into battle and is taken."

phetic word, of the Almighty. But isn't it a bit odd that an audience with a dead person, via a witch, is to be implicitly trusted? Doesn't the Law of Moses relate that no sorcerer or necromancer is to be found among the Israelites, much less heeded? But never mind any of that as long as it points to David as the rightful king.

After this incident, there is no doubt – as if there ever had been – that Saul's days are numbered. The great crescendo of these two rivals' stories is fast approaching, as the nation's foes from the coastal plain relentlessly struggle to overwhelm the tribal confederacy. While the Israelites had previously emerged victorious at the battle of Mishmash Pass (around 1010 B.C.), thereby regaining the land's central mountain ridge, the Philistines now plan a counterattack. They would cut across the Jezreel Valley to the north, outflanking Saul's forces, camped atop Mt. Gilboa.

Where is David while all this is going on? Where is the impetuous young man who slew the mighty giant with his trusty sling? Clearly, he knows something that all politicians learn at one time or another: "When your opponent is destroying himself, get out of the way." Accustomed to being "on the lam," he has retreated once again to Philistine country. This time, however, he is prepared to fight against Saul, on the side of King Achish. Some might call this "treason." In America he would be called "Benedict Arnold." Many are of the opinion that no matter how one is mistreated, even death is preferable to turning against one's own people. Patrick Henry's quip, "I only regret that I have but one life to give for my country," obviously didn't apply. In David's case, the Philistines themselves are taken aback, aware that this was the rascal who had felled their hero Goliath. In the final analysis, David is one politician who is not to be trusted. Not a few textual critics are convinced that this view of David is probably more accurate than the glorified sugar-coating through which he is approached in traditional circles.[21] King Achish tells him to mind the fort at home, while his forces advance against Saul.

Approaching Mt. Gilboa from three sides, the Philistines press the Israelites against the side of the hill, effectively blocking their ability to maneuver. Just when it appears that the Israelite troops might withstand the fierce assault, calamity strikes. The Bible records: "The battle raged around Saul, and some of the archers hit

---

21 Paul Borgman, op cit. An "A Source" is said to have denied that David ever served Israel's enemies, while a "B Source" is quite frank by comparison.

him, and he was severely wounded... The Philistines pursued Saul and his sons, and ... struck down Jonathan." The dying king turns to his weapons bearer and asks that he kill him, lest he fall into the hands of the uncircumcised. But the servant is unable to follow through with the order, leaving Saul to undertake a final act of heroism. He falls on his own sword. When, however, it fails to penetrate, the disconsolate king asks a nearby Amalekite to finish the job, which he does. At the end of the day, the Israelites go down to ignominious defeat. With a little chutzpah we might ask whether the outcome might have been different had David and his men decided to fight with his own people rather than consorting with the enemy. David is in any case forgiven for his "treason," because he is after all, David.

On the morrow, the victorious Philistines recover the bodies of Saul and his sons, decapitate them, and hang them upside down from the walls of the Galilean city of Beth-Shean. Such a shameful end for a king who perhaps deserves much more pathos than tradition has granted him. It will now fall to David to take up the crown, turn on all his enemies, and turn Israel from a "confederacy" of tribes to a true monarchy, and ultimately an empire. Israel has found herself a Caesar. America's Founders understood the lesson of how confederacies die. Maybe that's why, when the suggestion was made that George Washington be introduced as: "His Mightiness, His Excellency, His High Mightiness," he replied, "No, just call me 'Mr. President.'"

### Standing at Armageddon

Today's politicians instinctively recognize the importance of unity, and that "a house divided against itself cannot stand." There are plenty of examples in American history, looking back for instance at the contentious election of 1912. Two Republican candidates and former friends, William Howard Taft and the effervescent Teddy Roosevelt, in that year stood to battle each other. T.R., who assumed the presidency on the assassination of William McKinley, had vowed not to seek another term after standing for a single election on his own. It was a decision he would live to regret. He had handpicked Taft to replace him in the White House, but became deeply disillusioned with his successor's first term. This was especially true after seeing many of the bold initiatives of his "Square

Deal" abandoned. Taft, it seems, was not the same sort of "big government" leader (some would say "tyrant") as T.R. Taft, who preferred the idea of being an enlightened "judge" (recalling the Is-raelite Judges) to being an exalted Chief Executive, was a "Saul" to Roosevelt's "David."[22]

When it comes to leadership figures, there appear to be some universal character "types" (be it Saul and Taft, or David and Teddy) who are cut from the same cloth and who emerge repeatedly down through the centuries. Taft, not unlike the indecisive Saul, fretted and vacillated over every move, often procrastinating. Not unlike Saul, he became grumpy and depressed. He perceived the job of the president as doing nothing more than upholding the Constitution. This of course places him firmly in the "small government" camp – a defender of Federalism.

T.R., incensed at seeing much of his progressive agenda un-ravel, decided to challenge Taft for the Republican nomination. Taft may not have enjoyed being president, but he wasn't about to be bul-lied out of it by the mildly unhinged Roosevelt. It was a bitter con-test. When T.R. publicly called Taft a "puzzlewit," a "fathead," and a man with the brains of "three guinea pig power," the chief execu-tive, feeling devastated, broke down in tears.[23] In the end the party decided not to change their proverbial horses in midstream, perhaps recognizing that Roosevelt was more of a "big government" Demo-crat than a principled Republican. They renominated Taft.

Never one to back down, T.R. (doubtless channeling the spirit of David) became a renegade from his own party, running under the banner of the progressive Bull Moose Party and opening a third front in the presidential election of that year. Saved from an assas-sin's bullet that by chance grazed his wallet, Roosevelt, who was in the middle of a speech, famously quipped, "It takes more than that to kill a Bull Moose!"[24] T.R. even saw himself in David-like "mes-sianic" garb, declaring in the heat of the campaign, "We stand at Armageddon and we battle for the Lord!"[25]

When election day came, on November 5, 1912, the Repub-

---

22 See James Chace, op cit. Chap. 15: "The Authentic Conservative and the Red Prophet."

23 Neil A. Hamilton, Ian C. Friedman, *Presidents: A Biographical Dictionary* (New York: Facts on File, 2010), 226-7.

24 Alison Kelley, *Theodore Roosevelt* (New York: Chelsea House Publishers, 2004), 76.

25 Mark Harris, *City of Discontent* (Sag Harbor, NY: Second Chance Press, 1992), 162.

licans (like Saul and the Israelites) were trounced, since their vote was split, Taft finishing a distant third. Victory was ceded by default to the most "progressive" Democrat the country had ever seen, the "huge government" challenger, Woodrow Wilson. While Saul's death is depicted as bitter tragedy, Taft, by contrast, was relieved to step down. Now a happy ex-president, he later achieved his life's goal of becoming Chief Justice of the United States, a position in which he excelled as much as he enjoyed. Like King Saul, his legacy is overshadowed by his his ebullient challenger, T.R., who (like the charismatic David) loved the office as much as Taft despised it. But Taft's tenure as president did serve as a counterbalance and, in a sense, a warning against an emerging twentieth-century "imperial presidency," and its potential abuse of executive power and privilege.

Indeed, when David is ensconced on the throne, Israel will come face-to-face with an "imperial monarchy." The "Brutus current" goes down in temporary defeat, but it will surface again in open revolt against the centralization of power in the hands of one man, who would come to favor only his tribe. An increasingly disenfranchised and subservient population would never consent to being dominated by a freewheeling potentate, even one of such charm and perspicacity as David. Resistance was destined to rise, and their battle cry may well have been, "Don't tread on me!"

# 5

# MONARCHY or TYRANNY? THE DAWN OF EMPIRE

*"There is danger from all men. The only maxim of a free government ought to be to trust no man living with power to endanger the public liberty."* – John Adams[1]

A t the end of the great debacle on Mt. Gilboa, the Israelites are scattered and the strategic Jezreel Valley of the north lay in Philistine hands. The last leader standing on the Israelite side is David, whose behavior during the battle was enough to give his own people serious pause for thought. Here is a man who found himself ensconced in the enemy camp at the moment of his king's demise. To avoid the impression that David has gained Saul's crown through disreputable means, the Bethlehemite must demonstrate his deepest sorrow for the fallen king. Summoning his talents as a psalmist, he produces a lament that reverberates across the centuries: "How the mighty are fallen! Jonathan lies slain on your heights."[2] As poetry, it's classic; as politics, it's brilliant. Politicians know that if you ever lose the support of the public, you've lost it all, and David moves swiftly to bring about "damage control." As a result, readers of the Bible never think of David as a schemer or con-

---

1 John Adams, in notes for an oration at Braintree (Spring 1772).
2 2 Samuel 1:25.

102

niver, but as a pure heart, who is genuinely dismayed at the death of his king and best friend. But make no mistake; the "confederacy" is dying, to be supplanted by a new warrior-king, whose entire reign would be consumed with bloodshed.

## Old Soldiers

In the American experience another principle was becoming established. "Old soldiers never die; they head to the White House!" When Andrew Jackson entered the executive mansion it was after a struggle of biblical proportions. We have already drawn some brief parallels between "Old Hickory" and the ancient conqueror of Canaan, Joshua, but there are a good deal more to be drawn with the newly crowned King David. Jackson, like David, was a true war hero, the victor at the War of 1812's Battle of New Orleans and the darling of the "common man." But like David, someone else had been ruling as chief executive. His name was John Quincy Adams – another version of the hapless Saul.

When Jackson ran for the presidency in 1824, we can almost picture the crowds chanting, in biblical fashion, "Adams has slain his thousands, Jackson his tens of thousands!" 1824 was the first year in which the popular vote was counted, and Jackson was the clear favorite, well ahead of his challengers, John Quincy Adams, Henry Clay and William Crawford. But in the Electoral College, the race was too close to call, and ended up in the House of Representatives, which, under its speaker Henry Clay, ultimately picked Adams. Once inaugurated, Adams chose Henry Clay as his Secretary of State (a position conceived as a stepping-stone to the presidency). All of this led to the charge that a "corrupt bargain" between Adams and Clay robbed Jackson of the presidency.[3]

Jackson went into a David-like exile for four years, while his supporters waged an unremitting war of obstruction against John Quincy Adams, whose high-minded plans were dashed on the rocks of reality. Adams endured what may have been the most miserable four years of any chief executive in American history. Jackson bided his time in a David-like "wilderness," waiting for the next election cycle, which in turn would become the most brutal ever waged in the American republic. Politics, as we know, is personal, and Jack-

---

3 Harry L. Watson, *Liberty and Power: The Politics of Jacksonian America* (New York: Hill and Wang, 2006), 73ff.

son epitomized this more than anyone else. In the election of 1828 there were charges and counter-charges, revolving around the character qualities of the candidates. Jackson (like David) was accused of disreputable conduct. It was alleged that Andrew had married his wife Rachel before she had obtained a legal divorce from her previous husband. The charge, leaked by a Cincinnati newspaper editor, was true, but so old that no one had thought it consequential. Jackson was incensed, his people returning fire with a charge that Adams' wife was a "whore" and that Adams had personally "pimped" her for a Russian czar. These accusations were pure concoctions, but, like so much "spin," ancient as well as modern, the truth hardly mattered.[4]

This time around, Jackson trounced John Quincy Adams, becoming the new "David" of the growing American "empire." Would Federalism survive an "imperial president" like Jackson? Where, moreover, was Brutus?

### The Emperor's New Clothes

How many authoritarian governments arise at times of political instability? How unstable must the Israelite confederacy have been at the moment of Saul's death, and how "authoritarian" is the king-in-waiting hell-bent on becoming? For his part, David will have to face new, "Jacksonian" political challenges. Though he has taken Saul's crown, the charismatic new leader is hardly "out of the woods" when it comes to political battles. Saul, it seems, has one surviving son, by the name of Eshbaal. The Bible renames him, however, the pro-David narrative calling him Ishboshet ("man of disgrace").[5]

In those days the captain of Saul's army, Abner, decides to transfer the capital of the confederacy eastward, across the Jordan River, to a place called Mahanaim, where he crowns Eshbaal king. If David is really the godly character he's made out to be, why doesn't he step aside at this moment and let Saul's rightful heir take the throne? Unthinkable! Instead, David moves to consolidate power by persuading the elders of Judah to anoint him king in Hebron. David makes Hebron his capital, at least for the time being. Due to this link

---

4 Ibid., 91ff.

5 Baruch Halpern, *David's Secret Demons: Messiah, Murderer, Traitor, King* (Grand Rapids: Eerdmans, 2001), xv.

with David and with Abraham, who is buried there, Hebron would be destined to become a flashpoint in the Arab-Israeli conflict to this day. For determined Israeli settlers have bought property there, moved in, among not-so-friendly Arab neighbors, and have vowed never to leave.

Yet, we ask, what are they celebrating? David's privileging of a single tribe, Judah, because it happened to be his own?[6] At least Eshbaal in the north reigned over a league of five tribal regions. How odd, that Eshbaal, whose name is never remembered except, perhaps as a "bad guy," is the "Federalist," and David, the "emperor." Nonetheless, the political lessons get lost, as readers of the text hail David, simply because he's David. What seldom gets noticed is that his preference for and reliance upon this tribe alone will sow the seeds of division, that will (as in the American experience) plunge the nation into a brutal and protracted civil war.

Still a shrewd politician, David uses a bitter quarrel that breaks out between Abner and Eshbaal to overcome them both. Eshbaal is assassinated in the end, and David – Israel's "Old Hickory" – now rules as undisputed monarch. He will, however, live by the sword for the rest of his life. His first action will be to attack the Canaanite stronghold of Jebus, a move undertaken for purely political reasons. David recognizes something that America's Founders implicitly grasped – that in order to hold a "confederacy" together, a centrally located capital would be a key ingredient.

In early America, tensions between north and south (the latter often feeling trampled and taking up the mantra of "states' rights") were apparent from the beginning. In Israel, David, by appealing to the elders of his own clan to secure his throne, has stirred up a hornets' nest. By favoring his Judean kin he effectively marginalizes everybody else. That's why his stealthy capture of Jebus makes such good sense. Its location in the central hills of the tribe of Judah cements the political connections he needs with his own tribe, while capitalizing on the fact that Jebus is located smack in the middle of the land of Israel as a whole. That way, David can at least present the appearance of being neutral, and having the interests of all the tribes at heart.[7]

---

6 William Mackergo Taylor, *David, King of Israel: His Life and its Lessons* (New York: Harper & Brothers, 1874), 341; Haim Hillen Ben-Sasson, Samuel Ettinger, *Jewish Society Through the Ages* (New York: Schocken, 1973), 55.

7 Jonathan Kirsch, *King David: The Real Life of the Man Who Ruled Israel* (New York:

We can likewise understand why George Washington chose a piece of his own land conveniently located between Virginia and Maryland, between the northern and southern states, to become the location of the new American capital. For Washington, who surveyed the land himself, was a stroke of genius, that helped keep the fledgling states "united," in the face of tensions and divisions that were already manifest. Oddly enough, Washington was the only president never to live in the new District of Colombia. David, by contrast, has a starkly more "imperial" mindset. The Bible relates that he and his general, Joab, attack Jebus by stealth, gaining entrance to the city via an underground water channel that cuts directly beneath the walls and fortified towers. The unsuspecting inhabitants are taken by surprise and promptly massacred. David of course is never one to shrink from bloodshed.

The capstone of the victory will come in his renaming of the city, which will henceforth be known as Yerushalaim – Jerusalem – the "City of Peace." From this moment, Jerusalem will play a central role in Jewish history, from generation to generation. It will also become a major point of contention in world geopolitics. Ironically, and perhaps as part of David's legacy, it will never know peace. David may behave like an emperor, but as long as the "Brutus current" remains in the stories about him, he will be an emperor who is, at least on occasion, shown up to be wearing no clothes. Like the famous old fable of the little boy, who is the only one with the courage and honesty to point out that the "new clothes" the emperor thinks he is wearing are purely imaginary, and that he is in fact stark naked, it takes only one voice to reveal the truth.

## Leviathan

I don't wish to diminish David, and there is much to be said on his behalf. He was, arguably, a man with just the right qualities for ruling in a brutal age. Patriots, however, find the whole notion of "ruling" to be disquieting at best. For rulers invariably require "subjects." In David's case, the painful truth is that he wants absolute power. His major policy goal is to conquer the entire land of

---

Ballantine, 2000), 150ff. Jerusalem was to be an island of national identity in a sea of tribal squabbles. It arguably provided David with an independent power base, over which he exercise absolute power. Not surprisingly, he named it after himself – the City of David.

Canaan, a feat none of the previous judges, over the previous two centuries, was ever able to accomplish. This is David's version of "manifest destiny," the mantra of Old Hickory himself. It's a very different concept than "divine providence," to which America's Founders repeatedly appealed, for it wasn't just a reliance on God, but the hubris of conquest, coupled with the audacious claim that it was all willed by an unseen holy hand. Whereas Andrew Jackson began his administration with the Indian Removal Act, uprooting native Americans to make room for more white settlers, David twice trounces the very Philistines with whom he had previously consorted.

The Israelite ruler next sets his sights on Transjordan in the east, conquering the kingdoms of both Moab and Edom. According to the biblical account, he finds himself ruling over both major trade routes in the region, the Via Maris, hugging the Mediterranean coast from Egypt in the south, until it skirts across Galilee toward Damascus, and the King's Highway, passing through the eastern desert from today's Gulf of Aqaba and northward, east of the Dead Sea. We're even told that he conquers Damascus itself, and extends his realm all the way to the Euphrates River. Is this truth, or spin? Some modern critics allege that the extent of David's "empire" is wildly exaggerated, and a few go as far as to question whether King David was any more historical than King Arthur.[8] In any case, giving the Bible the benefit of the doubt, what makes us assume that great power and conquest makes a ruler great and/ or godly? Why, pray tell, do we forgive tyranny as long as it results in expansion? Tradition would have us believe that Israel reaches a high point of military and political dominance under David, becoming a major power in the ancient near east. Is the new "emperor" brilliant and far-sighted? Or is he an ancient "Napoleon"?

In nineteenth century America, similar questions were asked of Andrew Jackson, who was either adored as the hero of the "common man," or reviled as a new American tyrant. While Jackson called himself a Jeffersonian Democrat, Thomas Jefferson report-

---

8 A few remarkable ancient inscriptions have surfaced, referencing the name David, but no archaeological evidence bears witness to David's kingdom encompassing vast amounts of territory, stretching all the way to the Euphrates. See Iain William Provan, V. Phillips Long, Tremper Longman III, *A Biblical History of Israel* (Louisville, KY: Westminster John Knox Press, 2003), 230ff.

edly called Jackson "a dangerous man."[9] For whatever reason, people universally gravitate to "winners" – like Old Hickory, like Napoleon, and like David – but how many of those winners graduate to become tyrants? Napoleon was excused for his megalomania as long as he continued to conquer, but making excuses for tyranny was precisely what the Brutuses of history have always sought to prevent. The American patriots, well versed in Thomas Hobbes' Leviathan and determined to prevent the rise of such a potentate, understood what was at stake, which is why they were so insistent on limiting the power of their leaders.

In David's day there is still a semblance of "checks and balances," as long as the prophets are around to balance the otherwise unbridled authority of the sovereign. The very fact that God is referred to as "King" suggests that David is to be subservient to a higher authority. The Levitical priesthood should be the first to point this out, and should also act to "check" the king, at least in theory. We recall, however, that the priests are first commissioned by the "monarchical" Moses, and derive their power from whomever happens to be at the nation's helm. Moreover, since priests can easily be deposed by a despotic monarch, that essentially leaves the prophets to be God's mouthpiece, as well as the lonely proponents of the "Brutus current." Such will be the case when the "mother of all political scandals" erupts in the heart of David's court.

### Bathshebagate

Bill Clinton was faced with multiple "bimbo eruptions" during his tenure in office. For King David, only one woman is on his mind, and it's not his wife Michal. He spots her one day while surveying the growing grandeur of Jerusalem from the rooftop of his palace. She is gloriously sunbathing on the roof of her own house, in full view of the king, who is, to say the least, moved. The "Brutus current" resurfaces here, giving us more than a hint that megalomania has seized the "humble" harpist from Bethlehem. The suddenly infatuated David sends for her, presumably, "because he can." Her name is Bathsheba, and she is the wife of a Hittite mercenary currently off waging one of David's expansionist wars against the Ammonites. In ancient Israel, it's quite kosher for a man to have

---

9 Phillip Abbot, *Strong Presidents: A Theory of Leadership* (Knoxville: Univ. of Tennessee Press, 1996), 145.

multiple women. He can have as many wives and concubines as he pleases. But by an admittedly sexist double standard, a woman can have only one man. When David proceeds to sleep with Bathsheba, he is committing adultery, not against her, but against her husband, Uriah the Hittite. Worse still, Bathsheba becomes pregnant with his child.

Next comes "Part 2" in the playbook of political scandals – the coverup. Let's call it "Bathshebagate." David, unwilling to face the guild, the judgment, and verdict for his misdeed, now connives to hide his paternity. He invites Uriah home from the front and sends him to his wife, hoping that the child will appear to be his own. Unfortunately for David, Uriah refuses to sleep with his wife as long as his men are risking their lives and sleeping out in the open. In desperation, David decides he must be eliminated. He orders that Uriah be sent to the front line of battle, and that his comrades should withdraw when the enemy approaches. He correctly guesses that Uriah will be killed in the heavy fighting. David is clever enough to try to "worm out" of culpability for Uriah's death – "not guilty" by reason of a technicality. But for those who understand the essence of David's actions – the "Brutus current," uncannily preserved in the text – this is nothing less than conspiracy to murder.[10] Lord Acton's adage is epitomized in Israel's "greatest" king.

It's time for Israel's "minute men," the prophets, to leap into action. In this case, the "Johnny-on-the-spot" prophet is one Nathan, tasked with the job of insuring that King David does not become an ancient "King George." His weapon: old-fashioned Jewish guilt! Nathan approaches the king and tells him a story: There was a poor shepherd, who had a single prized ewe lamb that he dearly loved. Not far away lived a very rich man, with many herds of sheep and cattle. Once, when a guest came to visit, the rich man, rather than slaughtering any of his own cattle, sent for the poor man's lamb and prepared it for his guest.

"That man is a criminal!" David exclaims. "He must pay fourfold for the lamb and then be executed himself!"

"You are that man!" the prophet retorts. "And you have condemned yourself for your great crime!" The prophet goes on to condemn the child of David's sinful relationship, and the king is cut to the quick. He falls on his face, shouting, "I have sinned!" It's a clas-

---

10 Nahama Aschkenasy, *Woman at the Window: Biblical Tales of Oppression and Escape* (Detroit, MI: Wayne State Univ. Press, 1998), 106f; Halpern, op. cit., 34ff.

sic case of the Israelite "guilt culture" taking its toll on a king. David falls into deep mourning, praying and fasting and asking the divine will to spare the child of his beloved Bathsheba. But no amount of repentance will do the trick. When the child is born, he quickly falls ill and dies. At this point something very curious happens. Rather than continuing in a state of mourning (the usual Jewish practice after a death) David gets up, washes himself, and goes about his business, declaring that as long as there was hope, he would mourn, but now that the child is dead, there is nothing more to do. What a schmuck!

Nevertheless, he's officially "contrite," and he writes a very nice Psalm:

> To the Chief Musician. A Psalm of David, when Nathan the prophet came to him, after he had gone in to Bathsheba.

> Have mercy on me, O God, according to Your loving-kindness; according to the multitude of Your tender mercies, blot out my transgressions. Wash me completely from my iniquity, and cleanse me from my sin. For I confess my transgressions; and my sin is ever before me. Against You, You only, have I sinned, and done evil in Your sight; that You might be justified when You speak, and be clear when You judge.[11]

It's a deeply touching "mea culpa," but it's more than that. When a ruler has become authoritarian, when the priesthood has been emasculated and all other claimants to the crown (e.g. Saul's line) silenced, everyone nods approvingly, going as far as to depict David as the eternal model of repentance. On closer examination, though, David seems to deflect blame, as the psalm continues:

> Behold, I was brought forth in iniquity, and in sin did my mother conceive me [12]

David, you've got to be kidding! We understand you saying "The Devil made me do it," but are you honestly laying your mur-

---

11 Psalm 51:1-4.

12 Psalm 51:5

derous imperfections at your own mother's doorstep? Still, David gets away with it, so much so that the religious world ended up basing its complex and elaborate doctrine of "original sin" in part on this verse. David, we have to hand it to you; this is perfect "spin control" from a master politician.

Most American leaders were not as poetically gifted as David, and handled their own sexual peccadilloes differently. Thomas Jefferson encountered a firestorm in 1802, when a tabloid writer leaked an accusation of an illicit affair between the president and one of his slaves. Even more scandalous, the woman in question, Sally Hemings, was the half-sister of Jefferson's wife (whose father had himself had an affair with a slave). Jefferson wasn't a poet like the Israelite Psalmist, but he handled the press brilliantly. Adept at exercising power in such a way that people seemed oblivious to his use of it (a trait pioneered by King David), he never personally responded to any of the allegations, choosing simply to ignore the issue. The tactic worked, and the story simply faded away, at least until modern DNA analysis of the descendants of Sally Hemings supposedly verified the truth of the story.[13]

### Braveheart

According to the biblical prophet, there will be no end of strife and bloodshed in David's house, and this fearsome prediction is about to be fulfilled when in an episode that pits the king against his own son, Absalom, whose name ironically means "father of peace." David, as we have seen, has already exhibited signs of tyrannical behavior, in securing power by appealing to his own tribe, Judah, while marginalizing the others. Now, it's time to test the old adage, "like father, like son." Absalom's backstory involves the rape of his half-sister, Tamar, by her full-brother, Amnon, after which he dispatches his "hit men" to murder the vile rapist. King David, unable to inflict the death sentence on his son, instead sends him away for three years, before fully reinstating him.

It is then that Absalom begins his grand plot for power. He begins acting like one of the Judges of old, from the period of the Israelite confederacy. He pledges that if he were only made "judge in

---

13 The results of the DNA testing are still in dispute, however, and their veracity challenged. See William G. Highland, *In Defense of Thomas Jefferson: The Sally Hemings Sex Scandal* (New York: Thomas Dunne Books, 2009).

the land," he will bring about justice for all. The great prince humbly kisses those who approach him, in stark contrast with his father, in front of whom they must bow and scrape. "Small government" seems poised for a comeback, perhaps with a little help from the "Brutus current."[14] Over the next four years he builds enough support to make his move, which he consummates by sleeping with the king's concubines. Declaring himself king, he proceeds to Hebron, where he raises a standard of revolt. All Israel, including David's favored tribe of Judah, rallies to Absalom, and the rebellion is on.

As expected, Absalom gets a proverbial "bum rap" throughout the narrative, but discerning critics once again wonder whether the heavy hand of a later editor, in the employ of the Davidic monarchy, didn't rewrite the story in a way that favored David and turned his son into a misguided troublemaker.[15] How many times in history have William Wallace-like "rebels" uttered the cry of "Freeee-dom!"? The biblical redactors, however, are on the side of David/ "Longshanks," and will have none of it. We equally wonder whether the populace of the land favored Absalom, because here was a "king" who would act more like "Judge" – like the dearly departed Saul – and restore to them the kind of tribal confederacy that Thomas Paine so admired. We can only speculate, though the public acclaim for Absalom must have been enormous, as he next seizes Jerusalem itself.

The "spin" on Absalom is that he consorts with his treacherous adviser, the infamous Ahithophel, while David flees east to Transjordan. David gains the upper hand like any absolutist ruler, through intrigue and subversion. The Jerusalem priesthood, led by Abiathar and Zadok, is still in his pocket, and their sons act as spies on Absalom. David's servant, Hushai, also weasels his way into Absalom's court, persuading him not to attack his father while he is on the run, but to wait for a decisive battle. David now has the time he needs to regroup and prepare his army.

The final battle will take place in the Wood of Ephraim, and unfolds with as much pathos as the story of "Braveheart." David's forces have the strategic advantage, and the battle turns into a rout for Absalom. The comely young "traitor" ends up clumsily fleeing from the carnage on a mule, his long, Fabio-like hair flowing in

---

14 It has been noted that the Absalom story is one of a number of anti-David traditions preserved in the narrative. Lester L. Grabbe, *op. cit.*, 227

15 Halpern, op. cit., 94ff.

the breeze behind him. As he escapes through the thicket, his wavy locks get caught in a low-hanging oak branch. The mule continues on, leaving the Absalom dangling above the ground. David's general, Joab, through instructed not to harm the king's son, nonetheless stabs the helpless rebel with three spears, leaving his swordsmen to finish the job. David is cut to the quick, composing another of his immortal psalms to mourn his tragic loss: "O my son Absalom, my son, my son Absalom! would God I had died instead of you, O Absalom, my son, my son!"[16] We'd like to believe that David means it, but after everything we've witnessed, transparency is not exactly a character quality we expect in him. In any case, Absalom's rebellion will not be the end of disunity and dissent in the ranks of David's kingdom. It will on the contrary be a precursor of "a great Civil War" to come.

### The Absaloms of South Carolina

In America in the early nineteenth century, there were already signs that the Union was losing its fundamental integrity and might just fly apart. During Andrew Jackson's tenure in office, the brewing dissatisfaction over "states rights" almost came to a head. South Carolina, incensed about the high tariff on imported goods, benefitting New England manufacturers at the expense of southern planters, threatened to "nullify" the law.[17] Their position hearkened back to the spirit of the Constitution. What gave the "big government" in Washington D.C. the right to trample on the legitimate rights of a sovereign member of the American confederacy (South Carolina), and where would it end? What was the meaning of Federalism and what was happening to the "federal republic" championed by the Founders?

Then vice president of the United States, John C. Calhoun, came to the defense of his native South Carolina, forming the Nullifier Party. Their's was a position that Andrew Jackson might in theory have been inclined to support, since he was, like Calhoun, a southern planter. Jackson was like King David, however, in that he seemed to thrive on personal rivalries, and he personally despised Calhoun. Like the kings (or the Judges) of biblical days, he threat-

---

16 2 Samuel 19:1.

17 Richard E. Ellis, *The Union at Risk: Jacksonian Democracy, States' Rights and the Nullification* Crisis (New York: Oxford Univ. Press, 1987).

ened to raise an army, invade one of his own "tribes," and hang John C. Calhoun (his version of an Absalom) from the nearest tree. The Vice President was said to be genuinely concerned for his life. When Congress passed the Force Bill, Jackson went as far as to dispatch U.S. naval vessels to Charleston Harbor. South Carolina responded in kind by nullifying the Force Bill.

Calhoun at one point went as far as to argue that a state could overturn any piece of legislation it considered unconstitutional, suggesting that the nullification doctrine might in fact provoke secession. What might have resulted in a bona-fide civil war was narrowly averted when Senator Henry Clay put forth the Compromise Tariff of 1833, that managed to satisfy Calhoun. Nonetheless, the crisis was a clear indication of the tensions brewing beneath the surface that would one day (in a manner uncannily similar to what happened in the kingdom founded by the biblical hero David) catapult the nation into all-out civil war. Jackson, for his part, asserted that he was the nation's supreme leader (some would say "autocrat"). His heavy hand made it clear that the Union was not about to dissolve on his watch.

In the twenty-first century, there is still serious discussion about whatever happened to Federalism, and the fact that the sovereign states these days have less and less autonomy. Increasingly, state legislatures act as little more than conduits through which the all-powerful "nanny state" passes out "goodies" to a citizenry grown dependent on Uncle Sam for cradle-to-grave welfare. There's a "soft" kind of tyranny in today's America; in biblical times, however, David's heavy hand was fated to metastasize into a "hard tyranny."

### Egomaniac: "You Fill Up My Census"

Even after all of David's misfortunes, the Bible still isn't done with dumping on the great king. David's kingdom is about to be harshly judged. The reason? David takes a census. Do we read this correctly? The text declares rather enigmatically:

> And again the anger of the LORD was kindled against Israel, and he moved David against them to say, Go, number Israel and Judah.[18]

---

18 2 Samuel 24:1.

So, it is God who "inspires" David to number the people, then judges Israel because he did it. The troublesome detail is that elsewhere in the biblical narrative, the blame is laid at the door of "Satan":

And Satan stood up against Israel, and provoked David to number Israel.[19]

In both cases, it's David who's let "off the hook." First, God is angry with Israel; that's why the divine will "inspires" David to count the people. Then, it's the Devil who makes David do it. The only explanation is that the biblical editors – writing, as always, in employ of the Davidic monarchy – have to find someone to blame other than the great king himself. The next questions, that bedevil readers of the text, are: What's so bad about taking a census, why does David get into trouble for it, and why does blame need to be deflected? Might it have something to do with David's monstrous ego, and the danger of Israel becoming a monstrous military monarchy? After all, isn't a census used for counting the number of potential warriors?[20] Might the "Brutus current" be seen here, reporting on the king's maniacal desire for self-aggrandizement, for proving his greatness by proving, numerically, how many people he rules? In other words, for David it's about more than conquering territory. It's about adding more and more people to the official count of citizens he controls. He just needs them to "fill up his census." He commands his general, Joab:

Go number Israel from Beer-sheba to Dan. And bring the number of them to me so that I may know.[21]

No ego here, is there? He just wants to know.

And Joab gave the sum of the census of the people to David. And in all Israel there were one million and a hundred thousand men who drew sword. And in Judah were four hundred and seventy thousand men who drew

---

19 1 Chronicles 21:1.

20 Rayner Winterbotham, Thomas Whitewall, *Numbers: The Pulpit Commentary* (London: C Kegan Paul & Co., 1881), 3.

21 1 Chronicles 21:2.

sword.[22]

The Almighty, apparently, is on the side of "Brutus," for the text announces that this was "evil in the eyes of God," who promptly "struck Israel." We're not told exactly how the nation is "struck," but we are introduced to another "Brutus" in the ranks, a "seer" by the name of Gad, who announces to the egomaniac king three possible punishments from On High:

1) seven years of famine (according to 1 Samuel 24) or three years of famine (according to 1 Chronicles 21),

2) three months of war, or

3) three days of pestilence.

David declares to the prophet that he is "in great distress," meaning basically that he can't decide, only that he prefers to fall into God's hand rather than man's. (We shouldn't be surprised, given that even God can't decide between seven or three years of famine.) In the end, God selects the third option, whereupon seventy thousand men perish by plague. Oddly, no one bothers to count the women and children. Is King David, now properly chastised, now any less an egomaniac? Judging by his behavior down to the end of his life, he's awfully slow learner.

The Christian Bible famously begins with the story of another census, used by the Romans:

> And it happened in those days that a decree went out from Caesar Augustus that all the world should be taxed... And all went to be registered, each to his own city. And Joseph also went up from Galilee to be taxed (out of the city of Nazareth, into Judea, to the city of David which is called Bethlehem, because he was of the house and family line of David). And he took Mary his betrothed wife, being with child.[23]

"Never let a census go to waste," said the Romans. "Count 'em, then tax 'em." While the Bible says nothing about taxation as a motivation for David, let's not be fooled; with future kings of Israel, the levies will soon be on their way.

In the twenty-first century, big government loves taking cen-

---

22 1 Chronicles 21:5.

23 Luke 2:1-5.

suses no less than the ancients, because in order to control you, it needs to know as much about you as possible. Who are you? Where are you from? How big is your family? How much money do you make? But there's a catch. Instead of being used to collect taxes, the modern census is used to allocate handouts, all part of the liberal progressive agenda. Said Libertarian Party Director, Steve Dasbach, "The government uses Census information to dole out an estimated $180 billion in taxpayers' money, to justify and expand wasteful government programs, and to allow politicians to discriminate against Americans based on their racial or ethnic background."[24]

Thomas Jefferson put it this way: "The natural progress of things is for liberty to yield, and government to gain ground." To this he added, "As yet our spirits are free."[25] The question in David's day will continue to revolve around the degree to which the independent-minded spirit of the Israelites – forged at Mt. Sinai and galvanized in the days of the Judges – can remain free.

### The King of Sheba

For David the ongoing question will be how he can remain king of all the tribes while favoring his own, and a single city, Jerusalem. A new rebellion against David's "tyranny" breaks out over the preferential treatment of Judah. The all-powerful king, having returned victoriously after his defeat of his son Absalom, must face the dissatisfaction of ten of the twelve tribes, who resent Judah having taken the lead in bringing the king back to power. They make up the great majority of David's kingdom, and they apparently see a level of autocracy and favoritism in David that future generations of biblical commentators are content to gloss over. The disgruntled secessionists want to know what this David fellow is doing on the throne to begin with. Wasn't Saul the one originally designated to wear the crown? Can't we find a descendant of his who will be better suited to governing, in the tradition of the "good old days" of the tribal confederacy? A "limited monarchy"? A government of laws, not men?

Enter Sheba (not to be confused with the famous queen). He's the son of Bichri, and he hails from the family of Becher (son of Benjamin) therefore being of the lineage of Saul. Biblical spinmeis-

24 http://www.wnd.com/?pageId=4451
25 Thomas Jefferson, letter to Colonel Carrington (27 May 1788).

ters notwithstanding, it seems there is still considerable support in Israel for Saul's model of a less autocratic, smaller government, "kinder, gentler" theory of government. It's up to Sheba to shake things up, which he does by raising a new battle cry: "We have no part with David!" He raises a band of fellow malcontents and proceeds to the secessionist north, in what becomes yet another threat to the integrity of David's realm.[26] As usual, David responds with force, convinced that he is king of all his subjects, including Sheba. He dispatches his "mighty men" (doubtless the same "thugs" who accompanied him during his struggle for power), along with a contingent of troops, along with his general, Joab.

Realizing he is hopelessly outnumbered, Sheba takes shelter in a city of northern Galilee, Abel-bet-ma'acah. But the city will prove to be no safe haven. Joab and Abishai (David's nephew and another military commander) have gotten wind of where the king's adversary is hiding, and fear spreads that they will destroy the city entirely. A so-called "wise woman," whom the text leaves unnamed, convinces Joab to spare the city, since its inhabitants oppose the renegade Sheba, and will by no means grant him asylum. She convinces the people of the city to murder the unfortunate rebel. They not only kill Sheba; they decapitate him, tossing his severed head over the rampart, in full view of Joab.

Another rebellion crushed, David can carve another notch in his kingly girdle. But as with Moses before him, we can't help but wonder, given such a constant undertow of complaint against him, whether there might be much more to the "Brutus current" than casual readers are led to believe. As for David, he is never unsure of himself or his absolutist tendencies. He never negotiates, never offers compromise, never reconsiders the autocratic principle. And while this approach seems to have worked during his lifetime, it would eventually set the stage for ancient Israel's version of the Civil War.

### Old Rough and Ready

In early nineteenth century America, the rumblings of discontent, fueled by the cry of "states rights" were gaining momentum. While there was no one like a David on the scene, there was a quintessential pre-Civil War president by the name of Zachary Taylor,

---

26 Steven L. McKenzie, *King David: A Biography* (New York: Oxford Univ. Press, 2000), 169ff

known affectionately as "Old Rough and Ready" – as much a testimonial to his fighting prowess as to his disheveled appearance.

Most republics throughout the course of history had simply not survived, and America's Founders were well aware of this, even as they studied the Bible. Would the American republic end in tyranny? Would it break apart? As the young nation expanded to the west (as surely as David had annexed new territories to his own realm), the tensions between north and south intensified (in a way parallel to regional strife in David's day). While the northern states were far more populous and more developed, economically, the south still controlled much of the country's power structure – the Democratic Party, the Supreme Court, and the presidency. The crisis between the north and south was escalating to the point that an extraordinary president was required. Zachary Taylor (like Brutus' unflattering portrait of King David) hardly fit the bill.[27]

Taylor was, (again like David) a "celebrity," a war hero, who helped win more than half a million square miles for the young nation. Like the "humble" young Bethlehemite, he was a political unknown, who deigned to seek elective office himself. While the young David was discovered and anointed by the prophet Samuel, Taylor was approached by both parties (Democrats and Whigs) and coaxed into running, ultimately as a Whig. As a war hero, he appealed to the north, and as a Louisiana slaveholder he was the darling of the south.

But in spite of outward appearances, he was in many ways a Washington "insider." (Recall that David appeared to be an "outsider" while secretly developing a relationship with Saul's son Jonathan and marrying the king's daughter Michal.) Taylor's military position had been arranged by his second cousin, James Madison, and his fourth cousin once removed was Robert E. Lee. His son-in-law had been Jefferson Davis. Once in power, however, he found that his connections and sympathies would pull him in different directions.

Henry Clay's proposed solution, the Compromise of 1850 (admitting California as a free state, balanced by certain pro-slavery measures favorable to the south), Taylor threatened to veto, even at the risk of the secession of the southern states. "Old Rough and

---

27 Considering Taylor's enigmatic career, one wonders how he ever came to be elected president. See K. Jack Bauer, *Zachary Taylor: Soldier, Planter, Statesman of the Old Southwest* (Baton Rouge: Louisiana State Univ. Press, 1985).

Ready" was again like King David in his simplistic response to rebels in the ranks. At a conference with southern leaders, Taylor promised to personally lead the army against potential secessionists and hang them, possibly starting with his own son-in-law and senator from Mississippi, Jefferson Davis. Like the ancient Israelite king, he affirmed the nation's integrity in response to threats of disunion. But the "states' rights" movement, like the ancient "tribes' rights" outrage, could't be assuaged by heavy-handedness alone. Serious political skill was required, including the willingness to compromise, which Taylor lacked as much King David. We can't fault Taylor for evolving, barely a year in office, into an ardent Unionist. But as noble as opposition to slavery was, there were other issues that were just as troublesome to the south – some would say more so – relating to the role of a powerful central government and the quashing of the semi-autonomous nature of the state governments.

On a hot July Fourth in 1850, Taylor took a break from the Washington infighting to preside over the groundbreaking ceremony for the Washington Monument. He sought relief from the summer sun with a bowl of cherries and a pitcher of milk. Within a few hours he contracted severe stomach pains. Five days later he was dead. Was it a case of intestinal inflammation – gastroenteritis? Or was the nation by now so fragmented that sinister motives were in play? Troublesome rumors began to circulate. Might the heavy-handed and militant chief executive (a southerner who was now seen as the single greatest foe of the "states' rights" agenda) have been poisoned by arsenic? Might there have been a dark conspiracy to eliminate the president, as surely as the ancient "Unionist," King David, was surrounded by conspirators? It would take until 1991 for the truth to be established. A historian convinced Taylor's descendants to have the president's remains exhumed and tested for traces of arsenic. After extensive testing it was determined that the likely cause of Taylor's death was not poison, but a form of cholera. Case closed.[28] But the fact that arsenic poisoning might even have been suspected indicates just how fragile the Union had become and how formidable the "Brutus current" had grown in the American republic.

When it comes to the Bible, whoever opposed David or any of the other authority figures of biblical lore, was seen as seen as ungodly and rebellious, certainly not one of the "good guys." There's

---

28 Jeremy Roberts, *Zachary Taylor* (Minneapolis: Lerner Publications, 2005), 99.

never the slightest possibility that any of the "rebels" might actually have had a point. In the American experience, the "states' rights" controversy is so overshadowed by the slavery issue that it rarely gets a fair hearing. But let's remember that the concept of semi-autonomous state governments was so important at the nation's founding that the Constitution could only garner enough support to be ratified if it included an amendment – the Tenth – guaranteeing that the sovereignty of the individual states shall not be compromised:

> The powers not delegated to the United States by the Constitution, nor prohibited by it to the States, are reserved to the States respectively, or to the people.

It basically reiterated an earlier provision of the Articles of Confederation:

> Each state retains its sovereignty, freedom, and independence, and every power, jurisdiction, and right, which is not by this Confederation expressly delegated to the United States, in Congress assembled. (Article II)

The Tenth Amendment was exactly in-keeping with the warning issued by America's "Brutus," Robert Yates, who feared that true "federalism" might be drowned by an overly strong executive branch. As we look at America today, it's patently obvious that what Brutus feared has become the new reality. The federal government has become all-powerful. The Tenth Amendment has been shredded. And many ask, can the republic envisioned by the Founders long survive?

### David's "Temple of Doom"

Perhaps the worst thing students of Holy Writ do is simply to take for granted the way things panned out, as "meant to be." That certainly applies to the great king and psalmist, David, who brutally crushed all opposition, but who is universally forgiven and even adored. After all, he writes such nice psalms! But his motto might well be: "Resistance is futile!" He has centralized power in Jerusalem, but even that isn't enough for his monarchy. He must centralize worship as well. After all, a monarchy has come about when the people asked to be "like all other nations," with a king and a royal house. But don't those "other nations" also have permanent structures they call "temples." Why should Israel be stuck with a portable shrine – an "Ark" that has no fixed location?[29] David, being David, has to express his desire for centralization in a characteristically "humble" and "charming" manner:

> After David was settled in his palace, he said to Nathan the prophet, "Here I am, living in a house of cedar, while the ark of the covenant of the LORD is under a tent."[30]

First of all, David, what are you doing living in a palace? Did Abraham have a palace? Did Moses have a palace? Did any of the Judges have a palace? Is it any wonder that Thomas Paine admired the Judges and saw them as the governmental "ideal"? Once a monarchy is a reality, however, religion almost invariably gets wedded to the top-heavy state. Avoiding this was of course the motivation behind the Second Amendment's separation of Church and state. In David's case, he needs to make this "union" appear to stem from his genuine concern for the sacred shrine.

There's a problem with this, however. Wasn't the genius of the Ark of the Covenant the fact that it could travel anywhere among the twelve tribes? It's portability was key, for everyone could access the golden box that contained the original tablets of the Ten Commandments. When the tribes needed a visible symbol of unity, there was the Ark. When inspiration was needed for battle, there was the Ark, leading the troops. So what if it resided in a tent? Better there than in some gargantuan stone edifice, resembling a pagan Canaanite or Philistine sanctuary.

Notice how the prophet Nathan responds to David, in yet another textual echo of the "Brutus current":

> So says the LORD, You shall not build Me a house to dwell in. For I have not dwelt in a house since the day that I brought up Israel until today, but have gone from tent to tent, and from one tabernacle to another. Wherever I have walked with all Israel, did I speak a word to any of the

---

29 Roland De Vaux, *Ancient Israel: Its Life and Institutions* (Grand Rapids: Eerdmans, 1997), 329.

30 1 Chronicles 17:1.

judges of Israel, whom I commanded to feed My people, saying, Why have you not built Me a house of cedars?[31]

David is emphatically denied the privilege of building God a temple. Moreover, his penchant for "tyranny" is duly noted: "You shall not build a house in My Name because you have shed much blood to the ground before Me."[32] The passage goes on to declare prophetically that one of David's sons (who we of course recognize as Solomon) will be the one to build God a "house." Again, who is writing the narrative, but a court scribe, in the employ of the Israelite monarchy, perhaps working for Solomon himself? And since Solomon did in fact build the Temple in Jerusalem, this must have been the divine will all along, right? We'll see about that...

In any case, we have to wonder whether the prophet Nathan is being not just God's mouthpiece, but that of the Brutuses of his day, who remember the old tribal confederacy, and who seek to prevent the centralization of worship as well. The skinny on David is that he has too much blood on his hands to undertake such a holy endeavor, and this analysis is undoubtedly correct. David doesn't quibble with the divine verdict, and he leaves the Ark of the Covenant sitting in a portable tent for the rest of his days. That may well have been the best thing he ever did...

### "Not with a Bang but a Whimper"

In Cincinnati, Ohio, there is, not surprisingly, a statue of the ancient Roman aristocrat, Lucius Quinctius Cincinnatus, bearing the following inscription:

With one hand he returns the fasces, a symbol of power as appointed dictator of Rome. His other hand holds the plow, as he resumes the life of a citizen and farmer.

George Washington, like Cincinnatus, had no need to designate a successor. David, however, embodies a very different approach. Like all "tyrants," he must designate a worthy successor, who can be counted on to continue propping up the "big govern-

---

31 1 Chronicles 17:4-6; Gwilym Henry Jones, *The Nathan Narratives* (Sheffield, England: Sheffield Academic Press, 1990), 74ff.

32 1 Chronicles 22:8.

ment" mechanisms (the centralization of political power, military power, and religious power) he spent his reign putting in place.

His name is Solomon, his son by Bathsheba. The trouble is, Solomon isn't David's eldest son – a problem that often arises when monarchies supplant republics. As David lay dying, an elder son named Adonijah declares that he should be the rightful king. David orders that Solomon be brought to the Gihon Spring, where he has his priest anoint him, thus denying Adonijah his great ambition. As expected, intrigue follows. David's general, Joab, and the priest Abiathar side with Adonijah, who compounds things with the hutzpah-filled request of Solomon that he be given David's servant (also his old-age "cuddle-bunny") Avishag, as his wife. Correctly perceiving this as a veiled threat to his own succession, Solomon has Abiathar banished, and Adonijah and Joab, along with another of David's foes (Shimei son of Gera) put to death. Yet, David is forever revered for his godliness, and Solomon for his wisdom.

David may have built himself an empire, but he has also bequeathed a nightmare. To paraphrase T.S. Eliot, "This is the way republics end, not with a bang, but a whimper."

# 6

# TAX AND SPEND
# SOLOMON: KING OF THE
# BOONDOGGLE

*"If ye love wealth better than liberty, the tranquility of servitude better than the animating contest of freedom, go home from us in peace. We ask not your counsels or arms. Crouch down and lick the hands which feed you. May your chains set lightly upon you, and may posterity forget that ye were our countrymen."*
– Samuel Adams[1]

**W**hile David is known for his conquests, it is actually Solomon who builds a kingdom and an empire that conforms to the "standards" of the ancient near east. It is he who, for better or for worse, creates a truly centralized government, coupled with an absolute monarchy. Welcome, to the Empire of Solomon! Pretty impressive it is, stretching all the way from the border of Egypt to the Euphrates River. Nonetheless, when we think of the word "empire," positive associations are hardly what come to mind. Empires are harsh, cruel, often dictatorial and brutal. They rape, pillage and enslave, subjecting the hapless survivors of their conquests to forced labor and oppressive taxation. It is difficult to conceive of some-

---

1 Speech at the Philadelphia State House (1 August 1776).

thing more oxymoronic than the concept of a benign empire. Yet, the Bible would have us believe that the "empire" forged by David and consolidated by Solomon is quintessentially benign.

Of course empires down through history have often conceived of themselves in the most benign of terms, exercising a "divine right," as it were, to bring civilization to the lands of their conquest. The Romans with their *Pax Romana* were said to have brought "peace with a vengeance." The British empire, on which it was said that the sun never set, was depicted by its architects (including a host of colonists who circumambulated the globe) as bringing political stability and cultural and industrial advancement to multiple under-developed areas of the world. While today denounced the world over, the legacy of empire is (at least according to some, such as Dinesh DeSouza) mixed. Himself a product of colonial India, De-Souza argues that imperialism has essentially gotten a "bad rap."[2] Colonial rule did in fact increase education levels, hasten an end to the caste system, bring modern medicine and the like. And though unpopular to admit it, few can deny that a number of former colonies, subsequent to being granted freedom from imperial rule, have actually declined in their overall wellbeing.

How, then, do we look at the Bible's version of the *Pax Israelatica* – the Empire of Solomon?[3] Because the Bible is almost always read as a religious text and in a religious environment, serious questions about the "empire" it depicts are never even raised. If Solomon ruled an empire, we should see it as a testament to his greatness and to divine favor upon him, right? If David's hands were full of blood establishing it, well, righteous kings get to do those sorts of things, don't they? After all, it's in the Bible.

The Bible was certainly in the minds of America's pioneers and settlers, as they migrated westward, across the Alleghenies, through the Great Plains, and ultimately on to the west coast. America, the City on a Hill, the Light to the Nations, was also the New Israel, destined to re-create the legacy of its ancient counterpart. "God bless America" was more than a brittle slogan; it expressed a living faith in what became known as "American exceptionalism" – the idea that this land was fundamentally different from any other.

It is hardly coincidental that America's relentless expansion

2 Dinesh D'Souza, *What's So Great About America* (Washington, D.C.: Regnery), 36ff.

3 For an exposition of the term *Pax Israelatica*, see Norman Podhoretz, *The Prophets: Who They Were and What They Are* (New York: Free Press, 2010).

was couched in religious-sounding language, such as "manifest destiny." There was, as already mentioned, Andrew Jackson's uprooting of the Seminole Indians from Florida, resulting in the infamous "Trail of Tears." All was justified as part of America's God-given right to more and more territory. "What would Jackson do?" became the guiding principle of many an American expansionist, including James K. Polk, who, as previously noted, drove all the way to the Pacific and made the United States the New World's version of an "empire."

### Solomon's "Spoils" System

Let's, however, backtrack a bit and reflect on the fact that after David passes from the scene, it's all about consolidating the kingdom Solomon inherits and turning it into an empire. Solomon's real name, by the way, is Shlomo – a derivative of shalom – meaning, of course, "peace." But what that peace will be like and how he will attain it is all a matter of perspective. Also up for debate is whether the biblical description of this "empire" is in any sense accurate, or whether Solomon's domain is no more historical than the "minimalist" view of David's, i.e. wildly exaggerated.[4] But let's once more take the Bible at its word and assume that there really was a Solomon and that he really ruled the kingdom attributed to him. Do we cheer him for his "empire"? Or do we, like America's Founders, look askance at all power-hungry monarchs, even if they are the stuff of biblical lore?

According to the holy writ, Solomon is born under the luckiest of geopolitical stars, inheriting from his father a land-sea alliance with King Hiram of Tyre (the Phoenician city up the Mediterranean coast). Having ruthlessly liquidated his foes, one-by-one, he appoints his friends to key positions – in government, the military, and religious institutions. We forgive him, of course, and praise his wisdom, since this is the only way to solidify a stable regime in the ancient Near East. Religious "rationalizing" strikes again!

Millennia later, Andrew Jackson inaugurated the "spoils system," in the spirit of the adage, "To the victor belong the spoils."[5]

---

4 Israel Finkelstein, Amihay Mazar, *The Quest for the Historical Israel: Debating Archaeology and the History of Early Israel* (Atlanta: Society of Biblical Literature, 2007), 107ff.

5 David M. Kennedy, Elizabeth Cohen, Mel Piehl, *The Brief America Pageant: A History of the Republic* (Boston: Wadsworth Engage, 2008), 185.

The president who, by contrast, had refused to play the patronage game in Washington was none other than Jackson's arch-nemesis, John Quincy Adams, who wrote the handbook on "failed presidencies." The lesson: forget high-minded political ideals; it's all about cementing power and keeping it. Hardly the "republican" ideal, but who cares? (Only Brutus, but he seems conspicuously absent at this point in the biblical narrative.)

The tension between patronage and meritocracy was destined to become a permanent fixture of American political discourse, continuing to this day. In post-Civil War America nothing symbolized political cronyism more than appointments to the post of Collector of Customs at the Port of New York (the chief source of national revenue in pre-income-tax America). Such appointments were effectively controlled by the notoriously corrupt Senator Roscoe Conkling, head of New York's political machine. In a rare decisive moment, the usually indecisive President Rutherford B. Hayes sacked the head of the customs house – a Conkling crony and later president in his own right, Chester Arthur – and replaced him with a person of merit.

Hayes' successor, President James Garfield, likewise stood up to the patronage system by appointing one of Roscoe Conkling's rivals as Collector of the Port of New York. It was another salvo in the ongoing war to return America to its founding principles. Some considered the struggle as important as the Civil War had been, in purifying the nation's governance. Tragically, Garfield was cut down by an assassin's bullet, fired by a disgruntled federal office-seeker (Charles Guiteau), who symbolized the nature of the conflict. The fight would be carried on by Garfield's vice-president, who now ascended to the Oval Office, Chester A. Arthur.[6]

Himself a product of the patronage game, and a personal friend of Roscoe Conkling, Arthur was uniquely acquitted for the job of combatting cronyism and cleaning up Washington. Some have pointed out that it often takes a product of the "old system" to change that system and bring about meaningful reform. In this sense, Arthur has even been likened to Richard Nixon (the classic Cold Warrior) heading to China. Nonetheless, while serious efforts were made in the days of Garfield and Arthur to curb cronyism and fill government positions on the basis of merit – replacing a patronage-centered bureaucracy with a true "meritocracy" – who

6 Zachary Karabell, *Chester Alan Arthur* (New York: Times Books, 2004), 86ff.

can doubt that over the next century and down to the present, the war to reform government has essentially been lost?

The fact is, once statism gets established, it's nearly impossible to uproot. In today's America, there is considerable discussion about the extent to which the republic has lapsed into government by executive order, and, with political cronyism more rampant than ever, government by "czar." Some go as far as to suggest that America now has two distinct governments: an elected government that presents a "public face," and an unelected, "shadow government" of corrupt cronyism, where the choice federal jobs go to the biggest campaign "bundlers."[7]

In the beginning, the idea behind the American republic was, as we have seen, to mimic the pattern of the Israelite tribal confederacy, ruled by "part-time" leaders called Judges. It was to be a relatively small and focused government, with limited, enumerated powers. Over time, however, its leaders have chosen to emulate biblical empire-builders – David and Solomon (with a little FDR thrown in for good measure). The federal government today employs an army of over two million bureaucrats, presiding over a massive administrative state with considerable police powers. Operating as an unelected "fourth branch" of government, it has little if any regard for the nation's founding principles, and (unlike Thomas Paine) considers the very idea of looking to the biblical Judges as a model of governance to be at best laughable and at worst dangerous.

Solomon, for his part, seems to have morphed into quite the "statist." But then again, after David's legacy, not much "morphing" was required. David had followed the Near Eastern custom of using marriage for political ends (Michal being a case in point). Once his throne is secure, Solomon conveniently arranges marital alliances, and he does so "on steroids." He marries the daughter of Egypt's pharaoh, who, as the Israelite king's father-in-law, attacks and burns down the Canaanite city of Gezer, handing it over to Solomon as a gift. A burned-down city? Some "gift."

Solomon proceeds to go on a marrying frenzy, adding almost as many wives and concubines to his makeshift harem as modern presidents have czars and assistant-czars. The grand number listed is seven hundred wives and three hundred concubines. Doubtless, these numbers possess certain mystical qualities – seven representing

---

7 Richard McKenzie Neal, *The Compromising of America: An American Tragedy* (Bloomington, IN: AuthorHouse), 248ff.

"perfection" and ten recalling the Moses' famous commandments – and may be more symbolic than literal. On a practical level, Solomon is excused for such indulgences, since in antiquity marriages are considered a form of diplomacy, consistent with the image of an exalted monarch. As he marries the daughters and sisters of kings from across the region, he establishes pacts of trade and armament. In so doing, he is equally touted as creating a vast commercial and trade network. Trade and commerce? We should applaud him for that … or should we?

### No Adam Smith

Let's face it; Solomon is hardly a model for the early American merchant class, whose free-wheeling laissez-faire ideas ultimately created the wealthiest society on earth. In the final analysis, Solomon may sound like the quintessential ancient capitalist, but make no mistake; he's no Adam Smith. We can by contrast liken him to the economic theory that will later be called "mercantilism."[8] By this we mean the notion that financial prosperity derives from extracting the wealth of others. Mercantilism is all about monopoly. In its heyday, it connoted the economic doctrine by which foreign trade is controlled, not by the "free market," but by "big government." The security and prosperity of the state is supposedly ensured by such governmental meddling, but we should also note that mercantilism was the direct cause of many a European war, not to mention colonial expansion across much of the world.

Such an approach was harshly criticized by Adam Smith, the paragon of laissez-faire capitalism, who insisted that what causes national wealth to increase is labor, not just the nation's quantity of gold or silver, the latter being the basis for mercantilism. In Solomon's case it is in fact all about gold and silver, and copious quantities of the same. That in turn means control of the major trade routes – the Via Maris and King's Highway, conquered by King David before him. It also means using empire to drain wealth from subjugated peoples and to fill the royal coffers. And all of this of course requires Solomonic "big government."

This is hardly what we see in the genteel age of the patriarchs,

---

8 Lars Magnusson, *Mercantilism: The Shaping of an Economic Language* (London: Routledge, 1994). Magnusson elucidates the sharp distinction between mercantilism and nineteenth century laissez-faire economics.

who, as we've already noted, are antiquity's "venture capitalists." Abraham and Isaac are nomads and farmers, living in a remarkably unregulated world, where self-interest and individualism are key to survival. Jacob is a prosperity-seeking wheeler-dealer who's all about wealth creation (as he prospers under his uncle Laban) – quite the opposite of Solomon's monopolistic "wealth extraction."

The Bible declares: "King Solomon was king over all Israel."[9] How nice. It only mentions his status as "king" twice in a single verse. "And these were his high officials," the passage continues, priests, court secretaries, military commanders, district governors, royal advisers, and one fellow (Adoniram, son of Abda) in charge of the "forced labor." So, this is the legacy of King Solomon the wise? Forced labor? Hadn't the prophet Samuel warned about this if the people demanded a king "like all other nations"? Isn't this where "statism" inevitably leads? But fear not; the Bible explicitly states that Solomon didn't make slaves of the Israelites. It was conquered peoples – Canaanites, Amorites, Hittites, Perizzites, Hivites, and Jebusites – who were subjected to servitude; so we give Solomon a pass.

The text goes on to list a host of additional "bureaucrats" by name. "And Solomon had twelve officers over all Israel, who provided food for the king and his household. Each man had his month in a year to provide food."[10] Never mind the "foreign" slaves, suffering under cruel bondage as they labored on Solomon's building projects. Never mind the haunting similarity to Moses' day, when it was the Israelites who labored to make bricks for Pharaoh. Now, the pharaoh is Solomon, and the slaves are those he has vanquished.[11]

But all of this is forgiven as long as his own people (the nonenslaved ones) are proverbially fat and happy:

> Judah and Israel were many, as the sand by the sea in multitude; eating and drinking and making merry. And Solomon reigned over all kingdoms from the River to the land of the Philistines, and to the border of Egypt. They brought presents and served Solomon all the days of his life. And Solomon's food for one day was thirty measures

---

9 1 Kings 4:1.

10 1 Kings 4:7.

11 Isaac Mendelssohn, "State Slavery in Ancient Palestine," *Bulletin of the American Schools of Oriental Research*, 85 (1942), 14.

of fine flour and sixty measures of meal, ten fat oxen and twenty oxen out of the pastures, and a hundred sheep, besides harts and roebucks, and fallow deer, and fattened fowl. For he had the rule over all on this side of the River, from Tiphsah even to Azzah, over all the kings on this side the River.[12]

How many times in history has growing state "tyranny" gotten a pass, as long as it's accompanied by wealth, prosperity, and at least for a goodly period of time, peace?

And he had peace on all sides all around him. And Judah and Israel lived safely, every man under his vine and under his fig-tree, from Dan even to Beer-sheba, all the days of Solomon. And Solomon had forty thousand stalls of horses for his chariots, and twelve thousand horsemen. And those officers provided food for king Solomon and for all who came to king Solomon's table, every man in his month. They did not lack anything. They also brought barley and straw for the horses and mules, to the place where the officers were, every man according to his charge.[13]

From where does Solomon's great wealth derive? From free markets and free trade, a-la Adam Smith? Or from the subjugation of neighboring peoples and growing state tyranny over his own? These are the kinds of descriptions the likes of which have been applied to some of the great mercantilistic "tyrants" of history, from Julius Caesar to Napoleon and beyond. Julius Caesar of course had his Brutus. In Solomon's case it would seem that Brutus is still lurking in the shadows. Notice the earlier description that the Israelites were "eating and drinking and making merry." Is this a subtle commentary that has survived via the "Brutus current," likening this generation of Israelites to the earlier Hebrews who had come out of Egypt and found themselves worshipping the Golden Calf? Consider the phrasing of the Exodus passage, regarding the Israelites' idolatry:

---

12 1 Kings 4:20-24.

13 1 Kings 4:24-28

And all the people broke off the golden rings which were in their ears, and, brought them unto Aaron. And he received it at their hand, and fashioned it with a graving tool, and made it a molten calf; and they said: 'This is thy god, O Israel, which brought thee up out of the land of Egypt.' And when Aaron saw this, he built an altar before it; and Aaron made, proclamation, and said: 'To-morrow shall be a feast to the LORD.' And they rose up early on the morrow, and offered burnt-offerings, and brought peace-offerings; and the people sat down to eat and to drink, and rose up to make merry.[14]

While the heart of this passage involves a condemnation of idolatry, the emphasis is nonetheless on the accumulation of gold – a literary link with the legacy of Solomon and the "mercantilist" obsession with accumulating precious metals. It's been said that in the mercantilist world of the 1700s (the period when the American republic was taking shape), issues of morality and religion amounted to little more than trivial subtleties.[15] Well, in Solomon's ancient version of mercantilism, we can make a case that the same trend became entrenched.

His reign starts out promisingly enough, when the king requests from the divine will, not wealth and power but wisdom. Oh yes, Solomon is destined to be the great builder of Jerusalem's Temple. But the same text that lauds him for this achievement excoriates him for allowing his many wives – the women he had wed to cement his trading/ "mercantilist" alliances – to lead him into idolatry in his later years:

King Solomon, however, loved many foreign women besides Pharaoh's daughter—Moabites, Ammonites, Edomites, Sidonians and Hittites. They were from nations about which the LORD had told the Israelites, "You must not intermarry with them, because they will surely turn your hearts after their gods." Nevertheless, Solomon held fast to them in love... As Solomon grew old, his wives turned his heart after other gods, and his heart was

---

14 Exodus 32:3-6

15 Howard Morley Sachar, *The Course of Modern Jewish History* (New York: Vintage Books, 1990), 18ff.

not fully devoted to the LORD his God... He followed Ashtoreth the goddess of the Sidonians, and Molek the detestable god of the Ammonites.[16]

Is this description the voice of "Brutus," a faint echo of the anti-monarchy current, present from the days of Samuel, Saul and David, and now continuing in the narrative regarding the greatest "statist" of all? From a political standpoint, it's clear that by this point in Israel's history, "resistance is futile." What's left, then, for the "loyal opposition" but to harangue the king for his wives and his idolatry? It's remarkable that the later biblical editors chose to preserve this "Brutus current" ("B source") at all. In any case, they made sure that in doing so they maintained a line of consistent praise for David and his royal house.

The passage ends with the verse: "So Solomon did evil in the eyes of the LORD; he did not follow the LORD completely as his father David had done."[17] While David may have followed his God "completely," he also made autocracy a permanent feature of Israel's political landscape. Nonetheless, under Solomon, there was at least room for what today's "left" likes to call "diversity." With multiple deities being worshipped, there's no "religious test" in the king's court. How nice. But there's also a lack of cultural unity in the kingdom, that inevitably weakens the state, politically. That in turn precipitates even greater centralized government and coercive power.

### The Greatest Statist

Solomon is of course forgiven his abuse of power, as long as the majority are wealthy and prosperous, and as long as there is peace in the land. Never mind that a part-time militia has been converted to a permanent standing army. Never mind that Solomon has done exactly what the prophet Samuel had warned that a king would do:

He will make soldiers of your sons, while others will plough his fields. He will take a tenth of your harvests and of your flocks, and you will all become his slaves.[18]

---

16 1 Kings 11:1-5, NIV

17 1 Kings 11:6.

18 1 Samuel 8:12; author's paraphrase.

We're told that the king builds up a force of some 12,000 horses (the "cavalry divisions" and the source of considerable mythology about "Solomon's Stables") and 1,400 chariots (the "tank corps"). These he stations in the capital, Jerusalem, and in strategic "chariot cities" – Hazor, in the far north, Megiddo, guarding the Jezreel Valley, as it cuts a swath across Galilee, and Gezer, further south between the Judean hills and the Mediterranean coast.

But Solomon isn't done, even after creating a substantial army. He must have a navy to match. Far to the south, at Ezion-geber (today's Israeli city of Eilat, on the Gulf of Aqaba), he builds a fleet of ships. Since Israelites are not exactly the sea-faring sort, he relies on and one of his many foreign allies, King Hiram of Tyre, to supply an experienced crew of sailors.[19] They sail as far as Ophir (of uncertain location, though perhaps on the African shore of the Red Sea) and bring back for Solomon's coffers some sixteen tons of gold. They text doesn't tell us exactly how they acquire such treasure, but we can guess that they basically abscond with it. We can call them "Solomon's pirates."

But at least such plunder might have gone a long way toward funding Solomon's sizable standing army and navy. The other option might have involved the king simply confiscating the booty and supporting his troops through an ever-increasing tax burden. In the early American republic, there was great reluctance to accept a standing army. George Washington, the great general, nonetheless famously opposed the creation of a permanent military force, and did so on multiple occasions. Washington's ideal was an army of citizen soldiers, not a permanent mercenary class:

> "Standing Armies are dangerous to a state... The prejudice in Other Countries has only gone to 'em in time of peace – and then from their not having in general cases, any of the ties – the concerns or interests of Citizens or any other dependence, than what flowed from their military employ – in short from their being mercenaries – hirelings. It is our policy to be prejudiced against them in time of War – and tho they are Citizens, having all the ties – & interests of Citizens, and in most cases property totally unconnected with the military line. If we would pursue

---

19 1 Kings 9:26

a right system of policy, in my opinion, there should be none of these distinctions – we should all be considered, Congress – Army, as one people, embarked in one cause – in one interest; acting on the same principle, and to the same end."[20]

Washington, the American Cincinnatus, was akin to a biblical Judge, leading his part-time militia and sending them home when the conflict was over. He might have become America's Solomon, but such a role would have been profoundly distasteful to him. Since he well knew that armies travel on their stomachs, it would have been incumbent on the young nation to find a way to sustain its men in arms, and that of course would have meant (as it did for Solomon) increasing layers of taxation. By contrast, this federal republic was remarkable in terms of what it could not do, and by the strict limitations on its powers. In his oft-quoted Farewell Address of 1796, Washington counseled his compatriots "… to avoid the necessity of those overgrown military establishments, which, under any form of government, are inauspicious to liberty, and which are to be regarded as particularly hostile to Republican Liberty." Not coincidentally, Washington produced his address in collaboration with James Madison, who in his own right declared, "A standing army is one of the greatest mischief that can possibly happen." To this he added, "Keep within the requisite limits a standing military force, always remembering that an armed and trained militia is the firmest bulwark of republics – that without standing armies their liberty can never be in danger, nor with large ones safe."[21]

Solomon, however, is the quintessential statist, and everything he does, from his army and navy to his monumental building projects, is geared to the task of expanding the size and scope of the Israelite central government. Big governments require great monuments, and Solomon's building binge is destined to lead him into the history books, and his nation into the poor house.

### Temple Trouble

20 George Washington to John Banitster, April 21, 1778.

21 James Madison, First Inaugural Address, March 4, 1809; see John Robert Ireland, *The Republic, or, A History of the United States of America in the Administrations*, Vol. 4 (Chicago, Fairbanks and Palmer, 1886), 216.

America's Founders knew that centralized government, a standing army, and a lavish capital don't come for free, and Solomon should have known it as well. The District of Colombia, far from being envisioned as the capital of an empire, is really just a small Virginia town, that couldn't be farther removed from the image of Solomonic grandeur. The crown jewel of Solomon's capital is well beyond anything boasted by the city of Washington. It is the massive Temple, envisioned, but never constructed, by his father David.

Unfortunately, there's a human inclination to assume that because certain facts come to exist "on the ground," that's the way things were "meant to be." If Solomon builds a Temple, it must be the divine will. Is it possible, however, that just as God acquiesced to an Israelite king, the divine "stamp of approval" was ultimately given to a "Holy House"? Don't we see serious reluctance on God's part inasmuch as David's fervent desire for a Temple was officially denied? Leave it to theologians, however, to start rationalizing, noting that since the Bible later hails the Temple – arguably the greatest thing since "sliced manna" – it must at the very least been part of "God's passive will."

On a more philosophical level, it's been said that the only real way to define God is not by positive, but by negative attributes – not by what God is but by what God is not. That's because the very nature of monotheism separates God from the universe itself. Israel's God isn't like any of the pagan deities – the sun, the moon, the stars, the primordial waters, the atmosphere. God is above and beyond the cosmos, apart from materiality, and therefore sitting in judgment on the material world and all its inhabitants. Islam teaches this as well, declaring that there can be no "association" between God and anything on the earth. That explains the biblical command that there can be no "graven images" of God, no idols, no pictures, no statues; and that precept remains in both Judaism and Islam to this day.

Just as the Israelites were ideally not to have a king "like all other nations," they were not to have a temple "like all other nations." Temples, after all, invariably housed the statue of whichever deity was being honored. They were the physical "house" of a particular god or goddess, or, in the case of the Parthenon, a whole slew of gods and goddesses. Solomon seems to "get it," when he exclaims:

But who is able to build Him a house, since the heavens
and the heaven of heavens cannot contain Him? Who *am*
I then, that I should build Him a house, except only to
burn sacrifice before Him?[22]

All right, then, Shlomo! Why do you feel compelled to go
through with it? And don't just tell us that the prophet gave you
the go-ahead. We should't be surprised, though. In our own day,
once Congress makes an appropriation for a "bridge to nowhere,"
it doesn't matter that it's recognized to be a boondoggle; full speed
ahead!

When it comes to ancient Israel, the nation seems to have survived before a Temple existed. In fact, the true genius of the previous Tabernacle – the one constructed under the auspices of Moses,
in the days of the forty-year post-exodus wilderness sojourn – was
that it was portable. While housed in a tent made of animal skins,
there's certainly something to be said for such humble confines. It
could travel among the twelve tribes, giving all the people access to
the Ark of the Covenant and the sacrificial altar. It was perfectly
suited to the ancient governmental ideal of a loose "confederacy,"
where local leaders could solve local problems for local folk. There
was room for diversity within the larger national unity – "tribes'
rights."

All of that, however, must come to an end when, arguably, the
greatest boondoggle of all goes up on the hill to the north of David's
city, that will come to be called the Temple Mount. The Bible goes
into meticulous detail regarding its construction, though the first
thing it records is Solomon's message to King Hiram of Tyre, to the
north, spelling out his need for an alliance:

You know that because of the wars waged against my father David from all sides, he could not build a temple...
But now the LORD my God has given me rest on every side, and there is no adversary or disaster. I intend,
therefore, to build a temple... as the LORD told my father
David, when he said, "Your son whom I will put on the
throne in your place will build the temple for my Name."

---

22 II Chronicles 2:6.; see also 1 Kings 8: 27: "But will God indeed dwell on the earth?
Behold, heaven and the highest heaven cannot contain you; how much less this house
that I have built!"

So give orders that cedars of Lebanon be cut for me. My men will work with yours, and I will pay you for your men whatever wages you set. You know that we have no one so skilled in felling timber as the Sidonians.[23]

Solomon will pay a foreign king "whatever wages you set"? Money is no object? This is Solomon's version of fiscal responsibility? George Washington well knew that "foreign entanglements" are injurious to free republics, compromising a nation's sovereignty and its ability to pursue its own interests:

Against the insidious wiles of foreign influence ... the jealousy of a free people ought to be constantly awake, since history and experience prove that foreign influence is one of the most baneful foes of republican government.[24]

Solomon should have recognized that the kind of alliances he was forging would necessarily cause "partiality" toward certain nations, exactly what G.W. later advised against:

Excessive partiality for one foreign nation and excessive dislike of another cause those whom they actuate to see danger only on one side, and serve to veil and even second the arts of influence on the other. Real patriots who may resist the intrigues of the favorite are liable to become suspected and odious, while its tools and dupes usurp the applause and confidence of the people, to surrender their interests.

So, when Solomon makes his marital alliances, with various nations round about, and when he later gets himself "in hock" to King Hiram of Tyre on behalf of his precious Temple, he is actually on his way to surrendering the interests of his own people? Washington summed it up:

The great rule of conduct for us in regard to foreign nations is in extending our commercial relations, to have with them as little political connection as possible. So far

---

23 1 Kings 5:3-6, NIV.
24 George Washington's Farewell Address, Sep. 17, 1796.

as we have already formed engagements, let them be fulfilled with perfect good faith. Here let us stop.

However, when it comes to the influence of the Tyrians on King Solomon and his realm, there is destined to be no stopping point. The minute architectural details of the new Temple indeed make the structure seem to be a copy of the Temple of Melquart of Tyre. As in Phoenician shrines, Solomon's Temple is to have a central courtyard (heikhal), an outer chamber (ulam), and an inner sanctum or holy of holies (debir). Beyond the front entrance there is an annex housing rooms for the temple staff.

There is also the great bronze laver, a veritable "Sea of Bronze," as the Bible calls it, adorning the courtyard in front of the Temple proper. Symbolically declaring that Israel's God reigns, not just over the land, but the sea as well, it holds some ten thousand gallons of water. Used by the priests to attain ritual purity before officiating in the sacrificial offerings, it weighs in at a staggering two hundred tons.

The ancient Greek historian Herodotus describes the Tyrian shrine as having two great pillars – of gold and of precious stones – in a manner reminiscent of the two pillars at the entrance of Solomon's Temple. They are in essence phallic symbols, being regarded by the Phoenicians as emblematic of fertility. It is in fact a reasonable assumption that the Phoenician craftsmen hired by the Israelite king use the Tyrian temple as a prototype for the one they will construct in Jerusalem. Elsewhere we read:

> King Hiram of Tyre sent a trade mission to David; he provided him with cedar logs and with stonemasons and carpenters to build a palace.[25]

Solomon's Temple a copy of a pagan shrine? That's what "foreign entanglements" get you. They also get you indebted by degrees to your "allies." In order to feed Hiram's workforce, Solomon now has to scrounge up 100,000 bushels of wheat and 110,000 gallons of pure olive oil each year. Additionally, Solomon drafts thirty thousand "forced laborers" from all over Israel. They are divided into three groups of ten thousand, each group spending one month in

---

25 1 Chronicles 14:1, GNT.

Lebanon and two months back in Israel.[26] While the Bible calls them "foreigners," they aren't really foreign at all, but Phoenician residents of Judea. Again we find parallel with the Hebrews suffering under Pharaoh; only now the Israelites are the taskmasters. "Pharaoh" Solomon supplements these laborers with an additional eighty thousand stone cutters in the Judean hills, and seventy thousand more to haul the quarried ashlars to the Temple Mount and set them in place.

As for the interior of the edifice, it is covered with fine cedar wood panels from, of course, Lebanon. No expense is spared, as the king adorns the Temple furnishings – the altar of incense, the table of bread offered to God, and the ten lamp stands before the holy of holies with pure gold. Doubtless, all of this is spectacularly beautiful, but money, proverbially, really doesn't grow on trees. As the simplicity and portability of the Ark of the Covenant is lost, indebtedness to the kingdom of Tyre (Solomon's version of China), grows beyond measure.

Of course, readers of the Bible never worry about the Temple's considerable "down side," as the text describes the great commemoration ceremony, at which Solomon himself presides. The king offers a magnificent prayer, paragon of wisdom that he is, and slaughters twenty-two thousand head of cattle and 120,000 sheep. (Fortunately for him there's no ancient version of PETA.) The whole extravaganza is capped off by an unscheduled appearance of God, who warns Solomon that if the people fail to obey the divine laws, and worship other gods, this Temple, far from being hallowed, will be abandoned and become a pile of ruins. Never mind that the Temple has in fact been constructed, by and large, by people who worship other gods. Does all of this perhaps mask an implicit recognition that fixed temples don't cultivate piety, but sow the seeds of disobedience? In the end, the people's waywardness is destined to play out as discontent and jealousy, over who has access to the shrine and who does not. Far from unifying the land, this great Temple will sow the seeds of the kingdom's ultimate dissolution. In the meantime, however, how about three cheers for "Solomon the wise"?

### Solomon's "Executive Mansion"

Yet, there's even more "pagan" influence from Tyre, lurking

---

26 1 Kings 5:13-14.

in the background of Israel's "foreign entanglements." Beyond the need for a splendid Temple, shouldn't a king have an equally splendid palace? In Phoenician tales from ancient Ugarit, we find that after the god of the sea, Yam, becomes king, his craftsmen construct:

> ... a mansion for Yam... a palace for Judge Nahar
> ... they are building a mansion for Prince Yam
> they are constructing a palace for Judge Nahar

In near eastern tradition, a king had to have a palace in order for his rule to be considered legitimate. Solomon in his vanity will prove to be no exception. It takes him thirteen years, which at least proves that he's patient. Located on the Temple Mount, to the south of the shrine itself, it's one more testimony to the influence of King Hiram and the Tyrians. Its main feature is the one hundred fifty foot-long Hall of the Forest of Lebanon, boasting three rows of cedar pillars, supporting massive cedar beams and covering a series of storerooms. Then there is the Hall of Columns, seventy-five feet in length and supporting a covered porch.[27]

For Solomon himself we find an enormous throne room, covered from floor to ceiling with cedar rafters, where the mighty potentate sits in judgment on all manner of cases and disputes. The king's own quarters are in a separate structure behind the judgment hall. But as if all this isn't enough, there is a separate house for his wife, the daughter of Egypt's pharaoh. Readers are supposed to marvel at Solomon's version of "Camelot," but what about the dream of an Israelite confederacy? And what has become of Brutus?

Of course, a "chief executive" needs an impressive set of quarters, and George Washington knew this, as he personally surveyed the land for what would become the "City of Washington." However, the Executive Mansion, like the District of Colombia itself, would possess a measured sense of humility when compared with the dazzling palaces of continental Europe, and their distant antecedents in the days of Solomon. Designed by Irish-born architect James Hoban, the structure, completed in 1800, was occupied by every American president with one notable exception – George Washington, whose term ended in 1797.

Nor was presidential protocol at the White House particularly

---

27 Rivka Gonen, *Contested Holiness: Jewish, Muslim, and Christian Perspectives on the Temple* (Jersey City: NJ: KTAV Publishing House, 2003), 52ff.

pompous in the early American republic. Compare the biblical description of Solomon's regal quarters with those of America's Chief Executive, as described by a writer of the day:

> The President is accessible to all; there is not need of an official introduction; each introduces himself; all etiquette is reduced to this simple formality. Upon New-year's day, or on the fourth of July ... the White House is thronged with visitors of a more mixed character than usual. On these days of formal reception, it is not uncommon to see a hackman, who is in waiting before the door, entrust his horses to the care of a brother whip, and enter to clasp the President familiarly by the hand, and the latter returns his clasp with as much cordiality as if he were receiving a member of congress, or a foreign ambassador. Every Tuesday and Friday the President's doors are open to all visitors ... there are neither body guards, nor soldiers, nor even valets to interpose between the President and the lowest citizen... The saloon might be taken for that of a retired wood merchant. An old piano which has seen several generations of Presidents and Lady-Presidents, a few straw chairs, six mahogany arm-chairs, two sofas, a lamp, curtains of white muslin, a crystal luster, the portrait obligato of Washington – this is all.[28]

Indeed, the president sounds very much like an early biblical Judge, rather than the highest member of America's twenty-first century "ruling class." History in fact shows that as the American government grew, so did the White House. It shouldn't surprise us that the president who did the most to expand the role of government in the early twentieth century – the King-David-like Teddy Roosevelt – found it necessary to add the "West Wing" to what he now officially called the "White House." An "imperial presidency" presiding over a hugely bloated District of Colombia – exactly what T.R.'s friend, turned arch-nemesis, William Howard Taft feared – was destined one day to swamp and supplant the "old republic." Memories of an earlier – some would say more "genteel" – society, would, not

---

28 "French Critics and Yankee Foibles – Letters of the Baron Charles de Boigne," in Thomas Prentice Kettle, ed., *United States Magazine and Democratic Review*, Vol. XXI (New York: Publication Office, 1847), 499.

surprisingly, linger. The story is told that during a short walk on the White House grounds, President Calvin Coolidge was chatting with Missouri senator, Selden P. Spencer, who jestingly pointed to the Executive Mansion, saying "I wonder who lives there." "Nobody," returned President "Silent Cal." "They just come and go..."[29]

### When Taxes Aren't Enough

Solomon, for his part, may have built a monarch's dream, but he still hasn't paid the bill. For all of his wealth and his grandiose building projects, the reality is that his most desired materials, gold, silver, and cedar are commodities lacking in Israel. He is forced to look to other lands for his commodities, for which he must pay increasingly exorbitant prices. He therefore resorts to the one tool that members of the ruling class can always count on – taxation.

His realm is divided into twelve administrative districts (one for each tribe), and each is expected to pay him tribute – as if he is a "foreign" overlord. However, continuing David's policy of favoritism toward his own tribe, Judah is conveniently exempted. This of course gains him the tribe's unconditional allegiance, as surely as the modern legions of citizens who do not pay federal income tax are in the pocket of the "ruling class" in Washington. But Solomon's preference for Judah will cost him dearly, in the tension and jealousy that his actions spread among the other tribes. It is a tension destined to plunge the nation headlong into a war between the tribes, as surely as the American republic will erupt in a War Between the States.

As in modern America, Solomon ends up deeply indebted to other lands, Tyre being his version of China. In the American experience there have been no shortage of warnings, from the nation's founding to the present, about the peril of public indebtedness. John Adams once remarked, "There are two ways to conquer and enslave a nation. One is by sword. The other is by debt." Though from a different political party and a diametrically opposite political philosophy, Thomas Jefferson fundamentally agreed with his rival Adams on the question of debt:

I place the economy among the first and most important

---

29 Paul F. Boller, Jr., *Presidential Anecdotes* (New York: Oxford University Press, 1981), 2.

virtues... and public debt as the great danger to be feared. To preserve your independence, we must not let our leaders load us with perpetual debt. We must make our choice between economy and liberty... or profusion and servitude.[30]

In Solomon's case, sandwiched among all the lavish praise heaped upon his construction of the Temple and his palace is a brief verse that speaks volumes:

> King Solomon gave twenty towns in Galilee to Hiram king of Tyre, because Hiram had supplied him with all the cedar and pine and gold he wanted.[31]

The Bible makes this sound like a gift, but let us suggest something else lurking beneath the surface. The Bible may well be covering for the fact that Solomon's debt burden has become so heavy that he must resort to ceding his own territory – his sovereign land – to a foreign monarch.[32] Moreover, King Hiram doesn't even appreciate the "gift":

> But when Hiram went from Tyre to see the towns that Solomon had given him, he was not pleased with them. "What kind of towns are these you have given me, my brother?" he asked. And he called them the Land of Cabul (which sounds like the Hebrew word for "worthless"), a name they have to this day.[33]

Not only has Solomon lost entire cities, but they are officially considered "worthless" by their new foreign master. Could there be a greater measure of degradation, provoked by the folly of debt? Indeed, Solomon would have done well to read one of his own proverbs: "The borrower is servant to the lender."[34]

On a personal note, when I worked in Lebanon for an Ameri-

---

30 Thomas Jefferson to William Plumer, July 21, 1816.

31 1 Kings 9:11, NIV.

32 Such details indicate that the imperial structure Solomon inherited from David was beginning to crumble. See Brooks, op. cit., 170.

33 1 Kings 9:12-13, NIV.

34 Proverbs 22:7.

can news gathering organization, I daily drove the road from northern Galilee, passing by a sleeping mound, an un-excavated ancient city known in the Bible as Abel Bet Maacah. While mentioned several times in the biblical text, it was never a prominent site, and I paid little attention to it until I realized its connection with Solomon's debt. This ancient site, I learned was probably one of the cities surrendered by Solomon to compensate for his massive debts. No archaeologist's spade has ever touched it, and it remains a mute testimony to governmental "boondoggles" (temples and palaces not exempted) both ancient and modern.

All of Solomon's fortifications won't help him or his kingdom in the end. One of Solomon's own officials, Jeroboam by name, has an encounter with a prophet that will shape the course of future events:

> One day as Jeroboam was leaving Jerusalem, the prophet Ahijah from Shiloh met him along the way. Ahijah was wearing a new cloak. The two of them were alone in a field, and Ahijah took hold of the new cloak he was wearing and tore it into twelve pieces. Then he said to Jeroboam, "Take ten of these pieces, for this is what the LORD, the God of Israel, says: 'I am about to tear the kingdom from the hand of Solomon, and I will give ten of the tribes to you!'"[35]

We are told that Solomon, fearful for his rule, tries to kill Jeroboam, who flees for safety to Egypt. Exile, as we know on multiple occasions in history – Comrade Lenin being a prime example – is the incubator of civil war, the crucible of revolution. So it will be in ancient Israel, in Solomon's mighty wake.

---

35 I Kings 11:29-31, NLT

# 7
# THE WAR BETWEEN THE TRIBES

*"What country before ever existed a century & half without a rebellion? & What country can preserve its liberties if their rulers are not warned from time to time that their people preserve the spirit of resistance? Let them take arms..."*
– Thomas Jefferson[1]

I t takes little imagination to recognize, in Solomonic Israel, as in the American republic, serious debate about the role and scope of the central government, and the role of the leader within that government. In ancient Israel everybody knows that in theory the individual tribes should make their own decisions, of, by and for their own people, locally. "Don't tread on me" might well be the Israelite tribal mantra. But tread Jerusalem does, until the air is rife with rebellion. The dissolution of the biblical union has been simmering beneath the surface for quite some time when Solomon "the wise" finally passes from the scene. The official line of the biblical text is that the people have "forsaken" God and worshipped foreign deities, specifically Ashtoreth, goddess of the Sidonians, Chemosh the Moabite god, and Milcom, goddess of the Am-

---

1 Letter to William S. Smith, Nov. 13, 1787.

monites.[2] The monotheist is perennially looking for some spiritual/ religious reason behind every calamity. But in so doing, the most valuable political lessons of the sacred text are obscured if not lost sight of completely.

There is no greater case in point than the legacy of Solomon's son and successor, Rehoboam, who heads for the city of Shechem to be properly vested as the new monarch. But pomp and ceremony notwithstanding, the differences between Judah and Benjamin in the south and the other ten tribes in the north, unreconciled and growing during the reigns of David and Solomon, are destined only to be exacerbated under Rehoboam. The northern tribes in these days feel just as trampled as America's southern states felt in the period leading up to the Civil War. Rehoboam fails to realize that only broad and meaningful concessions, including reform of the Jerusalem-centric governmental apparatus, will be sufficient to preserve the disintegrating "United Kingdom." We no longer hear of massive building projects, or of the throngs of slaves needed to erect them. This, however, is hardly a measure of "reform," but merely a reflection of the fact that tribal tensions are such a diversion that Solomonic grandeur is now out of the question.

As the biblical narrative advances, who should seek out the new king but the exiled Jeroboam, who comes up from Egypt, now that the "tyrant" Solomon is out of the way? Arranging an audience with Rehoboam, Jeroboam wants to know what kind of ruler the new king will be. "Your father made our yoke hard," declares Jeroboam. Are we to understand that the "wise" Solomon, righteous judge and maker of multitudinous proverbs, was a harsh taskmaster? The Bible, by the fact that it openly quotes Jeroboam and doesn't attempt to censor him, seems to acknowledge this fact. The erstwhile exile adds a demand. "Now lighten the hard service of your father, and the heavy yoke which he put on us, and we will serve you."[3] The obvious reference is to Solomon's heavy-handed, "big government," high taxation, coupled with forced military conscription and forced labor. Enough tyranny! How about returning to the principles of limited government, the tribal confederacy we once had under our Judges, but lost to a royal house that did exactly what the prophet Samuel had warned it would do? Yet, Jeroboam doesn't demand the abolition of the monarchy, but merely that it undertake reforms.

2 1 Kings 11:33.

3 1 Kings 12:4.

Clearly, he sees the possibility for compromise. The "United King-dom" at this moment hangs in the balance.

Interestingly, Rehoboam doesn't respond immediately. He sends his petitioners away for three days, in order to consider his options. This might be the very moment that will save the "U.K." from dissolution. The king consults with a number of elderly advisors, who had served in the days of his father Solomon. They have seen first-hand the "corruption of power" that goes with the monarchical turf. Their advice: If you want the people to serve you, be a servant to them. Speak to them good words, and they will serve you.

The king, however, is not satisfied. He next speaks with his young advisors, who had served in his own day. Their advice is de-cidedly different, suggesting that he deliver the following message:

> My little finger shall be thicker than my father's loins.
> And now my father loaded you with a heavy yoke, and
> I will add to your yoke. My father has whipped you with
> whips, but I will chastise you with scorpions.[4]

The "scorpion" line is a true classic of biblical literature. It's the epitome of everything that might conceivably go wrong with a monarchy. A truly wise man might have asked, "Why is youth wasted on the young?" Rehoboam, however, goes with the "youth vote" and, when Jeroboam returns three days hence, responds to him precisely in this manner.[5] In this candid account of Rehoboam's tyranny, the Brutus current, submerged in the narrative since the days of Solomon, rises again. It is refreshingly rebellious, anti-estab-lishment, and contemptuous of authority.[6]

### Federalism vs. Nationalism: The Catalyst for Dissolution

In ancient Israel, the fundamental issue of "tribes' rights" is not unlike the tensions brewing in the American republic. The major difference, of course, is that in the biblical account it is the north that

---

4 1 Kings 12:10-11.

5 George Claude Orimer, ed., *The People's Bible History: Prepared in Light of Recent Investigations* (Chicago: Henry O. Shephard Co., 1896), 383.

6 In ancient Israel the power of kings was "checked" via illegal action, in that the people could revolt, even if a king was acting within his authority. See Miller, op. cit., 235.

breaks away. As America's Civil War takes shape, the two Israelite regions are conveniently reversed, as historical "mirror images" of each other. Washington D.C. under Lincoln is the equivalent of Jerusalem under Rehoboam. The question that dogs historians down to the present has to do with the "real" issue behind the outbreak of the Civil War. Was it purely slavery, which was after all the single most wrenchingly ethical ignominy in the entire American experience? Or was slavery, disgusting as it was, more of a "catalyst" that ignited the simmering controversy over "states' rights"?

Was America to be a Washington-dominated centralized state or a loose federation of sovereign states? Was the "republic" bequeathed by the Constitution still too weak (allowing certain states to believe that they could in fact withdraw from the Union) or (recalling the ominous harangues of Robert "Brutus" Yates) yet too strong? In the beginning there was general agreement that the role of the federal government was designed to be strictly limited and that powers not expressly delegated to it were to be reserved to the states – hence the Tenth Amendment. But to recognize fully what was at stake we need to take yet another look at the theory of government according to the Founders.

In the late eighteenth century a "federation" by definition entailed a relationship, as in an alliance, between independent, sovereign states or nation-states. However, the very term "federal," as in "federal government," shifted over time to mean the exact opposite of its original intent. Nowadays, it means "centralized;" in the 1700s it meant a localized "confederation." The Constitution's framers and supporters, who ironically called themselves the "Federalists," didn't really intend to create a "federal" government (as in a loose alliance of states), but a consolidated-federal "hybrid." Madison wrote:

> The proposed Constitution . . . is, in strictness, neither a national nor a federal Constitution, but a composition of both. In its foundation it is federal, not national; in the sources from which the ordinary powers of the government are drawn, it is partly federal and partly national; in the operation of these powers, it is national, not federal; in the extent of them, again, it is federal, not national; and, finally, in the authoritative mode of introducing amend-

ments, it is neither wholly federal nor wholly national.[7]

While it may sound a bit like gobbledygook, the Founders essentially created what historians call a "dual federalism" or "layer cake," namely, the concept of two separate and distinct spheres of government.[8] They were designed to consist of a national sphere and a state sphere, the government of each being autonomous and largely independent, one from the other. In the nineteenth century, however, the single issue of slavery would test the very essence of federalism and all that it entails. The result would be the greatest epic tragedy ever to unfold on American soil – the Civil War. It would signal the slow demise and ultimate obliteration of the federalist principle.

To be sure, secession had been discussed repeatedly during the nation's short lifespan, and it hand't always been connected with slavery and abolitionism. Back during the Monroe administration, New England felt directly threatened by the disruption of trade brought on by the War of 1812. Trade was, after all, the lifeblood of the region, and there was serious talk in 1814 of breaking away from the federal Union. So great was the resentment against centralized power coming out of Washington, D.C. that the Civil War might well have been fought decades earlier, over an entirely different set of issues.

We have already noted the near-secession of South Carolina, not over slavery, but over the issue of the protective tariff and Andrew Jackson's "authoritarian" federal response. When slavery finally erupted as a potential ground for secession, we saw Zachary Taylor's resolve in squelching any and all talk of rebellion, and even threatening to hang the rebels. What indeed were the limits of the federal government? How far could central authority go in squelching dissent? And did the federalism as a political theory go as far as to allow local governmental units – the states – to withdraw from the larger nation? The issues faced by the Israelite King Rehoboam and his nemesis Jeroboam returned with a vengeance to the American republic. The conundrum was daunting. To support federalism meant leaving the door open for the perpetuation of the evil of slavery. To oppose slavery entailed the risk of overturning the spirit of

---

7 The Federalist, No. 39.

8 Robert Singh, *Governing America: The Politics of a Divided Democracy* (New York: Oxford Univ. Press, 2003), 83.

federalism.

President Franklin Pierce, who served from 1853 to 1857, came face to face with these conundrums when Senator Stephen A. Douglas cajoled him into adopting the Kansas-Nebraska Act. The effect of this legislation was by-and-large to overturn the Compromise of 1820, that had banned slavery above the southern border of Missouri. The intent was to allow the new territories to decide for themselves whether or not they wanted slavery. Wasn't this in-keeping with the notion of a "federal republic" – exactly the system adopted by the early Israelite tribal confederacy and so admired by Thomas Paine? Maybe so, but there were by then plenty of abolitionists who felt that a moral imperative as important as the abolition of slavery trumps even the most "sacred cows" of political theory. That at least was the position of a little known Whig politician from Illinois, Abraham Lincoln, whom destiny would select to lead the charge in asserting federal power to overturn moral evil. Lincoln went on to help found a new political party – the Republican party – that would take up the abolitionist cause. Meanwhile, Kansas turned into "bleeding Kansas."[9] On May 21, 1856, pro-slavery forces burned to the ground the abolitionist settlement of Lawrence, Kansas.

Pierce was subsequently dropped by his own party, setting the stage for the election of James Buchanan, who has earned the dubious distinction of being perhaps the worst president in American history. By the time Buchanan was ensconced in office, the southern position of "states' rights" so well-articulated that the president himself leaned in the South's direction – so much so that he has been posthumously accused of near-treason. Let's bear in mind, however, that when it comes to political theory, the grotesque evil of the south's slavery culture is so abhorrent that we often lose sight of the principle of limited government that was simultaneously being argued by the southern states. On that score Buchanan has been defended, as one who favored compromise in respecting the rights of the southern states, so as to prevent the fracturing of the Union.[10] As far as the southern states were concerned (notwithstanding the abhorrence of slavery), the loose "Confederacy" they assembled was

9 Nicole Etcheson, *Bleeding Kansas: Contested Liberty in the Civil War Era* (Lawrence, KS: Univ. Press of Kansas, 2004).

10 Jack L. Pennington, *The Real Cause of the Civil War* (Bloomington, IN: iUniverse Books, 2011), 55.

a true reflection of what the Founders were after – a bona-fide republic, where individual states could determine their own destinies.

### Lincoln: "Messiah" or Tyrant?

In the historic election of 1860, slavery, couched in the mantra of "states' rights," was, as everyone expected, the single defining issue. With the election of Abraham Lincoln, it was only a matter of time until the fragile Union's disintegration was sealed. South Carolina became the first state to secede from the Union, on December 20, 1860, but was this due to the election of an anti-slavery president (the "normal" take on things) or a chief executive intent on fundamentally undoing the rights of the sovereign states? The lame-duck president, James Buchanan, himself a southerner, denied the legality of secession, but took no action to stop it. In the interim, prior to Lincoln's inauguration, eight more slave states left the Union. The saga of biblical Israel was replaying itself.

On February 9, 1861, the "Confederate States of America" elected as their president Jefferson Davis – America's version of Jeroboam, who led ten of the twelve tribes in "secession" from the "U.K." On his last day in office, Buchanan remarked to Lincoln, "If you are as happy to be entering the presidency as I am to be leaving it, then you are a very happy man." As far as the nation today is concerned, Lincoln and Lincoln alone had the "right stuff" to save the Union. But in the eyes of the South (as well as a few modern "revisionist" historians), he was an incorrigible tyrant. Few can quibble with Lincoln's core character qualities, his self-effacing wit, his commitment to honesty and virtue. But even in Lincoln's mind, there was much more at stake than the slavery issue alone. There remained a host of issues dating from the founding of the republic, regarding the role of the federal government vis-a-vis individual states and localities. Was Lincoln the font of all wisdom, with a "messianic" aura, as he is traditionally cast? Or was he America's Rehoboam, foreswearing moderation (as some "revisionist" historians argue)" and insisting on heavy-handed central authority, even at the cost of over half a million dead on the nation's battlefields? Lincoln may have been a self-taught scholar and avid student of the Bible, remarking, "In regard to this Great book, I have but to say, it is the best gift God has given to man."[11] But did he really grasp the

---

11 Noah Brooks, *Washington, D.C., in Lincoln's Time: A Memoir of the Civil War Era by*

political lessons of holy writ? The fact is, in spite of the flawed character of the southern "cause," most southerners in the Civil War era thought of Lincoln exactly as northern Israelites thought of Rehoboam – a tyrant.

Lincoln's detractors, then and now, point to his privileging of the central government over the individual states, which, they argue, was not necessarily consistent with the ideas of the Founders. He declared:

> The Union is older than any of the states and, in fact, it created them as States. . . . The Union and not the states separately produced their independence and their liberty. . . . The Union gave each of them whatever independence and liberty it has.[12]

He insisted that the individual states were entitled to final jurisdiction over only "those things that pertain exclusively to themselves—that are local in their nature, that have no connection with the general government."[13] To "libertarians" from that day to the present, this was heresy. The allegations against him are legion, and, most would say, undeserved. It is nonetheless argued that he didn't prosecute the most devastating war in American history in order to free the slaves, but rather to establish the precedent of national supremacy over the states.[14] He is said to have spent his political career in a "fundamental transformation" of America from having a strictly limited government to a highly centralized and activist state.

No wonder, it is alleged, that he had to crush the South, which was driven by resistance to centralized government, the independence of the sovereign states, and free and open commerce. Lincoln's strategy, according to his detractors, was dubious at best:

\* Trample the Constitution
\* Nullify the most important principle of the Declaration of Independence – that governments derive their just

---

*the Newspaperman Who Knew Lincoln Best* (Athens, GA: Univ. Of Georgia Press), 252.

12 Samuel H. Beer, "The Idea of the Nation" in *How Federal is the Constitution?*, Goldwin and Schambra, eds. (Washington, D.C.: American Enterprise Institute, 1986), 110.

13 Roy P. Basler, ed., *op. cit.*, 3:409.

14 See Thomas DiLorenzo, *The Real Lincoln: A New Look at Abraham Lincoln, His Agenda, and an Unnecessary War* (New York: Three Rivers Press, 2003).

powers from the consent of the governed
* Shred the rights of the sovereign states
* Enact protectionist tariffs
* Promote subsidies for railroad and canal-building mo-
nopolies
* Create a government monopoly of the money supply
* Launch a "total war" that would leave the old republic
"gone with the wind."

We need to temper all this with the fact that the majority of
modern historians would call such charges sheer hyperbole. Indeed,
only radical revisionists buy into this view of America's sixteenth
president. The South, in any case, surely did see Lincoln in such
terms, and the great "cause" for which they fought finds many parallels with the "civil war" in biblical Israel.

As for implementing "big government," it's true that Lincoln
was the one who brought about the implementation of Henry Clay's
"American System," a tripartite "Hamiltonian" plan that called for
a high import tariff for the protection of American industry, a national bank (despised by Andrew Jackson as well as modern "libertarians") to promote commerce and reign in "risky" state and
local banks, and federal subsidies for roads, canals, and "internal
improvements" designed to foster markets for agricultural products.
An important tenet of the Whig Party, the American System was
backed by the likes of the venerable Daniel Webster. But it was vehe-
mently opposed by the Democratic Party, including Andrew Jackson, James K. Polk, Franklin Pierce, and James Buchanan.

Lincoln, however, took advantage of the southern Democrats'
absence from Congress, implementing its provisions literally at gunpoint. The Morrill Tariff more than tripled import duties, to a staggering forty-seven percent. The National Currency Acts nationalized the banking system. Lavish subsidies doled out to the railroads
brought about the corruption that later erupted during the scandal-
ridden Grant administration. This was, arguably, big government
mercantilism at its worst. It generated a self-perpetuating centralization of power that forever changed the character of the American
republic. Again we think of King Solomon, who built an empire of
ancient "mercantilism," and alienated ten of the twelve tribes in the
process.

The anti-Lincoln vitriol continues, with the charge (outlandish though it seems to most traditionally-minded students of history) that he created nothing less than a "constitutional dictatorship."[15] While considered part of today's "lunatic fringe," the Anti-Lincoln camp nonetheless gives us a snapshot of what the South viewed as principled arguments, and what the biblical North felt about Jerusalem's/ Rehoboam's "tyranny." Among the specific accusations against the sixteenth president:

* He invaded the South without congressional authority.
* He declared martial law.
* He blockaded southern ports though lacking a declaration of war.
* He suspended habeas corpus.
* He imprisoned northern anti-war protesters, including hundreds of newspaper editors.
* He censored newspaper and telegraph communications.
* He nationalized the railroads.
* He created three new states in order to inflate the electoral vote of his own party.
* He ordered federal troops to interfere in northern elections to assure favorable vote tallies.
* He deported an Ohio congressman for opposition to his proposal of protectionist tariffs and an income tax.

The long-term results, it is argued, brought about military conscription for the first time in American history (shades of King Solomon) and, over time, a permanent system of income taxation.[16]

Lincoln is of course remembered for one of the most famous speeches ever delivered, the Gettysburg Address, wherein he famously declared "that government of the people ... shall not perish from the earth." Today's Jeroboam-like "Brutuses," however, are quick to cite H.L. Mencken's observations on the same:

It is difficult to imagine anything more untrue. The Union soldiers in the battle actually fought against self determi-

---

15 Clinton Rossiter, *Constitutional Dictatorship: Crisis Government in the Modern Democracies* (Piscataway, NJ: Transaction Publishers), 224ff.

16 Dean Sprague, *Freedom Under Lincoln: Federal Power and Personal Liberty Under the Strain of Civil War* (New York: Houghton Mifflin, 1965).

nation; it was the Confederates who fought for the right of their people to govern themselves. The Confederates went into the battle free; they came out with their freedom subject to the supervision of the rest of the country.[17]

At the end of the day, the vanquished South felt that the entire principle of federalism had collapsed into a brave new political world, "of, by, and for" Washington, D.C. The fears earlier echoed by John C. Calhoun (according to anti-Lincoln "libertarians") had now materialized in full:

> The great conservative principle of our system is in the people of the States, as parties to the Constitutional compact....[18]

> Without a full practical recognition of the rights and sovereignty of the States, our union and liberty must perish.[19]

And perish, they did.

### The Great Emancipator?

As for the "number one" issue of the day, slavery, the nation's Founders, it seems, had left a political legacy that included a potentially fatal deficit. Unfortunately, "liberty and justice" applied to "some," not "all." As in ancient Israel, slavery had been institutionalized, having been a harsh reality for generations. Of course Solomon's slavery didn't apply to Israelites, only to "foreigners" in the land, and on that basis many students of the Bible have always been content to give the "wise" king a pass. By the same logic, however, one could also excuse African American slavery, as many in early America did, even while sanctimoniously pointing to the Bible. But when it comes to Abraham Lincoln, he was certainly on the "right" side; or was he?

---

17 H.L. Mencken, *A Mencken Chrestomathy* (New York: Knopf, 1956), 223.

18 John C. Calhoun, To Virgil Maxcy, Sep. 1, 1831, Library of Congress; cf. Clyde N. Wilson, ed.,*The Essential Calhoun: Selections from Writings, Speeches, and Letters* (New Brunswick, N.J.: Transaction Publishers, 2000), 299.

19 John C. Calhoun, Public letter to citizens of Dahlonega, Georgia, Aug. 31, 1834; cf. Wilson, 301.

It has in fact been argued that Lincoln wasn't really an abolitionist at all. Truth be told, he was derided by many abolitionists, including the prominent voice of William Lloyd Garrison, who pronounced that Lincoln "had not a drop of anti-slavery blood in his veins."[20] Garrison, who knew Lincoln personally, repeatedly asserted that the president from Illinois didn't even believe in the equality of the races, either socially or politically. Specifically, he opposed interracial marriage, favored Illinois' ban on the immigration of blacks, defended in court a slaveowner seeking his runaway slaves, and advocated repatriating blacks to Africa, or sending them to Haiti or Central America. Lincoln detractors point out that he never even mentioned slavery in public until a speech delivered in 1854, which, according to one editor of his works, was insincere.[21]

Even Lincoln's staunch defenders, who hail him for his virtue, admit that he wasn't always the "Great Emancipator;" he only became the "Great Emancipator." All agree that his original intent was merely to halt the expansion of slavery into the territories to the west. He declared that if he could save the Union without freeing a single slave, he would. If freeing some, while leaving others in bondage would save it, he would equally take that course. He even made a pledge of "no interference" with state power over the slavery issue.[22] Rather than confronting slavery head-on, he felt that the best way to kill the institution of slavery was to contain it and allow it to suffocate from within. His greatest goal was the preservation of the Union as it had existed until that point. Nowadays, Lincoln is roundly praised for his willingness to compromise in order to shore up the disintegrating Union. Certainly, Lincoln recognized that compromise will often achieve what stubbornness won't. Others, however, see not an ounce of compromise in Lincoln's policy of nationalism and his willingness to pursue "total war," even at the cost of over 600,000 of America's sons.

Some modern historians call him a "conservative," in his desire to preserve the status quo of the "United" States. But he is seen

---

20 David S. Reynolds, *John Brown, Abolitionist: The Man Who Killed Slavery, Sparked the Civil War, and Seeded Civil Rights* (New York: Vintage Books, 2005), 5; David H. Donald, *Lincoln Reconsidered: Essays on the Civil War Era* (New York: Vintage Books, 2001), 32.

21 Roy Basler, *op. cit.*

22 Michael Les Benedict, "Abraham Lincoln and Federalism," *Journal of the Abraham Lincoln Association*, 10:1, 1988.

as being drawn increasingly to the "left" in his desire to overturn the evil of slavery. His position is said to have evolved, becoming "revolutionary," insofar as it required the complete demolition of the society of the old South. But all this analysis may be more than a tad anachronistic. What, after all, does "conservative" mean? If it means "limited government," then Lincoln's pro-Union stance was hardly conservative. If "left" implies the destruction of federalism and a much bigger national government, then on that score Lincoln qualifies as a "leftist" all along. It was the southern Confederacy that was "conservative" in that sense. What evolved in the end was a national government that was far more centralized than anything the Founders ever contemplated.

What about Lincoln's greatest edict, the Emancipation Proclamation? Did this amount to what some have hailed as the "Second American Revolution"? Most of us would like to think so, but isn't it odd, that when the Great Emancipator heard the news, in August,1861, that in the border state of Missouri Major General John C. Freemont had issued his own "emancipation proclamation," beating Lincoln to the proverbial punch, he fumed with rage? On a political level, Lincoln feared that this action would only incite slave holders in all of the border states to join the rebel cause. Consequently, Lincoln not only nullified Freemont's proclamation; he relieved the general of duty. Was this the behavior of an ardent abolitionist?

As for Lincoln's vaunted version of Emancipation, it is true that the Proclamation, delivered in January, 1863, didn't free the slaves universally. Rather, being enacted under Lincoln's war powers, it only freed slaves in ten of the states in rebellion at the time. While in theory it applied to 3.1 million out of 4 million slaves in the nation, it nonetheless exempted such territories that were currently occupied by Union forces, namely, the very areas where slaves might actually have been freed. Furthermore, it did not apply to the slave-holding states of Missouri, Kentucky, Maryland and Delaware, that had not seceded. Nor did it by itself outlaw slavery, or enfranchise the emancipated slaves ("freedmen") as citizens. It would take the Thirteenth Amendment, which only took effect after Lincoln's death in 1865, to do that.

Some question whether there might have been another way to end the evil of slavery. The libertarian abolitionist lawyer Lysander Spooner frequently chided Lincoln, who wanted no part of him, even though he waged a bloodless struggle against slavery on constitutional grounds.[23] Spooner's campaign reminds us of the efforts of William Wilberforce in England, who labored tirelessly against the slave traffic until its ultimate demise. It was in line with the route to emancipation taken by countries all over the world in the nineteenth century; it was peaceful. Peace, however, was not in the cards in the age of Lincoln.

There are of course many fine reasons, not only to admire Lincoln personally, but to hail his policies.

1) Lincoln's apparent lack of abolitionist credentials should be understood in light of his resolve to use war only as a last resort. His contempt for slavery as an institution was balanced by his reluctance to overreach, beyond his constitutional powers, in order to abolish it.

2) Saving the Union was a worthy and noble cause, without which succeeding generations would certainly have inherited two greatly diminished, mutually hostile regions – exactly the result of ancient Israel's civil war.

3) The only realistic way to save the Union (whatever the genuine points on the side of the secessionists) was through war, which is on certain occasions in history, a necessary evil. To that extent the Civil War, in spite of the horrific toll it exacted on both sides, was indeed "the good war."

### Lincoln v. Rehoboam: "Total Warriors"

What was the difference between Lincoln and Israel's King Rehoboam? The issues – central control from Washington/ Jerusalem vs. local sovereignty of the states/ tribes – were much the same, in spite of the two societies being separated by thousands of years. Rehoboam, arguably, lacked the grit and determination of Lincoln to wage ruthless, all-out, total war, regardless of the cost blood and

---

23 Jonathan J. Bean, ed., *Race and Liberty in America: The Essential Reader* (Louisville, KY: Univ. Press of Kentucky, 2009); Thomas E. Schneider, *Lincoln's Defense of Politics: The Public Man and hIs Opponents in the Crisis over Slavery* (Columbia, MO: Univ. of Missouri Press, 2006), 142.

treasure. But he would at least try.

In war-torn America, Richmond, Virginia was designated as the rebel capital; in biblical days Jeroboam's new capital would be in the north, Tirzah. In the case of both Israel and America, the War Between the Tribes/ States would not be resolved quickly. Lincoln is known for having been more than mildly frustrated with the conduct of his own generals, who offered him nothing better than a protracted stalemate, accompanied by untold bloodshed. The town of Winchester, Virginia, for example, changed hands over seventy times during the course of the war. Things went baldly for Lincoln from the get-go, the defeat at Fort Sumter prompting four more states to join the Confederacy. In the spring of 1861 Lincoln himself became commander-in-chief of the armed forces, giving himself a crash-course in military strategy and tactics. As in ancient Israel, war sapped the strength of both north and south. Over time, Union armies were able to secure impressive victories in the west, but in the east, humiliating losses were more the rule than the exception.

In April, 1862, the Union army won a critically important engagement at the Battle of Shiloh. We might even find here a "mystical connection" with the Bible, for the town had been named after the biblical city of Shiloh, the ancient shrine that was home to the Ark of the Covenant, prior to it being ensconced in its permanent residence in Jerusalem. The "butcher's bill," however, was horrific, as some twenty-four thousand men were killed, wounded or missing by the battle's end. Even in Lincoln's day there were those who suggested that the president should be content, as his ancient predecessors in Jerusalem had been, to let the rebels go their own way. But this was Abraham Lincoln, and this commander-in-chief would refocus his efforts on waging "total war."[24] He would not only have to defeat the South in battle; he would have to "fundamentally transform" it. In the short term, however, the stalemate continued.

### Stalemate of Biblical Proportions

While Abraham Lincoln is the only American president to find his administration totally consumed by war, in our biblical example, the War Between the Tribes lasts much longer still, becoming multigenerational. When Rehoboam passes from the scene, his son Abijah takes the throne, and Jeroboam (a cross between Jefferson Da-

---

24 George Stanley McGovern, *Abraham Lincoln* (New York: Times Books, 2009), 79ff.

vis and Robert E. Lee) attacks him as well. Abijah counter-attacks to the north, annexing the hill country around Bethel. As the Civil War's "see-saw" action continues to the next generation, the new northern king, Baasha, recovers the lost territory by attacking the southern king, Asa, whom the Bible hails throughout his long reign as an emblem of righteousness. According the the biblical editors, the southern kingdom is a "mixed bag" of good and evil kings; but the rebel North, as we would expect, is universally ruled by wicked rulers.

Is Asa, unlike Rehoboam, a monarch who is willing and ready to compromise, and not to "lord it over" his wayward subjects like an incorrigible tyrant? The Bible is silent about such matters of political science, defining good rulership only in terms of fidelity to Jerusalem's Temple and its deity. But one political lesson Asa knows instinctively – "the enemy of my enemy is my friend." The Jerusalemite king now appeals directly to a foreign ruler, King Ben-Hadad of Damascus, who presses Baasha from the east, seizing eastern Galilee and taking the pressure off Asa. Baasha for his part must retreat from Judah and return to Tirzah. Order and prosperity is restored to Judah, but the "United Kingdom" is "gone with the wind."

Back in the rebel North, there is a new dynasty, strong and vital, headed by a powerful king named Omri. He is little remembered, because he is, after all, a northerner, and northern kings are uniformly "wicked." But after a power struggle that lasts for years, Omri nonetheless fosters stability and strength, and makes his realm a serious rival to Jerusalem. He shifts the northern capital to a city called Samaria, building there an impressive palace to match Jerusalem's royal house. Some archaeologists go as far as to claim that many of the monumental structures attributed to King Solomon (specifically at Megiddo and Hazor), are in fact the work of King Omri, who, they maintain, is deliberately written out of much of the biblical narrative.[25] His dynasty, however, will rule over Israel – and even briefly over Judah – for the next forty years.

The man who inherits the new dynamic dynasty is so thoroughly bashed by traditional commentators, down through the centuries, that his very name lives in infamy – Ahab. Though son and successor of Omri, he is much better known as the husband of his

25 Finkelstein, op. cit., 102ff; Israel Finkelstein, Neil Asher Silberman, *The Bible Unearthed: Archaeology's New Vision of Ancient Israel* (New York: The Free Press, 2001), 343.

queen, the daughter of the king of Tyre, who gets an equally "bad rap" in biblical narrative – Jezebel. Most of what is said about Ahab and Jezebel is probably undeserved. True, Jezebel is a pagan, importing the worship of a foreign deity – Baal – into the northern tribal confederacy. But are they any more despotic than the southern kings, with their Jerusalem-centric government and Temple-centric religious system?

There is one sad episode that relates the despotism that is now commonplace, in the North as well as the South. We're told of the owner of a vineyard on the eastern slope of a hill not far from Ahab's palace. The Israelite king "covets" it, wanting to convert it to "a garden of herbs." More likely, it was to be a ceremonial garden for Baal worship, which means, as far as the southern editors of the narrative are concerned, that Ahab already has at least two strikes against him. Naboth, however, is forbidden by biblical law to sell, since he has inherited the land from his father and for that reason must remain in his family in perpetuity.[26]

Ahab returns to his ivory palace, overcome with depression, an obvious case of "overreaction." That's when Jezebel gets involved. "Is this how you act as king over Israel?" she mockingly asks, and goes on to pronounce that she will obtain the vineyard on his behalf. The conniving queen plots against the unsuspecting vinedresser, staging a mock trial:

> She wrote letters in Ahab's name, placed his seal on them, and sent them to the elders and nobles who lived in Naboth's city with him. In those letters she wrote: "Proclaim a day of fasting and seat Naboth in a prominent place among the people. But seat two scoundrels opposite him and have them bring charges that he has cursed both God and the king. Then take him out and stone him to death."[27]

On news that the grizzly deed has been perpetrated, Ahab (on his wife's urging) takes the coveted vineyard as his own. The lesson in all of this is that somewhere along the line, the spirit of localism, "tribes' rights," and regional autonomy has gotten lost in the rebel

---

26 Paul R. Abrasion, *Politics in the Bible* (New Brunswick, NJ: Transaction Publishers, 2012), 88.

27 1 Kings 21:8-10, NIV.

North, replaced (as in Jerusalem) by an all-powerful monarch. "If the South has a king, a kingdom, and a palace, then so must we northerners!" Only Ahab's palace must be ivory, and his lands must include a vineyard.

## Big Government, Private Property, and "Eminent Domain"

America's Founders were certainly familiar with the biblical story of Naboth, which gave them one more lesson in political science regarding the fragility of private property rights, once "big government" gets entrenched. Ever since the notorious Quartering Acts of 1765 and 1774, requiring American colonists to provide housing and provisions for British soldiers, Americans have been zealous for the protection and preservation of private property rights. Such protections were written into the U.S. Constitution, the Third Amendment stipulating that the peacetime quartering of troops without consent of the owner of the house will not be permitted. Nonetheless, private property issues remain in the forefront of American politics.

The expropriation of private property for the "public good," as long as the owner is duly compensated – known as "eminent domain" – has long and established precedents. But with the growth of big government has come more and more abuse of eminent domain, in tandem with a contemptuous attitude toward privately held property in general. One libertarian-minded attorney sounded the alarm as follows:

> We have documented more than 10,000 instances of government taking property from one person to give it to another in just the last five years.... It is fundamentally wrong, and contrary to the Constitution for the government to take property from one private owner, and hand it over to another private owner, just because the government thinks that person is going to make more productive use of the land....Everyone knows that property can be taken for a road. But nobody thinks that property can be taken to give it to their neighbor or the large business down the street for their economic benefit.... People are shocked when they hear that this is going on around the

country.[28]

Of course, in our own day, when the even Constitution is lost sight of, how can we expect anyone to hearken to the lessons of biblical lore?

At any rate, King Ahab seems to have learned his lesson, after being berated for his arrogance by the prophet Elijah. Oddly enough, he "gets it," going into deep repentance. It should come as no surprise that when Ahab subsequently finds himself besieged by Ben-Herded of Damascus (who, as we noted, has been invited by King Asa of Damascus to harass the North), he manages to hold his own against the Syrian invader. He holes up for safety in his ivory palace in Samaria, and survives the siege, much to the chagrin of Jerusalem. At the end of the episode, it becomes clear that the rebel North is not about to be vanquished.

### "If you can't beat 'em, join 'em."

As the story of the two kingdoms continues, we find a new monarch in the South, known for being wise and just. He is known as Jehoshaphat, and he spends the first years of his reign fortifying his realm against the North, as well as routing Baal worship by destroying the deity's cult images. We read:

And Jehoshaphat [Asa's] son reigned in his place. And he made himself strong against Israel. And he placed troops in all the fortified cities of Judah, and set troops in the land of Judah and in the cities of Ephraim which Asa his father had taken.[29]

By now, it's not a matter of reuniting the twelve tribes under Jerusalem's rule; it's all about protecting Judah against possible rout by northern armies. Clearly, the ten breakaway tribes are no longer "rebels"; they are an independent kingdom to be reckoned with. They have waged their "civil war," and they have emerged victorious. This doesn't of course mean that the "confederate" principles of local government and tribal autonomy have prevailed, for

---

28 Rebecca Laung, "Eminent Domain: Being Abused?," *60 Minutes*, CBS, http://www.cbsnews.com/stories/2003/09/26/60minutes/main575343.shtml.

29 2 Chronicles 17:1-2.

the North has an entrenched monarchy as well, under the dynastic house of Omri.

As far as Jehoshaphat is concerned, he realizes, politically speaking, that he and his northern counterparts are essentially on the same "wavelength." Therefore, instead of fighting each other, why not form an alliance? Since in antiquity this is generally accomplished through wedding nuptials, Jehoshaphat arranges a marriage between his son Jehoram and the daughter of the despised King Ahab, Athaliah.[30] It's the rough equivalent of the Lincolns marrying their son Robert to Jefferson Davis' daughter Winnie. All things considered, ancient Israel may well have been the place of origin of the observation that politics makes strange bedfellows. Is this perhaps the origin of the expression "Jumpin' Jehoshaphat"? For better or for worse, the marriage is consummated, and Jehoshaphat and Ahab now find themselves political and military allies against a common foe, the Arameans (Syrians). As a military alliance, it's a far cry from the old tribal confederacy, when a Judge would rally what amounted to a militia. Tyranny has replaced liberty on both sides, and the antiquity's "minute men" have morphed into permanent armies of mercenary warriors.

We recall that it was Jehoshaphat's father, Asa, who invited the Syrians (Ben Hadad of Damascus) to invade Israel to begin with. Now Judah joins with the "rebel" tribes to beat back the foreign foe. The battle is joined in a city to the northeast of the Jordan River, Ramot-Gilead, in territory belonging to the tribe of Gad. Suffice it to say, things do not go well for the Israelite alliance. Jehoshaphat flees in defeat, while Ahab, dressed as a foot soldier to avoid looking conspicuous, is struck between the breastplates by a stray arrow. He is propped up in his chariot, still bravely facing his troops, but dies that evening:

> And the blood ran out of the wound into the midst of the chariot.[31]

In the midst of foreign threats, the "Brutus current" may seem to have submerged again ... but not really. For Ahab's death is characterized as divine "payback" for his "big government" seizure of

---

30 John Bright, *A History of Israel* (Louisville, KY: Westminster John Knox Press, 2000), 252.

31 1 Kings 22:35.

Naboth's vineyard.

Back in the South, however, Jehoshaphat must from this point focus purely on survival. While the Israelite tribal league is fractured, foreign foes are able to adopt their own "libertarian" principles, organizing an anti-Israel "confederacy." The menacing Moabites join forces with the Ammonites and Edomites to trounce Judah and the Jerusalemites once and for all. As the alliance is camped opposite the Dead Sea, at the oasis of En Gedi, King Jehoshaphat heads for the Temple, uttering a piously worded prayer:

> We have no power to face this vast army that is attacking us. We do not know what to do; but our eyes are upon you.[32]

Oft quoted as the essence of humble piety, it might be more accurate to say that by now the kings of Judah have figured out that politics and religion go hand in hand, and that power comes through centralizing both in one place. A local Levite named Jahaziel is so stirred by the King's entreaty that he prophecies that the advancing adversaries will be doomed the very next day. The Levites, of course, have been in the service of the "man at the helm" ever since the days of Moses, who selected them as his "Praetorian Guard." The deal continues to work well, as Judges morph into monarchs. By contrast, loose confederacies seldom stand the test of time. In this case, the tripartite pact (Moab, Ammon, and Edom) rapidly disintegrates, their troops quarreling to the point of slaying each other. As the Levite has foretold, it happens on the following day. There is nothing left for Jehoshaphat's forces to do but gather the spoils of the slain.

### John Wilkes Booth

Not long after this great victory, "Jumpin' Jehoshaphat" dies. He is succeeded by his son Ahaziah, who continues the policy of allying with, rather than battling, the North. We're reminded of the Democratic Party's challenge to Abraham Lincoln in the election of 1864, involving a pledge to end the Civil War via a negotiated settlement with the southern states. While Lincoln and his "war hawks"

---

32 2 Chronicles 20:12, NIV.

won reelection in a landslide, it's the "peaceniks" who carry the day in Israel's case. King Ahab has proved that reconciliation with Jerusalem is possible. However, his son and successor, Jehoram, comes face to face with a determined assassin, antiquity's version of John Wilkes Booth. His name is Jehu, and he goes on a murderous rampage against the house of Ahab.[33] Ahaziah happens to be visiting his northern counterpart, Jehoram, in the northern city of Jezebel, when Jehu arrives on the scene. The assassin murders Jehoram, depicted as additional divine retribution for Ahab's sin against Naboth. We can almost imagine him shouting "*Sic semper tyrannis!*" Some biblical critics speculate that the emphasis on "avenging the blood of Naboth" cloaks a "Brutus-like" dissatisfaction with the need to grow the northern kingdom into a regional power – a yoke that is too heavy for its libertarian-minded citizenry.

As for King Ahaziah of Judah, he is also wounded in the attack. We recall in the saga of Lincoln's assassination that one of Booth's henchmen repeatedly stabbed Secretary of State William Seward. The secretary survived the attack, but Ahaziah is not as fortunate. He flees across the valley to Megiddo, where he dies from his wounds. Jehu, unlike Booth, continues his killing spree. He next targets Ahab's queen, Jezebel. Hearing that the assassin is on his way, the queen adorns herself and presents herself at the window. Jehu commands, "Throw her down!" In utter ignominy, the narrative tells us that her flesh is eaten by dogs, who leave nothing more than her skull, her feet, and the palms of her hands. On a political level, there's a price to pay for the murder of the queen, for she was the daughter of the king of Tyre, and her marriage to Ahab had cemented an alliance with the Phoenicians. But from this point, good relations between Israel and Tyre will come to an end.

How do we assess Jehu, whom the Bible also calls a prophet? A hero? A true "libertarian"? Another biblical "Brutus"? Or a pathological killer-tyrant, who, after all, goes on to take the crown for himself? The Bible's own verdict on Jehu is schizophrenic, alternately praising and berating him. On the Bible's "plus" side: Once ensconced in power, he summons all the worshippers of Baal to Samaria, slays them, and proceeds to destroy their temple. Freedom of religion, a true libertarian tenet, has never been an element of "big government" tyrannies, and Jehu proves that in spades. On the

---

33 Samuel J. Schultz, *The Old Testament Speaks* (San Francisco: HarperCollins, 2000), 193ff.

"minus" side: The same anti-Baal monarch openly tolerates golden calves being set up at Dan and Bethel. By the end of his reign, Jehu has left the biblical narrators with a decidedly bitter taste in their mouths. One tyranny, it seems, has been exchanged for another.

In the meantime, one ignominious incident sums up the chaos of the age. After King Ahaziah's death at the hands of Jehu, his mother, Ahab's daughter Athaliah (widow of Jehoram, who had died some time earlier), succeeds in taking the throne of Judah for herself. She attempts to wipe out every descendant of the house of David in a murder spree rivaling Jehu. Perhaps there's a bit of "Brutus" in her, since she sees David's dynasty, not as glorious, but tyrannical. Her plot is foiled, however, when one lone descendant, a boy named Joash, is rescued by Athaliah's sister and raised in secret by the priest Jehoiada. When, six years later, Jehoiada proclaims Joash king, Athalaiah rushes in to crush the budding rebellion, only to be captured and put to death. So much for the "wicked" usurper-queen.

In Jehu's wake, two new monarchs rise in Israel and Judah, respectively. In the North we have Jeroboam II (a dynastic descendant of Jehu); in Jerusalem the illustrious King Uzziah takes the throne. Historians see both as wise and skillful rulers, who usher in a period of expansion and prosperity for both realms.[34] In fact, the borders of their kingdoms, taken together, resemble the grandeur of David's and Solomon's "United Kingdom." True enough, tyranny can bring about wealth, power and grandeur, which many tyrants down through history have proved. But once ensconced in power, tyranny seldom retreats. One tyrant is merely exchanged for another.

In the eighth century B.C.E., both the northern and southern kingdoms are at their zenith. Both, however, will go into ignominious decline. Jeroboam II's son Zachariah is murdered, and the dynasty of Jehu comes to an end after ruling Israel for a century. Subsequent northern kings make alliances with Damascus and with Egypt, trying to keep at bay the dominant new power of the near east, Assyria. But all attempts to forestall the inevitable are of no avail. In the year 722 B.C.E. the northern kingdom falls to the Assyrians, who take the ten tribes into captivity and resettle foreigners in the heart of biblical Israel. They will never be heard from again, giving rise to endless speculation about the "ten lost tribes" of Israel.

---

34 James Maxwell Miller, *A History of Ancient Israel* (Louisville, KY: Westminster John Knox Press, 1986), 307ff.

## The South Shall Rise Again

The South hangs on longer. The Assyrians fail in an assault on Jerusalem, their troops being slain in the field – according to biblical tradition – by the "angel of death." Having been divinely rescued from the fate that befell the North, a new king, Josiah goes on to become one of the South's most able rulers. He orders the Temple to be cleansed and refurbished. During the renovations, the High Priest Hilkiah discovers a long-lost "Book of the Law" in the Temple and presents it to the king, who tears his garments in anguish over the people's lack of fidelity to holy writ. Josiah embarks on a program of religious reform, tearing down pagan altars across the land and slaying idolatrous priests. It's all a part of centralizing worship in one place – Jerusalem – and strengthening monarchical power.[35] Tyrants through history have known that one way to increase political power is through religious "revival." Control the "opiate of the masses" and you control the hearts and minds of the people. We may therefore ask whether Josiah amounts to an enlightened monarch, or a "Stalinist" with his own religious-oriented "purge."

Whatever the verdict, it will take more than a century for another regional power – the Babylonians – to finish off Jerusalem. In any case Josiah's sons are not so successful in consolidating and maintaining power. The end comes in stages. First, Babylonia demands tribute from Jerusalem. They subsequently appoint "puppet kings" who they hope will do their bidding. But as rebellion grows, they opt to seal Jerusalem's fate. Babylonian King Nebuchadnezzar burns Solomon's fabled Temple to the ground and completely destroys the city, taking its inhabitants into far-away exile. It ends where it all began, near the Tigris and Euphrates Rivers – the same territory from which Abraham and his family made their long trek to the land of Canaan, so many centuries before.

This ignominy, however, will not put an end to the Israelites as a people. The "Brutus current" is still alive, even in exile. The exiles will return one day, and rebuild their ruined Temple. They will also establish a new form of government, local in character and strictly limited. They will create ... a republic.

"The South shall rise again!"

---

35 Richard H. Lowery, *The Reforming Kings: Cults and Society in First Temple Judah* (Sheffield, England: Sheffield Academic Press, 1991), 208.

# 8
# PROPHETS – CHECKS AND BALANCES

"*The degree of our worthiness to become a free people shall be determined by our ability to respect a lawful leader, to agree to the existence of an opposition, to listen to its arguments, and especially to put the nation's good above all party prejudices and private interest. Liberty is not one of man's inalienable rights; it is a desirable but difficult acquisition, and must be contended for constantly.*" – André Maurois[1]

America's Founders well understood the corrosive aspects of power. No leader, however well-intentioned, is incorruptible. Therefore, some counterweight to raw, centralized authority is indispensable. The Founders knew this instinctively, but they were also students of history ... and the Bible. When it came to the "divine right of kings," they were convinced that no earthly potentate had such a right. The Bible for its part contains multiple examples of how monarchs are "checked" in their power. They do not rule absolutely. The "Brutus current," though shoved to the side in many of the biblical narratives, persists for centuries, acting as a hedge against the excess of even the most celebrated of biblical monarchs. Bearing that in mind, let's take another look at the Bible's version

---

1 André Maurois, *The Art of Living* (San Francisco: Harper, 1960), 185.

171

of the "separation of powers." As in the American experience, we find three distinct "branches" of biblical government. They are represented by three spiritual currents in ancient Israel: the monarchy, the priests, and the prophets.

With regard to the monarchy, there's no question that Scripture acknowledges the need for a national leader, ideally a Judge, and later, with considerable acquiescence from the Almighty, a king. The biblical chief executive, however, is not to run roughshod over the rights of individuals or their respective tribes. Even a king of David's stature is required to respect tribal self-determination or face revolt – which he does on more than one occasion. The king, while fostering social cohesion, must be "checked," and his power "balanced" by other biblical institutions.

Enter, the Levites. While originally commissioned by Moses as a brutal "Praetorian Guard," whose role involves considerable bloodletting, they evolve over time – during the period of the Judges – into a stable, governmental institution. Their domain is the Law, the Torah – the five books of Moses. If the monarchy represents the Bible's "executive branch," the Levites are the "judiciary," who interpret the Torah in the same way that America's courts, the Supreme Court in particular, have been charged to interpret the Constitution. Like today's Supreme Court, their term of service is for life. In that sense they represent an elite legal hierarchy, immune (at least in theory) from corruption. The "interpreters-in-chief" among the Levites are the priests, the *cohanim* in Hebrew (*cohen* being the singular). They're the "culture keepers" of the land, who have attended to the Tabernacle and the Ark of the Covenant, as it has traveled from one sacred shrine to the next: Shiloh, Bethel, Gilgal, and finally the Temple in Jerusalem. They communicate universal truths about God and humanity, in the same way the the Supreme Court's nine "men in black" were charged to discover and interpret "Natural Law" from the founding of the republic.

Long after the Temple is razed to the ground – by King Nebuchadnezzar of Babylon in 586 B.C.E. – and after seventy years of "Babylonian captivity," the High Priest Ezra will come forth as the "great redactor"/ "editor" of the Torah. It is he who will gather the people together in the heart of Jerusalem and read aloud the words of the Law, establishing it as a constitution for all time. Thanks to Ezra and his priestly successors, the democratic character of Judaism will forever be fixed in Jewish tradition. Great rabbinical academies will sprout up around the world, wherever there are Jewish communities, to wrangle over Torah precepts, including the voluminous commentaries of the sages, the Mishnah and the Talmud. All of that activity – which will cultivate countless generations of great legal minds – is the direct legacy of the ancient Levitical priesthood. In practice, however, neither king nor priesthood will prove to be "incorruptible," any more than the French Revolution's "incorruptible" Robespierre.

### The Bible's "Congressmen"

Enter, the prophets. Some have likened them to America's "fourth branch" of government, the free press. One renowned critic called the prophet an "open-air journalist, reciting his own article, adding to and often interpreting it by some symbolic act."[2] Another commentator declared the prophet to be "a publicist not less than a preacher, a politician not less than a theologian."[3] For our purposes, it makes sense to view them as consummate politicians. They, more than anyone, comprise the "representative" branch of biblical government. It is they, perhaps uniquely, who understand the moral will of the people, and who are just as uniquely suited to carry both the vision and the burden that the people's "will" entails. The prophets, unlike the priests, who constantly tend the Tabernacle-turned-Temple, have no fixed locale. The whole nation is their domain, just as Congress must of necessity return to the localities they represent. Given that many are vagabonds by nature, there's nothing serene about the prophetic calling. On the contrary, it involves pain, travail, anguish, and on occasion the complete denial of normal human experience. They are known for entering self-hypnotic trance-states, brought on by uttering the ineffable Divine Name. While close to the common folk, they are just as likely to be feared, often being seen as a cross between beggars and lunatics. For the role of the prophet is invariably confrontational, and fundamentally at odds with temporal political and spiritual authority. Isn't that what the Founders had in mind, when they designed a bicameral legislative body – Congress – to "check" both the president and the courts? We shouldn't be surprised, considering the American experi-

---

2 E. Renan, *History of the People of Israel*, II (Boston: Roberts Brothers, 1896), 356.

3 G.P. Gooch, *History and Historians in the Nineteenth Century* (London: Longmans, Green, and Co., 1913), 485.

ence, that President Harry Truman got himself reelected in 1948 by running against a "do-nothing Congress." It's a charge echoed by Barack Obama in his own reelection bid, as if to lament the fact that the Constitution entails such a "messy" process. But isn't a healthy degree of governmental "gridlock" exactly the lesson of the Bible, as it details the exploits of prophets, and the bulwark they erected against tyranny? In ancient times, as long as the prophets roam the countryside, no one, neither priest nor king, is immune to their moral authority. In that sense, the prophets function as the equivalent of an independent "branch" of biblical government.

From time to time in the narrative, the Bible's Brutuses come to the fore, in the form of these raving "sages," whose moral authority directly challenges the man on the throne. Centuries later, biblical precedent of this sort would become an important part of political theory, famously elucidated by Montesquieu as a system of "checks and balances."[4] Still later, it would become the guiding principle of the government established by the U.S. Constitution. Some have tried to prove that Montesquieu was directly influenced by the Bible, particularly by a verse in Isaiah: "The Eternal is our judge, the Eternal is our lawgiver; the Eternal is our King." While this is difficult to establish, Montesquieu is quoted as observing that biblical religion "is a stranger to mere despotic power."[5] Moreover, there's no doubt that American political theory was, in a general sense, deeply inspired by biblical lessons on the limitation of power, and its "division" among multiple "branches." Let's consider, then, some specific examples of biblical prophets and the specific "check" on the other branches they represent.

### The Biblical "Tea Party"

Back in the days of the biblical Judges – the very period so admired by Thomas Paine and his fellow patriots, the first of the prophets rear their collective heads. They sprout, quite literally from Israel's "grassroots," wandering the Judean hillsides like the Greek oracles, delivering their divinely inspired messages in states of ecstasy. There are, apparently, loose-knit "schools" or "guilds" of these

---

4 Thomas L. Pangle, *The Theological Basis of Liberal Modernity in Montesquieu's "Spirit of the Laws"* (Chicago: Univ. of Chicago Press, 2010), 38.

5 Isaiah 33:22; see William Federer, *America's God and Country* (St. Louis: Amerisearch, 2000), 453-4.

early prophets, whose divinely inspired babbling is part of growing counter-culture in ancient Israel. While we've already cast them as the Bible's version of Congress, we can also think of these ancient holy men as history's first "Tea Party," for it's up to them to stand against the oppressiveness of centralized government.

They're the ones who stand in the gap between liberty and tyranny, serving as the nation's conscience. Like modern Tea-Partiers, they have no special pedigree, no unique education or training. No one knows where they come from or why they speak with such authority. But everyone recognizes that without them, the nation would be rudderless. Among them is a venerable prophet/Judge named Samuel. He is the direct answer to the anguished plea of his mother Hannah, who beseeched God out of her barrenness and asked for a child. Having been dedicated to divine service from birth, young Samuel is raised in the courts of the Temple, one day growing up to judge Israel in his own right.

Then there is Saul, Israel's unlikely first king, who, as we noted, behaves (at least at the beginning) more like a Judge than a monarch. We're told that the prophet Samuel, upon selecting Saul as king-designate, gives him some curious instructions. He orders him to head for Gibeah, where the Ark of the Covenant is ensconced among the priestly House of Eli:

> And it will happen to you when you come there to the city, you shall meet a company of prophets coming down from the high place with a harp and a tambourine and a flute and a lyre before them. And they shall prophesy. And the spirit of the LORD will come powerfully on you, and you shall prophesy with them, and shall be turned into another man.[6]

"Another man"? As odd as the sentence sounds, it's not a case of Saul losing his identity and becoming somebody else. It's that he "morphs" into a leader officially sanctioned by the prophetic class. In the American experience, the chief executive is not only checked by Congress and the Judiciary, but presidential nominees, including *"ambassadors, other public Ministers and Consuls, Judges of the Supreme Court, and all other Officers of the United States"* are subject to the "ad-

---

6 1 Samuel 10:5-6.

vice and consent" of the Senate.[7] Read politically, we recognize the biblical text's great lesson – that only with the "advice and consent" of the prophets can Saul possibly be a "*kosher*" king. The strange tale continues:

> And it happened when he had turned his back to go from Samuel, God changed him with another heart. And all those signs came on that day. And they came there to the hill, behold, a company of prophets met him. And the Spirit of God came on him, and he prophesied among them.

Readers wonder what exactly this "prophesying" amounts to. Most likely, it consists of ecstatic babble – something akin to the Pentecostal practice of "speaking in tongues." But these babblers aren't a bunch of "hicks from the sticks," straight from the mountains of Appalachia. They're an integral part of governing the land, in a pre-monarchic age, which explains why Samuel, and now Saul, are among them. Their presence is exactly what makes sure that tyranny will not rear its head again, even if it's under the renowned authority of a Moses-like figure. To this end, Saul must learn the mystical art of prophesy in his own right:

> And it happened when all who knew him before saw him, behold, he prophesied among the prophets. And the people said to one another, What is this that has happened to the son of Kish? Is Saul also among the prophets? And a man from there answered and said, And who is their father? Therefore it became a proverb, Is Saul also among the prophets?[8]

Such is the moral authority of Israel's prophets that simply being in their presence transforms even the king into "another man" – or, as the case may be, a real *meshuggeneh*. The story is a hint, that the prophetic class, far from a passing "fad," is destined to stay around, as a permanent "check" against the growing power of the monarchy ("imperial presidency").[9] Perhaps this helps explain why

---

7 U.S. Constitution, Article II, Section 2, Clause 2).

8 1 Samuel 10:9-12.

9 S. David Sperling, *The Original Torah: The Political Intent of the Bible's Writers* (New

the story is virtually repeated somewhat later in the narrative. When Saul appears to overstep his kingly authority, sliding into tyrannical behavior, we see him stumble upon the prophetic "Tea Party" movement once again, even as he pursues his arch-rival, David:

> Saul sent messengers to take David. And when they saw the company of the prophets prophesying, and Samuel standing as appointed over them, the Spirit of God came on the messengers of Saul, and they also prophesied. And they told Saul, and he sent other messengers, and they also prophesied. And Saul sent messengers the third time, and they prophesied also. And he also went to Ramah... And the Spirit of God was on him also, and going on he went and prophesied... And he stripped off his clothes also, and prophesied before Samuel... And he lay down disrobed all that day and all that night. Because of this they say: Is Saul also among the prophets?[10]

While as mentioned, considerable sympathy is to be found for Saul among modern commentators, the story in its present form deals with that "other" Saul – who becomes by degrees an absolutist monarch bent on eliminating his arch-rival, David. It's the perfect illustration of the Bible's "check" on the unbridled power of a chief executive. But he's stopped in his tracks – at least deterred and delayed from his mad pursuit of David – by the "populist party" of the day. As he runs around naked, babbling ecstatically, he appears himself to have joined Israel's ecstatic prophets.

But his transformation to prophetic leader will be short-lived, for he will by degrees turn to the "Dark Side," losing the crown he has fought so diligently to retain. As mentioned earlier, after the conniving David finally becomes king, he is confronted by another member of the prophetic class, a wandering sage named Nathan, over the notorious Bathsheba incident. Though David is arguably no less a tyrant after his humiliating transgression is exposed and punished, the prophet has earned himself a permanent place in the royal court. Later, in true "Brutus" form, Nathan forbids David, in God's name, to build a permanent Temple for the Ark of the Cov-

---

York: New York Univ. Press, 1998), 122f. Saul is at this point depicted in a thoroughly positive manner.

10 1 Samuel 19:20-24.

enant. Discerning readers wonder: who is this Nathan to announce to the king what he can and cannot build? And why doesn't the king simply ignore the prophet, have him locked away, or worse? How odd, by modern standards, that David doesn't raise an iota criticism against the "do-nothing prophets," bent on blocking a public works/ "jobs" bill. That's because it's exactly the prophet's place to "check" the chief executive, to actively foment "gridlock" when necessary, for the grand purpose of preventing big government "boondoggles" like a permanent Temple instead of a portable shrine. The prophetic "Tea Party" strikes again.

### Elijah's Chair

The most illustrious of the early brand of prophets is doubtless Elijah, around whom an entire folklore is destined to arise. Together with Samuel and Nathan, Elijah forms a trifecta of early prophets who firmly establish that God is "no patron of kings."[11] It is Elijah who, as noted earlier, confronts the despotic King Ahab over monarchal tyranny. As Ahab stands contemptuously in the vineyard he has effectively pilfered from a simple vinedresser named Naboth (executed on trumped-up charges), the prophet declares:

> Have you killed and also taken possession?... In the place where the dogs licked the blood of Naboth, dogs shall lick your blood, even yours.[12]

It is Elijah who, while the land is in the grip of a terrible drought, begins wandering through the hills, bedecked in a hairy mantle and loincloth, to bemoan the mounting disloyalty to Israel's God. In a direct challenge to the Baal worship imported into the land by Queen Jezebel, the prophet summons King Ahab and all the people to the summit of Mt. Carmel, where a great contest will be orchestrated, to demonstrate once and for all who is God and who is not. Two altars are constructed, one for Baal and one for the God of Israel. Two bulls are slaughtered and placed, one on each altar. Next, they beseech their respective deities to consume the offerings by divine fire. A crowd of four hundred fifty prophets of Baal shout and wail for half a day, cutting themselves with knives and spears

---

11 Abraham Joshua Heschel, *The Prophets* (New York: Harper & Row, 1962), 524.
12 1 Kings 21:19.

– all in vain. Elijah mocks them: "Either he is meditating, or he is pursuing, or he is in a journey; perhaps he is asleep and must be awakened!"[13]

Now, it's the prophet's turn to call on his God, who promptly sends down a torrent of flame, consuming not only the sacrifice, but the entire altar, including the wood, hay, stubble, and water in the trench. As all the people acclaim Israel's God as the true God, Elijah commands that the prophets of Baal be seized. What ensues amounts to the "Great Tea Party Massacre." Elijah, with the help of a mass of likeminded insurgents, immediately has them dragged to a valley nearby, where he slays one and all.

Commentators have opined, that monotheism appears to suffer, throughout its long history, from the sin of intolerance, and they point to Elijah's bloodletting as a case in point.[14] While there's certainly some merit to this criticism, another way to look at it is as open rebellion to the ever-growing power of the state and its cult-oriented legitimacy. Clearly, however, the grand scheme doesn't work, for the prophet ends up fleeing for his life to a cave on Mt. Sinai, to hide himself from the wrath of Ahab and his humiliated dynasty. There on the holy mountain, a number of "special effects" manifest themselves to Elijah – a mighty wind, and earthquake, a fire – but God is in none of them. Finally, a gentle breeze blows. This is how the prophet meets his God.

Elijah's great "reform" has ended in failure, but his legacy will linger forever. According to tradition, he is taken up into heaven on a chariot of fire, but will return one day to usher in the "anointed one" – the Messiah. That's why every year at Passover, an empty chair is set for Elijah, and why, at the end of the festive meal commemorating the Exodus from Egypt, the door is opened, to see whether Elijah may have come to this home on this day.

In modern America, Elijah's Chair is collectively occupied by a "populist" group of libertarian-minded folk from the grassroots who, like the prophets of old, are alternately feared and derided, as raving lunatics who dare to challenge the entrenched governmental status quo. There are a number of parallels between the prophets and the modern Tea Party, including a fervent love of country, and

---

13 1 Kings 18:27.

14 Karen Armstrong, *A History of God: The 4,000 Year Quest of Judaism, Christianity and Islam* (New York: Ballantine, 1993), 26-7.

a passion for ethics and morality.[15] The prophet addresses societal ills, speaking the truth unequivocally, and calling out those who do harm. On such counts the Tea Party passes muster. Modern critics of the left naturally lambast them as false prophets, but that's to be expected. Who can doubt that the spirit of the Tea Party is very much in line with that of the early American "patriots," who opposed the tyranny of the ruling class in their own day? And to the extent that those patriots were in line with the biblical prophets, so are the Tea Party folk of the twenty-first century. Moreover, if not for libertarian-minded folk, in whatever century, who is to stop the steady encroachment of the rulers over the people? In other words, the bigger the government, the smaller the citizen.

As Elijah is transmuted into the heavens, he drops his mantle to his trusty sidekick, Elisha, who will embark on his own prophetic career, inheriting a "double portion" of Elijah's spirit. Elisha will go on to perform many wonders and miracles, during his tenure as an "ecstatic prophet." Over time, however, the role of the prophet will itself be transmuted, from that of the wandering ecstatic/ seer, to a higher-type of social critic – whose words of profound poetry will be written down, copied and recopied from generation to generation. As the "civil war" continues over generations, their disciples, and the prophetic schools they establish, will become just as much an institutional fixture in Israelite culture as Congress is in modern America. And like Congress, they will "check" the chief executive in no uncertain terms. Coming from every social strata, they derive their authority from their direct communication with God. Unlike the Levites, who can occasionally be co-opted by unscrupulous monarchs, this new breed of "writing prophets" cannot be bribed or manipulated. It is they who carry the divine burden of making sense of the political catastrophe that ultimately falls on both the northern and southern kingdoms, as both are eventually gobbled up by foreign empires.

**Famous Amos**

First, however, the excesses of the Israelites themselves must be addressed, especially those of centralized government, in both

---

15 Mark Meckler, Jenny Beth Martin, *Tea Party Patriots: The Second American Revolution* (New York: Henry Holt, 2012), 182. Some major tenets of the Tea Party movement include championing American greatness and exceptionalism.

civil and religious spheres. We're told specifically of a cantankerous vinedresser/ herdsman from the southern city of Tekoa, who heads north, to the cultic shrine of Beth-El, where he barges in on the local priest with a message of harsh condemnation. Is Amos a member of an ancient "Occupy Beth-El" movement? On the contrary, he might more accurately be called a "conservative radical," since he doesn't reject the religious shrine itself, or the religion, but only demands that it clean up its proverbial act.[16] In a classic verse he announces: "I was not a prophet, nor a member of any brotherhood of the prophets." It's the most direct statement we have, that the role of the prophet has in fact evolved, from glorified "soothsayer" to ethical voice, on the level of Gandhi, or Martin Luther King.

Not surprisingly, today's left likes to view the prophets as paragons of "social justice," as they agitate for increasing involvement on the part of the federal government, to "level the playing field" and redistribute wealth. Very well, then. Let's look for Amos' demand for big government collectivism, and see what we find. At the outset, Amos rails against idolatry and paganism, viewing morality as inseparable from religion and castigating the pagans, not for what they have done to Israel, but for what they have done to each other. But those who want to turn the prophets into prototypical left-wingers had better think twice.

After berating the nations round about, he specifically turns his attention to Judah, where the people have not kept the commandments, but have despised divine teaching. That's the accusation. But where's the socialist imperative in all of this? Where's the demand for the centralized collective? On the contrary, doesn't it all come to the individual, and personal responsibility for the collective failure?

Next, he turns to Israel, where people who cannot pay their debts are sold into slavery. They trample the weak and helpless. At sacred shrines, men sleep on clothing confiscated from the poor, as security for their debts, and they drink wine taken from those who owe them money. Those are the damning charges against the North. But who is responsible for this? Greedy ancient capitalists? That's what the left would like us to believe. Moreover, who was supposed to bring about the great social reforms demanded by the prophet? The king, via the North's version of Solomon-like taxation?

Setting aside for a moment the narrative of modern liberalism, aren't the real culprits a cabal of religious and governmental/

---

16 Norman Podhoretz, *op. cit.*, 134.

monarchical authorities, who, having rebelled against a tyrannical monarchy in the South, move to create one of their own among the northern ten breakaway tribes? That's why Amos pronounces divine judgment upon them. Because, having had every opportunity to re-create the egalitarian society of the period of the Judges, they have created yet another hierarchy of centralized power, where religious authority is fused with state power. This is one more reason America's Founders were careful to separate religion from the state, for they realized that a cohesive alliance between the two epitomizes state tyranny.

### Isaiah the Nay-Saya'

About the same time that Amos is active up in Beth-El, another prophet of the new variety – a writer, poet and literary giant in his own right – comes to the fore in Jerusalem. He's a member of Jerusalem's elite class – the very "big government" goons that Amos has railed against. Nonetheless, it has been observed that Isaiah and Amos are "on the same page" in checking, not just the monarchy, but the Israelite equivalent of the judiciary as well. Specifically, they inveigh against the fact that the innocent are condemned and the guilty exonerated. What this amounts to are crimes carried out under cover of judicial corruption.

Isaiah opens his work with a broadside against his own people, especially the ruling class:

> Woe, sinful nation, a people heavy with iniquity, a seed of evildoers, sons who make others rotten! ... They have gone away backward... You will revolt more and more; the whole head is sick, and the whole heart faint.[17]

The great prophet goes on to compare the ruling class with the rulers of Sodom. The Temple cult, in bed with the monarchy, is the epitome of corruption:

> Hear the word of the Eternal, rulers of Sodom; give ear to the law of our God, people of Gomorrah. To what purpose is the multitude of your sacrifices to Me? says the Eternal; I am full of the burnt offerings of rams, and the

---

17 Isaiah 1:4-5.

fat of fed beasts; and I do not delight in the blood of bulls, or of lambs, or of he-goats.[18]

The "religious left" (just as dominant as its alter-ego, the "religious right") loves to quote Isaiah, as the ancient example par-excellence of a voice for "social justice."[19] Here was a "true leftist," addressing income inequality, lambasting the affluent – the ancient equivalent of modern "corporatists." Greedy capitalists; they've been the supreme culprits from time immemorial, right? Then there's "liberation theology," which is outright Marxist, favoring the overthrow of capitalist systems and their replacement by a utopian classless society. Let's not forget the Reverend Jeremiah Wright, who fancies himself as a latter day prophet in the mold of Isaiah, famously declaring, "America's chickens have come home to roost!"

But wait a second. While Isaiah does rail against the expropriation of small landholdings by estate holders, who exactly are these dastardly robber barons?[20] Does ancient Israel have "big business" as we think of it today? Ancient oil companies, perhaps? Other ancient "corporate interests"? Ancient stock brokers, perhaps … from "Wailing Wall Street"? Or, are the real exploiters of the poor of Isaiah's day the religious/ governmental cabal that has turned the Promised Land from a tribal confederacy to a hierarchical monarchy and attendant bureaucracy?

A case can be made that ancient Israel is paralleled by modern America, where the governmental ruling class consists of the true robber barons, who incessantly persecute those who work the hardest and contribute the most. Take small business, whose earnings are expropriated by a ravenous tax system that systematically robs the productive elements of society, for the supposed purpose of redistributing income to the unproductive elements, i.e. the poor. In reality, however, little of the revenue thus generated ever reaches the needy, and most ends up enriching the bureaucrats and their agencies – the real "ruling class" of the modern era. C.S. Lewis famously wrote:

Of all tyrannies, a tyranny exercised for the good of its

---

18 Isaiah 1:10-11.

19 Walter Houston, *Contending for Justice: Ideologies and Theologies of Social Justice in the Old Testament* (London: T&T Clark, 2006), 77ff.

20 Podhoretz, *op. cit.*, 187.

victims may be the most oppressive. It may be better to live under robber barons than under omnipotent moral busybodies. The robber baron's cruelty may sometimes sleep, his cupidity may at some point be satiated; but those who torment us for our own good will torment us without end, for they do so with the approval of their own conscience.[21]

So, would Isaiah, transported to the twenty-first century, be standing with the "occupy" movement? Or would he be among the Tea Party "patriots," enraged at the corruption of an out-of-control government ruling class, that keeps the poor in poverty (all the while pretending to care for them) while enriching itself? We can almost hear the righteous indignation of the Tea Party crowd in Isaiah's scathing denunciation:

Your rulers are rebellious, and companions of thieves; everyone loves a bribe, and is pursuing rewards; they do not judge the orphan, nor does the cause of the widow come to them.[22]

The plight of the widow and the orphan is stressed repeatedly by the prophets – not by Isaiah alone – and becomes a theme of sorts in biblical literature. But who is blamed for their oppression? The ruling class, the government. And who will step up to help the needy and the unfortunate? In Israel, it will be the prophetic "schools" themselves, who privately organize what amounts to an ancient social safety net. In fact it's been observed that Israel is the only ancient society on the planet that institutes an elaborate system of social welfare. But it's all due to the efforts, not of the ruling class, but the common folk – what one modern commentator has called the "Country Party."[23] In ancient Judea they are the prophetic class, though someday they will become known, collectively, as the Pharisees.

### Mr. Speaker

21 C.S. Lewis, *God in the Dock* (Grand Rapids: Eerdmans, 1994), 292.

22 Isaiah 1:23.

23 Angelo M. Codevilla, "America's Ruling Class – And the Perils of Revolution" in *The American Spectator*, July-August, 2010 issue.

Of all the prophets in the Israelite "House of Representatives," Isaiah is the chief. Call him "Mr. Speaker." And considering just how substantial is the biblical book he writes, he certainly has a lot to say. We might nonetheless ask why this cantankerous prophet isn't dismissed, as a nay-saying "nabob of negativism." The answer comes down to the man on the throne, of whom there are several during Isaiah's long career: Uzziah, Jotham, Ahaz, and Hezekiah. Surprisingly these chief executives decide to heed the people's representative, given that he seems to be in touch with a "higher power." In spite of being called out for corruption, they seem to recognize that the executive branch genuinely needs to be checked by the prophetic class, who give voice to the concerns of ordinary folk. In due consideration of this, Isaiah subsequently delivers some strikingly positive, even "jingoistic" messages for Israel's political front.

Whereas modern Tea Party activists chant "U.S.A." in unison, Isaiah is entranced by the idea of Israelite triumphalism. The same prophet who declares that the people's abundance will one day be taken away, people hiding in caves and holes in the ground to escape the divine wrath, turns his entire message to hope and restoration. When the armies of Syria swoop down from the north, in league with the breakaway tribes of Israel, he declares to King Ahaz that he has nothing to fear. A sign will be given: A young woman (the ancient Greek translation of the Bible renders the word "virgin") will be with child, and you will call him "Immanuel" – "God with us."[24]

A second utopian prophecy follows: "Unto us a son is given; unto us a child is born."[25] Commentators are divided as to whom these cryptic messages refer. Some see reference to the son of Ahaz, the next king in line, Hezekiah, while Christians obviously prefer to see allusion to some future Davidic king – an "anointed one."[26] But in looking for hidden religious links, pointing to Jesus, people generally miss the political meaning; for regardless of the reference, the message of triumphalism, of an "Israelite peace" (or "*Pax Israelatica*") to extend around the world, could't be clearer. When the executive branch pays attention to the people's representatives, all will be well. No foreign power will prevail over Jerusalem.

The prophecy continues: And the government will be upon his shoulders." "The government"? What kind of government? "Big

---

24 Isaiah 7:14.

25 Isaiah 9:6

26 Podhoretz, op. cit.

government"? Cradle-to-grave welfare government? That's the way today's leftists like to read Isaiah. But what the prophet actually envisions is a powerful Israel, a force to be reckoned with, fully capable of taking on its foes. That's the real role of government ... not to redistribute wealth, but to defend the nation against all enemies, foreign and domestic.

Over the decades to come, the prophet's messages to Hezekiah in particular will be one of encouragement and optimism, especially as an existential threat presents itself, right on Jerusalem's doorstep. The Assyrians, the evilest of "evil empires," have invaded the northern kingdom with full fury, taking the ten breakaway tribes away in shackles. They have been dragged into exile, far to the east, never to be heard from again, except in the legends about them. They will become the "ten lost tribes" of Israel.

Isaiah insists that Jerusalem will withstand the Assyrian juggernaut, and that their great commander, Sennacherib, though he prepares to lay siege to the city and choke it off, will leave the battlefield and go home in disgrace. The great prophet, with his "morning in Jerusalem" message, is of course been proven right. Not only does Sennacherib retreat; the whole Assyrian "evil empire" collapses.

### Ronaldus Magnus

Fast-forwarding to the present, no American president epitomized this positive, can-do message of American triumphalism (a *"Pax Americana"*) more effectively than Ronald Reagan. "It's morning in America," Reagan's famous television ad proclaimed. And right from the start Ronald Reagan "got it." He saw America as a force for good in the world. At the Republican National Convention in 1980, when he secured his party's nomination, he declared: "They say that the United States has had its day in the sun, that our nation is passed its zenith. My fellow citizens, I utterly reject that view."[27] Donald Rumsfeld, Reagan's Middle East envoy, later observed, "Ronald Reagan had a well-developed philosophy, that was elevating, and it caused people to nod and say, 'I understand that.'"[28] We read in the book of Isaiah the audacious statement that

---

27 *Tear Down this Wall: the Reagan Revolution - a National Review History* (New York: Continuum International, 2004), 18.

28 See "Fox News Reporting: The Right, All Along: The Rise, Fall & Future of Conservatism," Dec., 2010

all nations will one day honor Jerusalem:

> And it shall be, in the last days the mountain of the LORD's house shall be established in the top of the mountains, and shall be exalted above the hills; and all nations shall flow into it. And many people shall go and say, Come, and let us go to the mountain of the LORD, to the house of the God of Jacob. And He will teach us of His ways, and we will walk in His paths. For out of Zion shall go out the Law, and the word of the LORD from Jerusalem. And He shall judge among the nations, and shall rebuke many people; and they shall beat their swords into plowshares, and their spears into pruning-hooks. Nation shall not lift up sword against nation, neither shall they learn war any more.[29]

Ronald Reagan likewise saw America as the preeminent world power, bringing peace through strength and an end to the domination of the "evil empire" of his day, the Soviet Union. Curiously, according to the vision of both prophet and president, it will come about without brandishing a sword (in Isaiah's case) or firing a single missile (in Reagan's). Reagan said to his national security adviser, Richard Allen, "I'd like to tell you my theory of the Cold War; it's we win, and they lose."[30] Publicly, Reagan proclaimed, "The West won't contain Communism; it'll transcend Communism."[31] Going beyond the role of president, Reagan spoke as a prophet in his own right, especially in what was perhaps the greatest speech of his presidency, at Britain's Westminster Palace:

> What I'm describing now is a plan and a hope for the longterm – the march of freedom and democracy which will leave Marxism-Leninism on the ash-heap of history.[32]

---

29 Isaiah 2:2-4.

30 Michael R. Beschloss, *Presidential Courage: Brave Leaders and How They Changed America 1789-1989* (New York: Simon & Schuster, 2007), 378.

31 Steven F. Hayward, *The Age of Reagan: The Conservative Counterrevolution: 1980-1989* (New York: Random House, 2009), 114.

32 Natan Sharansky, Ron Dermer, *The case for Democracy: the Power of Freedom to Overcome Tyranny and Terror* (New York: Public Affairs, 2004), 136.

As reports of his bold declaration circulated around the world, it was said that prisoners in the Soviet gulags passed his message from cell to cell, rejoicing that someone was at last coming to their aid. And we're again reminded of Isaiah's heartening proclamation:

> The Spirit of the Lord GOD is upon me, Because the LORD has anointed me To bring good news to the afflicted; He has sent me to bind up the brokenhearted, To proclaim liberty to captives And freedom to prisoners...[33]

Reagan went on, using Marx's own thoughts to prophesy the collapse of communism:

> In an ironic sense, Karl Marx was right. We are witnessing today a great revolutionary crisis. . . . But the crisis is happening not in the free, non-Marxist West, but in the home of Marxism-Leninism, the Soviet Union. It is the Soviet Union that runs against the tide of history by denying freedom and human dignity to its citizens. . . .[34]

Of course the left doesn't much care for "I'm right and you're wrong" kind of talk, that might (God forbid!) imply a moral judgment of some kind. Modern biblical critics are just as dismissive of the "Pax Israelatica" as their political counterparts are of the "Pax Americana." One of the minor prophets of the Bible, Nahum, is almost universally scorned by contemporary critics, and for good reason. Nahum is entirely devoted to heaping contempt on Israel's chief enemy, the "evil empire" of the day – Nineveh, capital of Assyria. Today's commentators on the left prefer to see the prophets as promoting a governmental system sensitive to social welfare, and deemphasizing government's role in national defense. Yet, the prophets appear to be arguing just the opposite – castigating the ruling class (i.e. the government) as incapable of addressing social ills, while advocating the defense of the nation, its role as a regional, even a world power, and doubling down on the wickedness of their enemies and the need to defeat them.

As for Reagan, by the time his term in office ended – in Janu-

---

33 Isaiah 61:1, NAS
34 Hayward, *op. cit.*, 255.

ary, 1989 – the *Pax Americana* seemed to be winning the day.[35] Within a year the first free and open election had taken place in communist Poland, and the Berlin Wall had come down, as Germany was on its way to reunification. Within two years, the Cold War would be won, as the Soviet Union's "evil empire" itself fell apart. As Reagan entered what he called the "sunset" of his life, the entire world began to experience a sunrise of freedom.

## "Undoing" Isaiah

Isaiah's life, at least according to tradition, doesn't end on such a satisfactory high note. For a cruel monarch named Manasseh rises in Hezekiah's wake. He decides he doesn't care for "checks and balances," and that he'd be better off without the people's representatives getting in the way. Manasseh unleashes a bitter persecution against the prophetic class. Isaiah, according to one apocryphal text, is tied to a tree and sawn in two.

Not surprisingly, when Isaiah passes from the scene, the tone of the prophetic class turns decidedly more negative, as yet another "evil empire" rises in the east. The new kids on the block are the Babylonians, who will swoop down on the southern kingdom of Judah and ultimately do to them what the Assyrians did to the breakaway North. The message of two new prophets, Jeremiah and Ezekiel, is that Israel will indeed fall, that it's too late for any kind of national salvation. We can liken them to the more pessimistic among today's Tea Party activists, who see America's decline as inevitable, but nonetheless hope for individual salvation, for a righteous "remnant."[36]

Jeremiah's has the unenviable task of "undoing" Isaiah. He must shatter the aura of invincibility around Jerusalem and convince king and people alike that this ship of state (like the Titanic, twenty-four centuries later) really can sink. Not even the Temple and the presence of the hallowed Ark of the Covenant will save her. In

---

35 Gary Dorrien, *Imperial Designs: Neoconservatism and the New Pax Americana* (New York: Routledge, 2004); John P. Diggins, Ronald Reagan: Fate, Freedom, and the Making of History, (New York: W.W. Norton & Co., 2007), 202.

36 Glenn Beck, Kevin Balfe, Broke: The Plan to Restore Our Trust, Truth and Treasure (New York: Threshold Editions, 2010), 255; Bill Miller, *The Tea Party Papers: The American Spiritual Evolution Versus the French Revolution* (Bloomington, IN: Xlibris, 2011), 107. It is argued that there is no such animal as "collective salvation."

ancient Israel the existential threat is now Babylonia; in twenty-first century America, it's the ballooning debt. Human nature, however, is what it is, and, no matter what day and age, prefers comfortable illusions to hard reality.

"Deficits don't matter!" said one contemporary pundit, regarding trillions of dollars in red ink as far as the eye can see. As long as the federal government continues to print money, there's nothing to worry about. Oh, really? Some call it a Keynesian illusion; but even John Maynard Keynes, renowned patriarch of the economic theory of deficit spending, would be revolving in his grave to see what today's big government has done. Keynes urged moderate deficit spending during economic downturns, with the understanding that the resulting debt would be paid off when the economy improves. America's modern debts, however, are beyond calculation, and, unless some drastic measures are taken to curb spending (especially entitlements), are destined to engulf the entire economy, leaving future generations in a permanent state of national decline.

Today's ruling class is likely counting on the fact that the debt burden is so utterly enormous that most ordinary people can't begin to comprehend it, preferring not to bother themselves with predictions of economic Armageddon. As in Plato's famous "cave" analogy, it's much easier to live in the shadows than face the uncomfortable light of day.[37] Jeremiah, for his part, is bound and determined to be the great illusion breaker. However, as the scroll Jeremiah dictates is read to the man on the throne in those days, Jehoiakim, the monarch cuts it off, piece by piece, and throws it into the fire.

In order to spell out the hopelessness of the situation, Jeremiah goes as far as to fashion an ox yoke, slip it around his neck, and parade through the streets, to dramatize the inevitable fate of the city. Just as modern "false prophets" ignore the financial calamity on the horizon and counsel others that deficits are unimportant, Jeremiah has to face his own cadre of optimistic fools, telling both king and people not to worry, that the budding rebellion being fomented against the Babylonians will succeed. One false prophet named Hananiah meets up with Jeremiah in the Temple precincts, grabs the yoke from his neck, and breaks it in pieces, announcing that the yoke of the Babylonians will likewise be broken.

---

37 Louise Nelstrop, Kevin Magill, Bradley B. Knish, *Christian Mysticism: an Introduction to Contemporary Theoretical Approaches* (Surrey, England: Ashgate Publishing, 2009), 24.

Modern Tea Partiers are regularly blasted as "extremists," just as the prophets of old. The adage is, if you can't attack the message, attack the messenger. In the days of Judah's last king, Zedekiah, the prophet himself is seized and thrown into muck-filled cistern, only to be rescued at the last minute by a Cushite official at the palace. The nation at large, however, will not be rescued. As the prophet predicted, their doom is sealed. If we compare Jeremiah with his predecessor, Isaiah, it's easy to see the prophets as a whole as a conflicted lot, torn between two visions, one of triumphalism, the other of national catastrophe. In the near term, as Jeremiah and another prophet of doom, Ezekiel, bear witness, the catastrophic vision wins out. King Zedekiah lends his support to the anti-Babylonian uprising, only to be captured and blinded, as his sons are slaughtered before him. Then he is sent away into exile. In his place the Babylonians set up a puppet governor, named Gedeliah; but he is murdered by the rebellious faction, who still believe they can regain their independence. This sets the stage for the final invasion by the armies of Babylon, who, in the year 586 B.C.E., put a final end to the kingdom of Judah.

What has their desire for monarchal grandeur under an ancient "big government" banner gotten them? They had wanted a king, "like all other nations." They had wanted a centralized capital with a permanent Temple. They had wanted to be a regional power, even an empire, to boast of. But all of this was idolatry as far as the prophets were concerned. For people who are oppressed by their own rulers can hardly do their best to defend their homeland. In the end, the city is destroyed, the magnificent Temple burned to the ground, the fabled Ark lost forever. And the once proud citizenry of Jerusalem are taken into exile, in far away Babylonia.

Millennia later, the patriots of the American colonies must have had all this in mind, especially as one of them, Patrick Henry, delivered a classic address to the Virginia House of Burgesses, in which he directly quoted Jeremiah:

> Gentlemen may cry, "Peace, Peace – but there is no peace."[38] The war is actually begun! The next gale that sweeps from the north will bring to our ears the clash of resounding arms! Our brethren are already in the field!

---

38 "They have also healed the hurt of the daughter of my people slightly, saying, Peace, peace, when there is no peace" (Jeremiah 6:14).

Why stand we here idle? What is it that gentlemen wish? What would they have? Is life so dear, or peace so sweet, as to be purchased at the price of chains and slavery? Forbid it, Almighty God! I know not what course others may take; but as for me, give me liberty or give me death![39]

Henry's intent was of course to stir the fledgling nation to resist the invading British, as they, like the Babylonians, swooped down from the north. The ancient prophet's burden, by contrast, was to convince as many as he could that the cause was already lost. So it is, that prophets, patriots and Tea Partiers alike are caught between conflicting visions, of national resilience and catastrophic decline. We can almost hear the mournful side of Jeremiah's refrain in certain contemporary conservative crusaders for small government, who warn that it really is too late to halt the nation's downward trajectory.[40] As the ancient prophet counseled his listeners to turn inward, toward a higher spirituality and ethical sensitivity, so these modern prognosticators urge today's "patriots" to get ready for a time of intense dislocation and hardship, all the while holding fast to family, friends and faith. As the prophets certainly knew, it's precisely out of the crucible of suffering that a "greatest generation" may well arise.

---

39 Patrick Henry, March 23, 1775.

40 Mark Steyn, *After America: Get Ready for Armageddon* (Washington, D.C., Regnery, 2011), 174. Steyn points to a whole society in decline: economic, cultural, spiritual, and demographic.

# 9

# OUT OF BABYLON
# DÉJÀ VU ALL OVER AGAIN

*"They who can give up essential liberty to obtain a little temporary safety, deserve neither liberty nor safety."*
– Benjamin Franklin[1]

With the final demise of Jerusalem, we see that the end result of generations of civil war between Israel and Judah is extinction for both. The lesson? When any "civil society" is fundamentally weakened from within, it eventually succumbs to invaders from without. Sometimes external invaders aren't even needed. The gloomiest of modern prognosticators have warned that the United States may one day fracture in pieces, hopelessly burdened by unsustainable debt and having forfeited the fabric of its "civil society."[2] Some declare that the American "republic" is in fact already gone, having been replaced by a "soft tyranny." But history also shows that extremity sows the seeds of rebirth, rekindling venerated old ideas and spawning bold new ones.

In the case of the Israelites, while ten of the original twelve

---

1 Benjamin Franklin, William Temple Franklin, *Memoirs of the Life and writings of Benjamin Franklin*, Vol. 1, (London: A.J. Valpy, 1818), 270.

2 Andrew Osborn, "As if Things Weren't Bad Enough, Russian Professor Predicts End of U.S." in *The Wall Street Journal*, Dec. 29, 2008.

tribes have now vanished, two of the tribes (Benjamin and Judah) remain uncannily intact in Babylonian captivity. Along the banks of the Tigris and Euphrates Rivers, not far from where Abraham and his family had begun their long journey, the Judean exiles are forced to make their new homes. The Bible records some of their lamentations:

> By the rivers of Babylon, there we sat down, yea, we wept, when we remembered Zion... If I forget you, O Jerusalem, let my right hand forget her cunning.[3]

Nevertheless, the bitterness of exile gives rise to an explosive, creative impulse, culminating in the faith we today call Judaism, and a reborn "civil society." Ironically, it's the loss of their national identity, as a free people living in their own land, that causes idolatry to vanish and promotes a new identity and a formally recognized faith – Judaism – to reign supreme in their hearts. With no earthly potentate to guide them, the Torah itself, as God's earthly representative, becomes King. Perhaps by a fluke of history, the two surviving tribes, Judah and Benjamin, are not assimilated into the surrounding population, but are actually encouraged to maintain their distinct cultural identity. Had not the prophet Jeremiah admonished them about how to behave in such a situation?

> Build houses and live in them; and plant gardens and eat their fruit. Take wives and father sons and daughters. And take wives for your sons, and give your daughters to husbands, so that they may bear sons and daughters, that you may be multiplied there and not become few. And seek the peace of the city where I have caused you to be exiled...[4]

They therefore learn to sanctify the smallest details of life, including the foods they can eat and how they must be prepared. In addition to circumcising their children, they perform various purification rituals, and recite multiple blessings relating to almost every aspect of their daily affairs. They also create a sanctified past, of blessed memory, and imagine a glorious future.

---

3 Psalm 137:1,5, KJV

4 Jeremiah 29:5-7.

They idolize Moses, and King David, in the same way that modern Americans all but deify George Washington (or, for those on the left, FDR). Forgiving past heroes of their "tyranny," or simply ignoring it, they dream of a new David – a "Messiah" – to sit on his throne and set things right once and for all.

## The New "Constitutional Convention"

Seventy years will pass, as captives in a strange land. The Babylonian empire will itself fall to foreign invaders – a coalition of Medes and Persians. In the end a dynamic new emperor will take the helm of a dominion that makes even Babylonia pale by comparison. His name is Cyrus of Persia, and his progressive policies will change everything for the Jewish people. He will even be hailed as the "Messiah" in Isaiah's prophecies, for he is the one who will issue a magnanimous decree allowing the Jews to return from exile and rebuild their shattered land and their ruined Temple.[5] The impossible is about to become the new reality.

Just as their exalted patriarch Abraham had left Babylonia some fifteen hundred years earlier, they embark afresh for the Promised Land. It is the journey of the Pilgrims once more. It is *déjà vu* all over again. This will not of course be an independent state, but rather an obedient colony under the auspices of Persian rule. It will be called Yahud, and it will comprise, at first, only Jerusalem and its general precincts. It will evolve, however, into a new nation that will help shape the course of western, and world civilization.

During the span of only a few decades, in the early sixth century before the Common Era, they accomplish some remarkable things, including the rebuilding of their holy Temple, on the ruins of the old, and erecting a new set of walls for Jerusalem's protection and defense. A series of "later prophets" – including Haggai, Zechariah, Joel and Malachi – encourage them in these formidable tasks, though modern liberal scholars tend to shun them, as being too focused on Israel alone and the *"Pax Israelatica."* Of course, anything that smacks of "Zionism" is too egocentric for today's universalist-minded left.

Still, the prophets of these days are unsurpassed "motivational speakers," who focus the people's energy, not on Solomon-like grandiosity, embarked upon through bloated bureaucracy and funded

---

5 Isaiah 44:28.

by crushing taxes, but on a national symbol and "community center," supported by the tithes and voluntary contributions of the local citizenry. When this Second Temple is finally dedicated, in the year 515 B.C.E., we're told that the old men in the crowd, who actually remember Solomon's Temple, weep, inasmuch as this one pales by comparison. But the young people rejoice, and the prophet Haggai declares: "The glory of this latter house shall be greater than that of the former."[6]

In the meantime, however, their challenges are not less than anything they have suffered in the past. They learn afresh the hard lessons of overbearing government, for while the crushing taxation of Solomon's dynasty is only a distant memory, Persian taxes are steadily increasing:

> And some said, We have borrowed money on our lands and vineyards for the king's tax... And, lo, we bring our sons and our daughters into bondage, to be slaves, and some of our daughters are brought into bondage. And there is no power for our hand, for other men have our lands and vineyards.[7]

The language of the passage hauntingly evokes modern discussion, not only about the tax burden, but the crushing debt that amounts to "generational theft." It's the closest thing we can imagine to bringing "our sons and daughters into bondage." Since the Israelite monarchy is long defunct (a good thing in the eyes of America's biblically grounded Founders) the Judeans will look for leadership to a single individual with neither royal pedigree nor kingly power, their high priest, Ezra.

The high priest, notably, isn't an absolute ruler. Though we're hampered by a lack of historical source material for this period, there is a long and well-developed Jewish tradition, known as the Oral Law, that tries to fill in the gaps. The Oral Law tells us of a council of elders, a "Great Assembly," that functions alongside Ezra and forms a small but effective government during these days.[8] Tra-

---

6 Haggai 2:9.

7 Nehemiah 5:4-5.

8 Scholars are divided on when this assembly comes into existence and whether it is present at all in Ezra's day. We can therefore only report on what Jewish tradition affirms. See Sidney Benjamin Hoeing, *The Great Sanhedrin: A Study of the Origin,*

dition also refers to it as the "Great Synagogue" – an assemblage of 120 scribes, sages, and the last of the prophets (including Haggai, Zechariah and Malachi, among others). Not all of them, however, live at the same time or in the same place. Nor do we know how its members are selected. It may sound like a representative body of some sort, but it's more like a wise, aristocratic oligarchy – a "House of Lords." According to rabbinic literature, "Moses received the [Oral] Torah from Sinai, and transmitted it to Joshua, and Joshua to the prophets, and the prophets to the men of the Great Synagogue."[9]

To this day Orthodox Judaism lavishes much praise on these sages, who are credited with transmitting the Oral Torah, handing it down from teacher to student, eventually being recorded in the great compendium of Jewish law known as the Mishnah.[10] They additionally fix the written "canon" of the Hebrew Scriptures (twenty-four books by their count, corresponding to twenty-four rotating groups of priests in the Temple) – basically, the "Old Testament" we know today. They also translate it into the vernacular language of the near east in this period, Aramaic.[11] Jewish tradition declares that the men of the Great Assembly gather the people together in the heart of Jerusalem, where the High Priest Ezra reads aloud the words of the Law:

> And Ezra the priest brought the Law before the congregation, both of men and women, and all that could hear with understanding, upon the first day of the seventh month. And he read in it before the street in front of the Water Gate from the morning until noon, in front of the men and the women, and those who could understand. And the ears of all the people listened to the Book of the Law.[12]

According to traditional Judaism, this is no less a momentous occasion than the original receiving of the Torah on Mount Sinai.

---

*Development, Composition, and Functions of the Bet Din ha-Gadol during the Second Jewish Commonwealth* (New York: Boch Publishing Co., 1953), 12ff.

9 Mishnah Avot 1:1.

10 Nissan Scherman, Meir Zlotowitz, eds., *History of the Jewish People: The Second Temple Era* (New York: Menorah Publications, 1982), 34-6.

11 Ibid., 36-7.

12 Nehemiah 8:2-3.

It is routinely assumed that during the subsequent "glory days" of Kings David, Solomon, and their progeny, the "law of the land," so to speak, remains this Torah of Moses. But let's not be naive. It's doubtful that most people know anything at all of the Torah in those early days, much less how to live their daily lives according to its precepts. Some scholars argue that the books of Moses, as we think of them, didn't exist at all until Ezra, except as a hodge-podge of independent sources in the hands of the priesthood.

This assembly in Jerusalem, however, is a sea change in the life of ordinary Israelites. This is Jerusalem's version of a "Constitutional Convention," the Torah itself being the newly ratified Constitution. Ezra, as he stands before this mass of people, is no less a statesman and political theorist than Benjamin Franklin, who, when asked what kind of government he and his colleagues had created, a republic or a monarchy, quipped, "A republic, if you can keep it."[13] The Torah, while it doesn't create a "republic" as we think of one, does promote a value that will become ensconced in the heart of western democracies in the millennia to come, and engraved on the front of the U.S. Supreme Court building – "equal justice under law."

### A Declaration, and its Ratification

The biblical book of Nehemiah hints at something more than just religion going on in all of this. Recognizing the need for wise and frugal government, a pact is drawn up, binding all its signatories to live in accordance with various precepts, deriving from On High, that give order to the society:

> We are cutting a sure covenant, and write it, and our princes, Levites, and priests are sealing it…. And the rest of the people, the priests, the Levites, the gatekeepers, the singers, the temple-servants, and all those who had separated from the people of the lands to the Law of God, their wives, their sons, and their daughters … entered into a curse and into an oath, to walk in God's law which was given by Moses the servant of God, and to be careful to do all the commandments of … our Lord, and His judg-

---

13 James McHenry, *American Historical Review*, vol. 11 (1906), 618.

ments and His statutes.[14]

Tradition relates that the people's resolve is recorded on a special scroll, bearing some eighty-four names, the leaders' signatures, and called the "Covenant of Trust" (*Brit Amanah*).

What a remarkable political idea! A government of laws, not men. It reminds us of those early days when Joshua (as we discussed earlier) gathers the people at Shechem and establishes an "ordinance," duly recorded in the "book of the law of God."[15] It's as though Israel has come full circle to the "tribal confederacy" of the period of the Judges, when "there was no king in Israel." We're also reminded of the experience of the early American colonists under the English, enjoying freedom of religion and a measure of political self-determination, though likewise struggling under an increasing tax burden.

When, in the American experience, the Continental Congress assembled to ratify the Declaration of Independence, they must have been aware of the Scriptural precedent, as they sealed their own covenant, likewise grounded in God's law, or, as they put it, "divine Providence." It was of course Thomas Jefferson who wrote the draft of the Declaration (cited above, Chapter 2), but Congress insisted on appending certain words (indicated in bold):

> And for the support of this declaration, «**with a firm Reliance on the Protection of divine Providence**,» we mutually pledge to each other our lives, our Fortunes, and our sacred Honor.

As one modern religious thinker put it, America achieved freedom without chaos, because there was a "form" – a heritage of justice based on biblical law.[16] Of course ratifying a covenant implies responsibility in carrying out its mandates. When it comes to jurisprudence, it is ordained in ancient Judea that judges should hold court on Tuesdays and Thursdays, when villagers come to town and go to market. The judges are admonished to be cautious in their judgments, not rendering a verdict without careful deliberation.[17]

---

14 Nehemiah 9:38; 10:28-29.

15 Joshua 24:25-26.

16 Francis Schaeffer, *op. cit*, 109.

17 Mishnah, Avot 1:1.

On those days at least three verses of the Torah are to be recited publicly, three being called to do the reading.[18]

While the main concern of the Great Assembly is the "judicial" realm of the new society, it is most likely also tasked with overseeing the general welfare of the people, including the distribution of charity to those in want; but whatever it's composition and its mode of operation, today's left had better think twice before branding it as heading up an ancient "entitlement society." One noted religious historian argues that the Jewish society of this period spawns an "egalitarian and socialist ethic."[19] Socialist? Perhaps the religious left needs reminding that caring for the poor and needy – something that this ancient society is proudly doing – does not a socialist make.

Rabbinic literature does go into detail about charity (*tzedakah*, by its formal Hebrew term), citing various levels of giving, ranking them from lowest to highest. Though the source is medieval, make no mistake, it has much to say about Jewish attitudes toward charity going all the way back to antiquity. The third highest level is when the donor is aware of the recipient's identity, but the recipient is unaware of the source. The second highest is when both donor and recipient are unknown to each other. The highest level of charity, however, is to help sustain someone before that individual becomes impoverished, by helping the person find employment or some form of business, so that dependance on others becomes unnecessary.[20] In any case, the pressing need, and Jewish obligation, to distribute charity to the needy strongly hints that the Great Assembly must be playing an important role during this challenging historical age.

### Culture Warriors

Politically speaking, it appears that during the course of time, a "democratic" tradition of sorts takes root in the land of Israel. Jews have been known, all through their history, for having a vibrant heritage of egalitarian self-governance, which continues to this day in the state of Israel – a lone bastion of democracy in a sea of tyrannical regimes that pepper the Middle East. A well-known adage says it all: Put two Jews together, and you'll have at least three opinions!

---

18 Scherman and Zlotowitz, *op. cit.* 37.

19 Karen Armstrong, *op. cit.*, 48.

20 Hayim Donin, *To Be a Jew: A Guide to Jewish Observance in Contemporary Life* (New York: Basic Books, 1972), 50.

During the Second Temple period, the next few centuries will see the Israelites fine-tune their government. They will adopt (as did their later American counterparts) many of the ideas (including the political theory) of their neighbors, especially those of a dynamic new power that will burst upon the scene in the early fourth century before the Common Era, the civilization of the Greeks.

When a charismatic young leader from Macedonia named Alexander comes marauding though the land in the early 300s B.C.E., the culture of Greece, Hellenism, is destined to come with him. The Judeans in Jerusalem and its surrounding territories are by now well accustomed to foreign domination, seeking only regional autonomy, enabling them to run their own affairs. They are pleasantly surprised when Alexander does just that, confirming the High Priest in his office and affirming their right to live under their ancestral laws. The ancient Jewish historian Josephus Flavius writes:

> Alexander asked the people what favors he should grant them; and, at the high priest's request, he accorded them the right to live in full enjoyment of the laws of their forefathers.[21]

The irony is, that continuing in the "laws of their forefathers" means, on a practical level, adopting significant elements of Hellenistic culture, some of it constructive, some not only foreign, but pagan. The society finds great allure in the art, architecture, theater, athletic competitions, and especially the political ideas of the Greeks. But what to embrace and what to reject?

Following the death of Alexander the Great, in 323 B.C.E., tradition recounts that the great high priest known as Simeon the Righteous (*Shimon Ha-Tzaddik* in Hebrew) comes to the fore. As a political leader, he uses his power to strengthen the community in the face of its challenging encounter with Greek culture.[22] Part of that encounter involves fine-tuning their high council, by adapting the "democratic" idea of an assembly of the people, who cast votes on important issues facing the citizenry, such as to whom to grant citizenship and when to go to war. The Spartan model of such a council of elders is called a *Gerousia*. It is composed of thirty members, twenty-eight being sixty years old and above. The name will be

---

21 Josephus, *Antiquities*, XI.8.4-6.
22 Scherman and Zlotowitz, *op. cit.* 40-1.

adopted, oddly enough, by pious Jews in Jerusalem, who will now use it to describe the Great Assembly. Other than its name, however, it amounts to a direct continuation of the council of the elders of Judah that has been in place since the Persian period.[23] Only its character will change, as both political leadership and land ownership end up in the hands of a small number of priestly families.

For almost a perfect century – during the third century B.C.E. – the land of Israel will be ruled by the Egyptian branch of Alexander's successors, the dynasty of the Ptolemies. Once again the Judeans will find themselves under "new management." It's the beginning of what one researcher calls a "core-to-core culture confrontation," that will one day pit the civilizations of Israel's God (Yah—) and Zeus in bitter conflict with each other.[24] One family in particular, the Tobiads, exert inordinate influence on the land, being in the vanguard of hellenistic culture. Many conundrums now face the Israelite populace, including whether to go to the theater, which is wedded to the worship of pagan deities, and whether to participate in athletic games, which also celebrate the gods and involve the "lewd" exhibition of gloriously unclad youths.

As the high priesthood itself becomes captive of hellenistic elements, the proud Jewish society of the days of Ezra morphs into a "soft tyranny," destined to metastasize into a "hard tyranny." What's wrong with the theater? many Judeans wanted to know. What's wrong with athletics and sport? The priest-led government in those days is able to "entrap" its own population by luring them with Hellenism's "goodies," in much the same way that modern "big government" ensnares its people with promises of more and more benefits. Governments throughout history have understood the trick of building domestic consensus by offering something that few can refuse.

### "Soft Tyranny" to "Hard Tyranny"

But some in Israel do refuse, specifically a group of pietists known as Hasidim – the "Hasidic" Jews, who first arrive on the stage of history during these tumultuous times. In them the long-

---

23 Abraham Malamat, Haim Hillel Ben-Sasson, eds., *A History of the Jewish People* (Tel Aviv, Dvir, 1976), 191-2.

24 Chaim Potok, Daniel Walden, ed., *Conversations with Chaim Potok* (Jackson, MS: University Press of Mississippi, 2001), viii.

submerged "Brutus current" will again raise its collective head. In 198 B.C.E., the land once more changes hands, as Egypt's Ptolemies lose to another branch of Alexander's successors, the Seleucid dynasty of Syria. The land of Israel has, geographically, been a "buffer zone" between Egypt to the south and Syria to the north. Now, after a critical battle in northern Galilee, the buffer belongs to the Seleucids. At first they seem respectful of their Israelite underlings, their great king, Antiochus III confirming Jewish ancestral traditions. His decree reads:

> Let all of that nation live according to the laws of their own country. And let the senate, the priests, the scribes of the temple, and the sacred singers be relieved from the poll tax, the crown tax, and other taxes also.[25]

Tax relief sounds good in any age, and the Jews hail this as an opportunity to manage their own affairs. Their government will be limited, not tyrannical, with power distributed between the high priest and the Great Assembly. But this generation's relative freedom is, paraphrasing Reagan, less than a generation from extinction. When a new Seleucid ruler, Antiochus IV, takes the stage, "hard tyranny" comes with him. In cahoots with a radical Hellenist Jewish high priest named Menelaus, he outlaws the practice of Judaism. A pagan statue is set up in the temple. A swine is sacrificed on the holy altar, and the juice of its boiled flesh sprinkled inside the Holy of Holies. Jewish tradition calls these acts "the abomination of desolation." Scrolls of the Torah are seized and burned. Circumcised infants are thrown from the walls of Jerusalem. In other cases, women are crucified, their circumcised babies hung from their necks. Jerusalem itself is being turned into a Greek-style city-state, a polis. It is the first true religious persecution in history.

In the centuries to come, the denial of the free practice of religion will become an oft-used tactic of totalitarian regimes. Karl Marx wrote:

> Religion is the sigh of the oppressed creature, the heart of a heartless world, and the soul of soulless conditions. It is the opium of the people. The abolition of religion as the illusory happiness of the people is the demand for their

---

25 Josephus, *Antiquities*, XII, 142.

real happiness.[26]

More recently, Barack Obama is quoted as saying, "And it is not surprising when [people] get bitter, they cling to guns or religion..."[27] Religion, we know from history, gets in the way of the absolute rule that tyrants seek to impose, and on that score it's not surprising that the Seleucid ruler, Antiochus IV, does what he does.

As for the pious Jerusalemites and their compatriots across the land – those who have not succumbed to Hellenism's lure, the Jewish faith is neither their sigh nor their illusion; it is a call to arms. The year is 168 B.C.E. In a little town called Modiin, on the border of the region of Samaria, a certain Israelite is ordered by a Syrian emissary to carry a swine to slaughter. Thereafter, the locals of the town are to be forced to eat the flesh of the animal as a test to determine whether they have abandoned their Jewish observance. The Israelite complies, but the episode is observed from a distance by an elderly priest named Mattathias. One thing is clear to this wise old man. This is no time for equivocation and appeasement. The old man grabs a spear close at hand, and in a moment of unparalleled spiritual dynamism, impales the young Israelite, along with the Syrian emissary who accompanies him, upon the very altar where the mock sacrifice was to be offered. He calls his five sons to his side and raises a standard of revolt. He cries out to the whole town: "Let all those who are fervent for the Law and faithful to the Covenant follow me!" They head off into the hills, to fast, to pray and to wait for the inevitable engagement with the enemy. The first religious persecution history is met with the first guerrilla war. "Brutus," we ask, "where have you been?"

Soon after the events in Modiin, the old patriarch Mattathias dies, passing the torch to his sons. The eldest of the five, named Judah, now takes up the sword on behalf of his oppressed people. A massive Syrian army, commanded by an infamous commander, Apollonius, musters against the Judean renegades. They're like the British troops of King George, descending upon the patriot militia. And they have no more luck against a vastly inferior force than the "Red Coats" will have, two millennia later. Marching in fine col-

---

26 Karl Marx, Joseph O'Malley, ed., *Critique of Hegel's Philosophy of Right* (New York: Press Syndicate of the Univ. of Cambridge, 1982), 131.

27 As quoted in Sharon Angle, *Right Angle: One Woman's Journey to Reclaim the Constitution* (Bloomington, IN: Author House), 175.

umns, their armor gleaming under a brilliant sun, the Syrians are attacked from nowhere by the sons of Mattathias, who have organized a militia of freedom fighters. The Syrians are cut to ribbons. Apollonius' sword is taken up by Judah, who now wields it as a symbol of defiance, pursuing the fight for the liberation of Jerusalem.

In response, the head of the entire Syrian army, Seron, heads south toward Judea to crush the resistance. Judah rushes into battle against Seron and his men, who are utterly routed before the Israelites. Antiochus IV, furious at such humiliation, dispatches an additional force, headed by another esteemed general, Nicanor, who takes on the Maccabee brothers. The fate of Nicanor's army, however, is the same as that of the first army. Nicanor himself is slain, and his troops flee in blind panic.

Judah, the hero, comes to be known as the "Maccabee," parroting an ancient Hebrew word meaning "hammer;" for he strikes hammer-blows into the flanks of the Syrian forces. Tyrants, nonetheless, are not accustomed to giving up so easily. Antiochus sends yet another army, which is likewise annihilated, their remnants fleeing into the plain, while those who stay in the rear are slain. After four grueling years of battle, in 165 B.C.E., the ragtag army of the Maccabees marches into the city of Jerusalem.[28] The Temple is cleansed and rededicated, in an eight-day festival known as Hanukkah. A cry of freedom goes up, that has not been heard since the days when Moses led the people out of Egypt.

### Patriots, Maccabees, and Sectarians

Once again we find parallel in the American experience, the United States having likewise been born in the crucible of rebellion. In a speech before the Virginia House of Burgesses, in May 1765, Patrick Henry would reference Colonial America's own "Brutus current":

Caesar had his Brutus, Charles the First his Cromwell; and George the Third — ["Treason!" cried the Speaker] — may profit by their example. If this be treason, make the most of it.[29]

---

28 Peter Schafer, *The History of the Jews in the Greco-Roman World* (New York: Routledge, 2003), 45ff.

29 Paul Aron, *We Hold These Truths...: And Other Words That Made America* (Latham,

Many years later, after the revolution had been won, Henry would be cited as trumpeting the principle of limited government in no uncertain terms:

> The Constitution is not an instrument for the government to restrain the people, it is an instrument for the people to restrain the government - lest it come to dominate our lives and interests.[30]

It would take America two full centuries to evolve from a constitutional republic of limited government, to something else – a "soft tyranny," as some today call it. It will take the victorious Maccabees less than a generation to get to the same place.

Following the liberation of Jerusalem and festival of Hanukkah, the Syrians (like the British in their dealings with the American colonies) are still unwilling to let Judea go its own way. Additional generals will be dispatched, and more battles fought. It will take years of additional struggle before this "revolutionary war" can bring about a new and independent Israel. In the interim, one of the five Maccabee brothers, Jonathan, comes to the helm of leadership, using the internal rivalries that erupt in the Syrian ranks to assume for himself the mantle of the high priesthood. The trouble is, he's not of the right priestly family to become high priest. According to Israelite law, that honor is reserved for members of the family of Zadok; Jonathan is of the House of Hashmon – a "Hasmonean." Oddly, most of his countrymen don't object, and are more than willing to trade their religious principles for political security, which they're sure this "war hero" will bring.

Only the Hasidic sect "gets it." Like some modern religious denominations in their struggle against government encroachment, they are not about to sacrifice principle on the altar of expediency. They realize that Jonathan's usurpation of the high priesthood is only one remove from the very tyranny they had all been fighting against. Consequently, they withdraw their support and defect from the government altogether. Before, the tyrant king, Antiochus IV, had attacked them bodily; now, it's the soul that is threatened by

---

MD: Rowman & Littlefield, 2008), 83; based on William Writ's biography of Henry, first published in 1817.

30 Brion T. McClanahan, *The Politically Incorrect Guide to the Founding Fathers* (Washington, D.C.: Regency, 2009), 254.

stealth.

As for Jonathan, the great Maccabee warrior, his motives shift from purely religious (when he fought to retake Jerusalem from the Syrians) to political, as he reaches out to cement an alliance with a new and growing power to the west, Rome. Tyrants, like birds of a feather, flock together. In what some Judeans see as a divine judgment, Jonathan is not destined to live much longer. He is kidnapped and subsequently murdered in continuing rumbles with his Seleucid foes.

In his place, another Maccabee, Simon, will take absolute power, not only as high priest, but king. This is double tyranny, in the minds of some. Not only is he from the wrong family (the Hasmoneans) to be high priest; he isn't from the line of David (by now rehabilitated in the minds of his people) and therefore is on the throne illegitimately. The society starts to come unglued.

### Judeo-topia

At some point a newly formed renegade sect heads east into the Judean desert, to create an alternate society, so to speak, on the shores of the Dead Sea, eagerly awaiting divine rescue by the promised Messiah. They are known as the Essenes, and their claim to fame is the literary product they produce, an enormous cache of documents that have come to be called the Dead Sea Scrolls. These texts comprise the oldest copies of the Hebrew Bible known in all the world, as well as hundreds of additional texts and assorted parchments, including their own rule books on how their sect should be organized, politically.

According to precept, they establish their own quasi-democratic assembly – the Council of the Community – consisting of twelve Israelite men and three priests. This council legislates on behalf of the whole sect, also called the Many. Lording over the community and presiding over its assemblies, is a supreme teacher called the Guardian or Overseer. It is he who examines every potential member for entrance into the community, while another office called the Bursar supervises the group's finances and property, which is held in common.[31] In some ways it sounds like a utopian society along the lines of Plato's *Republic*, and it quite possibly represents the direct

---

31 James VanderKam, *The Dead Sea Scrolls Today* (Grand Rapids: Eerdmans, 1994), 112.

influence of Greek political ideas, that have come in along with the tide of Hellenism.

In any case, this "state within a state" is hardly the kind of free society that would later inspire America's Founders. On the contrary, while responding to their Hasmonean liberators-turned-autocrats, they've created yet another autocracy, on a very localized level. Every detail of their daily lives is under the close scrutiny of the Overseer. As in other utopian societies down through history, they put an end to private property rights and ultimately sublimate the will of the individual to that of the whole. Today there is a debate about the degree to which contemporary society suffers from the same tendencies, replacing "America" with "Ameritopia."[32] The great political theorist Alexis de Tocqueville summed up this kind of tyranny as follows:

> When tyranny is established in the bosom of a small state, it is more galling than elsewhere, because acting in a narrower circle, everything in that circle is subject to its direct influence. It supplies ... exasperating interference in a multitude of minute details ... to meddle with the arrangements of domestic life. Tastes as well as actions are to be regulated at its pleasure; and the families of the citizens ... are to be governed by its decisions.[33]

The Essenes may imagine that they've escaped the tyrannical power of the king in Jerusalem, but the local government they've created is even more intrusive than the authoritarian rule of the Hasmoneans. In America today, those who think that local government is the answer to a bloated federal government had better consider the explosive growth of what may be called the "local leviathan." State and local governments have more than half a million elected officials on their payrolls, and an additional thirteen million

---

32 Mark R. Levin, *Ameritopia: The Unmaking of America* (New York: Simon & Schuster, 2012), 167. Levin elsewhere comments on various blueprints for utopian societies, from Plato's Republic, to Hobbes' Leviathan, to Marx and Engels' Communist Manifesto. The ancient Essenes should be considered, not just as a hypothetical, but as a real, historical example of a failed "utopia."

33 Alexis de Tocqueville, *Democracy in America*, Chapter VIII: The Federal Constitution – Part V.

appointed officials.[34] Needless to say, the level of local micromanagement touches nearly every aspect of the citizen's life.

Clearly, the Judeans are faced with some very poor choices – a large and growing tyranny on the part of their newly minted Hasmonean dynasty, or the smaller and even more intrusive tyranny of the Dead Sea "Judeo-topia." Either way, the "good old days" of Joshua's tribal confederacy are destined not to return.

### The New Revolutionaries

Liberty must instead be found in other ways, sought through other means. When the Hasmonean king, Alexander Jannaeus (*Yannai* in Hebrew) comes to the throne in the year 103 B.C.E., a new despotism comes with him. It is met by a new grassroots movement that has crystallized in opposition. Lacking priestly pedigree, material wealth, or political power, they, like the prophets of old, represent the common people. Their authority derives solely from their level of knowledge, and their scrupulous devotion to Torah precepts. They are called the Pharisees, and they are yet another expression of the ancient "Tea Party" spirit.

Not surprisingly, they come into sharp conflict with Jannaeus over a matter of ritual observance in the Temple, which the king (who like his royal predecessors also holds the office of high priest) is performing incorrectly. Acrimony turns to violence, as the Pharisees begin pelting the monarch with citrons. It's the ancient equivalent of the Bostonians who threw snowballs at the British troops, inadvertently prompting the Boston Massacre. King Jannaeus responds with more violence, unleashing his troops on the mob. The "Jerusalem Massacre" ensues, the king's troops slaying over six thousand people in the courtyards of the Temple.

The result is civil war, as the Pharisees (the patriots of their day) rise up in rebellion. While it's a supreme measure of hutzpah, the goal is refreshingly libertarian: the overthrow of the monarchy under the banner of divine law ... and doing it two thousand years before the age of revolution in Europe and America. It sounds pretty good, and it's enough to bring a smile to the face of any Brutus. The early part of the campaign goes badly for the rebels (as it did for Washington's Continental Army). The Pharisees, like their colonial

---

34 Clint Block, *Grassroots Tyranny: The Limits of Federalism* (Washington, D.C.: Cato Institute, 1993), 6ff.

American counterparts, are going to need a little help from foreign allies. Benjamin Franklin went to Paris, to enlist the French in the revolutionary cause; the Pharisees turn to the old nemesis of the Judeans, the Seleucids of Syria.

In 1777 the Marquis de Lafayette arrived to help the American colonists in their drive for independence, ultimately playing a major role in besieging the British at Yorktown. In ancient Judea the Seleucid king, Demetrius III arrives to take on Jannaeus. They defeat him in a major battle at the northern city of Shechem (the Israelite equivalent of Yorktown) and forcing him to retreat to the mountains. But then something unexpected happens. The Pharisees have a change of heart, most likely being smitten with the ages-old phenomenon of "Jewish guilt," for having supported a foreign power over their own nation. Besides, it's probably better to live under homespun tyranny than foreign tyranny. They return to Jannaeus, who now gains the upper hand, saving his skin and his throne. Unfortunately for the Pharisees, Jannaeus brings eight hundred of them to Jerusalem and has them crucified. He has their wives' and children's throats slit before their eyes, as Jannaeus dines with his concubines.

The Pharisees will have to surrender their political aspirations for the time being, turning inward and cultivating small "cell groups" (*Havurah* groups) where they can develop personal piety. While the Dead Sea sect has withdrawn from society altogether, the Pharisees create a new popular culture, across the length and breadth of the land. The synagogue is a Pharisee innovation, serving as a multipurpose "community center" with a remarkably egalitarian local government of sorts.[35] It's unfortunate the the Pharisees have been so maligned through the centuries, as they assiduously assert the principles of religious democracy and progress. Since the priesthood is in the hands of the Hasmoneans, in cahoots with the sect known as the Sadducees, the Pharisees declare that "God gave all the people the heritage, the kingdom, the priesthood, and the holiness."[36]

The Pharisees themselves have no hierarchy, no authoritarian structure, no single leader. The synagogue is the closest thing the nation has to a "democratic republic." A common observation is that the synagogue actually transforms the face of Judaism, making

---

35 Mordecai Avian and William Scott Green, "The Ancient Synagogue: Public Space in Judaism," in Jacob Neusner, William Scott Green, Alan Jeffery Avery-Peck, eds., *Judaism from Moses to Muhammed: an Interpretation* (Leiden: Brill, 2005), 183ff.

36 2 Maccabees 2:17.

it more communal and democratic. It has also been called a "universal" institution under local control. Lacking a formal clergy, its leadership is open, so that any congregant may be called upon to lead worship.[37] An ancient inscription uncovered in Jerusalem lists the functions of the synagogue as follows: "...for purposes of reciting the Law and studying the commandments, and the hostel, chambers and water installations to provide for the needs of itinerants from abroad."[38] In other words, the Pharisees are creating a functioning society within a society. Charity and compassion flow from a network of what we would today call "private institutions," not from the central government, certainly not the Hasmonean monarchy.

But with the death of Jannaeus, and the accession of his widow, Queen Salome Alexandra – *Shlomtzion* in Hebrew – peace will come between the Pharisees and the Hasmoneans. The new queen orchestrates an ingenious compromise, by which one of her two sons, who has strong Pharisee leanings, is given the high priesthood, while the other, a Sadducee, is given charge of the army. In yet another parallel with the American republic, it amounts to a tripartite division of power between:

* the "executive" branch (Queen Shlomtzion herself),
* the military (her Sadducee son Aristobolus II as "Chairman of the Joint Chiefs of Staff"), and
* the "legislative"/ "judicial" branch (her Pharisee son Hyrcanus II in charge of interpreting the Torah). The Pharisees suddenly have one of their own at the helm of the Temple itself. Moreover, the Great Assembly is reorganized, favoring the Pharisees. As a permanent legal body, it is composed of seventy-one members, who vote on the most important civil and criminal matters, and other issues of great import, such as declaring war. Meeting in the sacred precincts of the Temple (we think of the imposing Supreme Court building in Washington, D.C.) it is known as the Great Sanhedrin.[39] Across the land, every city has its own small Sanhedrin, of twenty-

---

37 Lee I. Levine, *The Ancient Synagogue* (New Haven, CT: Yale University Press, 1999), 1-2.

38 The so-called Theodotus Inscription, found at the bottom of a well, dates from the first century B.C.E. to the first century, C.E., and, notably, does not mention prayer as one of the functions of the synagogue. The picture it conveys is of a communal center. See Dan Urman, Paul Virgil, McCracken Fleshe, *Ancient Synagogues: Historical Analysis and Archaeological Discovery* (Leiden: Brill, 1995), 33.

39 David M. Goodblatt, *The Monarchic Principle: Studies in Jewish Self-Government in Antiquity* (Tubingen: J.C.B. Mohr, 1994), 106ff.; Sidney Benjamin Hoeing, *op. cit.*

three judges, who decide all manner of local cases.

Yes, it's still a monarchy, not a republic. But Queen Shlom-tzion (whose name means "peace of Zion") is the one Hasmonean monarch who is so revered that even today, a street in downtown Jerusalem bears her name.

### Hail Caesar!

The years 76 - 67 B.C.E. amount to a "golden decade" for this war-ravaged land. Internally, the queen's political acumen has made power sharing/ "checks and balances" a reality, in a way that would make Montesquieu proud. Externally, she increases the size of the military, provisioning many fortresses, so that neighboring king-doms dare not harass her realm. She instinctively grasps the modern argument, that the most important role of the central government is the defense of their citizenry (implying a strong military), while leaving social welfare to those closest to the people (oft times religious institutions) and best suited to caring for them – in this case the Pharisees. Her government is strong, but not overly so. She has found what America's Founders would later call the "balanced center."

Unfortunately, her death will bring on strong rivalry between her two sons, whose forces end up in bitter combat with each other.[40] Neither seems aware of the looming threat to the west, a republic with growing despotic tendencies, Rome. In the year 63 B.C.E., Pompey the Great, political and military leader, and member (along with Marcus Licinius Crassus and Julius Caesar) of the First Triumvirate, comes marauding through the Levant. On his way to Egypt, he must of course subjugate the squabbling little kingdom of Judea and take it into the Roman orbit. In short order a century of Jewish struggle for an independent land, with fledgling, quasi-democratic institutions, comes to an end.

Hyrcanus II will be confirmed as high priest, but only as a miserable lackey under the Romans. A worse fate, however, will be in store for the people of the land in the years to come; for one of Hyrcanus' friends, by the name of Antipater, has a son, who will finagle his way to absolute rule, with the full consent of his pals in Rome. His name will ring through the ages as a symbol of repression and

---

40 Peter Schafer, *op. cit.*, 76ff.

brutal tyranny – Herod.

# 10
# ROMANS, JESUS, AND THE
# MEGA-STATE

*"Liberty lies in the hearts of men and women; when it dies there, no constitution, no law, no court can save it; no constitution, no law, no court can even do much to help it..."* – Learned Hand[1]

**K**ing Herod the Great has been diagnosed posthumously as a "manic depressive, paranoid schizophrenic with aggressive tendencies." Of all the kings, potentates and despots to have ruled over the Israelites, Herod uniquely lives in infamy. His dubious career begins when his father Antipapter (friend of Hyrcanus II and lackey of the Romans) gets him appointed governor of Galilee. But all is not well in this region to the north. The "Brutus current" has woken up again, and now turns to ousting the occupiers, and "proclaiming liberty throughout the land" (Leviticus 25:10). The Zealot party, that happens to be headquartered in Galilee, began as yet another ancient expression of "Tea Party" sentiment, but has quickly morphed into a serious revolutionary movement. In Herod's new capacity as governor, he has the ringleader of these anti-Roman "freedom fighters," Hezekiah the Galilean, brutally slain.

Unfortunately for him, the Sanhedrin, far from disappearing,

---

1 "The Spirit of Liberty" - a speech at "I Am an American Day" ceremony, Central Park, New York City (May 21, 1944).

continues as the "judicial branch" of government, even under the Romans. Herod is hauled before the august body and convicted of murder. Fleeing for his life to Rome, he uses his considerable political acumen to convince his pals – Octavian and Mark Antony – to appoint him King of Judea. Now, Judea in these days is actually a drain on the resources of Rome. It's is of no particular strategic value; nor does it produce anything of material value. Its native population is hostile. It is far removed from the seat of power, and therefore difficult and expensive to send the necessary troops and civil servants to govern it. Herod is known in Rome to be incompetent, and his posting in this insignificant scrap of desert may well be regarded as a way simply to be rid of him.

The gist of the directive from the Roman leaders: "We have made you king; now go conquer your kingdom."[2] Returning to Jerusalem with a Roman legion in tow, Herod does just that. After incredible carnage and bloodletting, the new king reigns supreme. He will never, however, be accepted by the people he rules. For one thing, he isn't even Jewish. His father is an Idumean, and governor of that nearby province (situated southeast of Judea) under the Hasmonean dynasty. Not surprisingly, Herod is viewed as a usurper of monstrous proportions. He will therefore go to great lengths to justify his regime and gain legitimacy in the eyes of the Judeans. This will unleash his "manic" side, as he builds palaces of grandeur from the desert dust. In his "depressive" state, his cruelty will know no bounds. The one thing certain is that Herod's kingdom will amount to nothing short of "big government" on steroids.

### Mega-States: Yesterday and Today

Josephus, the ancient historian, writes in detail of the state tyranny of King Herod the Great, evocative in some respects of the modern tyranny of big and bloated government. Specifically he notes...

\* The violation of private property rights:

When he took the kingdom, [though] it was in an extraordinary flourishing condition, he had filled the nation with the utmost degree of poverty; and when, upon unjust pre-

---

2 Josephus, *Antiquities*, xiv.l.i.4-5

tenses, he had killed any of the nobility, he took away their estates; and when he permitted any of them to live, he condemned them to the forfeiture of what they possessed.

* Increasing tax burdens:

And beside the annual impositions which he laid upon every one of them, they were to make liberal presents to himself, to his servants and friends, and to such of his slaves as were promised the favor of being his tax-gatherers, because there was no way of obtaining freedom from unjust violence without giving either gold or silver for it...

* Ruination for the whole land:

That Herod had put such abuses upon them as a wild beast would not have put on them, if he had power given him to rule over us; and that although their nation had passed through many subversions and alterations of government, their history gave no account of any calamity they had ever been under that could be compared with this which Herod had brought upon their nation.[3]

As one modern pundit put it, "The bigger the government, the smaller the citizen."[4] John Locke, himself a student of the biblical legacy, and whose political theory became the bedrock of the American republic, observed:

[A common man] the subject, or rather slave of an absolute prince... whenever his property is invaded by the will and order of the [absolute] monarch, he has not only no appeal, as those in society ought to have... [but he is also] denied a liberty to ... defend his right; and so is exposed to all the misery and inconveniences, that a man can fear...[5]

3 *Antiquities*, 17, II (307-310), in Flavius Josephus, William Whiston, Paul L. Maier, *The New Complete Works of Josephus* (Grand Rapids: Kregel, 1999), 579.

4 Dennis Prager, http://townhall.com/columnists/dennisprager/2009/09/01

5 John Locke, *Of Civil Government and Toleration*, Chap. VII, "Of Political or Civil Society," 1688 (London, Cassell & Co., 1905), 57.

Today there is serious discussion about the trampling of private property rights, as wealth and assets are routinely transferred from those who've earned them to those who haven't. The burden of taxation has been proudly touted as "redistributionist" by nature, and, who can deny it, considering that the top 1% of the population now pays more in taxes than the bottom 95%?[6] Capital gains taxes, property taxes, death taxes, all can be seen as interminable encroachments on private property and the lawful accumulation of wealth. How different is this from what authoritarian regimes have always done vis-a-vis those who have accumulated wealth, dating all the way back to biblical times (and of course, King Herod)? But ironically, while this level of taxation is nowadays supposed to be benevolent, alleviating the suffering of the poor, it has only succeeded (as in Herod's day) in keeping the poor in poverty, and perpetually dependent on the "ruling class" – the army of more than two million bureaucrats (including "tax-gatherers") who are the real beneficiaries of the mega-state. Financial and cultural prognosticators alike routinely warn of looming ruin, even the end of America as we have known it.[7]

In the case of Herod, the tyrant still tries to please his subject Israelites in a manner evocative of how despotic regimes have always tried to ensnare and entrap their populations – passing out "benefits" in the form of massive public works projects. On the Mediterranean coast he builds a spectacular new port city, Caesarea, to this day considered a masterpiece of engineering. The massive artificial harbor employs the Romans' breakthrough construction technique of underwater concrete. It boasts of a Hellenistic-style theater, of perfect acoustics, facing the ocean, a great hippodrome where chariot races are conducted, an underground sewer system, periodically flushed by the tides, and an elaborate aqueduct, channeling a torrent of water from the distant hills. Its centerpiece is an enormous temple to the emperor Augustus, visible far out to sea.

---

6 Obama "Green Czar" Van Jones, Berkely, California, Feb. 26, 2009. Jones commented that Rosa Parks might have made a stronger demand: "...We want redistribution of all the wealth." It is noted that the U.S. – not Sweden or France – has the most progressive tax burden among all OECD nations; http://www.taxfoundation.org/blog/show/24944.html.

7 Steyn, *op. cit.*, 12, 20. Steyn notes that "for dominant powers, ruin comes by the express lane." He also observes, "America is ruled not by a meritocracy but by a cartel of conformicrats imposing a sterile monopoly of outmoded ideas."

But who cares about these trappings of high civilization, when the people are continually oppressed by a usurper-king?

Back in Jerusalem, the Temple built in the days of Ezra needs a facelift. But a facelift won't be enough. Herod will launch his greatest public works project of all, completely remaking, not just the Temple, but the very hill on which it stands. It remains the largest human-made platform on earth, nearly five hundred meters by three hundred meters in area. It's the rough equivalent of twenty-four football fields, eclipsing in sheer area even the Pyramids of Egypt. It essentially squares off a sloping hillside by means of a vast network of subterranean vaults, supported by rows of arches in four levels, each vaulted room being twenty feet tall by twenty feet wide.

Even today, the ruins of the structure are guaranteed to amaze and stupefy the visiting pilgrim. Standing before the Western Wall of the great plateau, you are given pause for thought as you realize that you are actually treading on roughly forty feet of compressed rubble, that would have to be cleared away to reach the level of Herod's pavement. Yet, all of this is only the retaining wall. You would have to imagine a freestanding wall of the same dimensions, basically doubling the height of the retaining wall, to appreciate the original height of the structure.

As for the Temple itself, it is gone today, replaced by the Muslim shrine known as the Dome of the Rock. But words cannot describe its grandeur in Herod's day, topped by castings of solid gold, its white marble gleaming in the Judean sun. It is the physical emblem of Herod's mega-state. But is it really necessary to have such a colossus in the heart of Jerusalem? Or is it really just an ancient "bridge to nowhere"? Moreover, even this gargantuan monument will not satisfy a populace that much prefers self-determination to grandiosity. If Solomon's Temple might in retrospect be considered a "boondoggle," this beautiful "monstrosity," bearing an idolatrous Roman eagle at its pinnacle, perfectly epitomizes the new tyranny.

### The Pharisees and the Flat Tax

In the Judean countryside, the Pharisees are still around, and more active than ever. Some dream of redemption from the yoke of oppression, both foreign (Rome) and domestic (Herod), becoming at least comrades, if not comrades-in-arms, of the growing Zealot movement. Others, however, counsel patience, and trust in the coming of a peaceful, not militant, Messiah. They believe that for those who take upon themselves the yoke of the Torah, the yoke of Rome will fall off of its own accord. To this end they have put in place a vibrant, lively infrastructure, whose dual aims are to encourage the "people of the land" (in Hebrew *am ha-aretz*) to be observant of their religious obligations, and to provide comfort and care for the neediest of the people.

Paying Herod's and Rome's taxes is a something they debate and that some try to avoid, but there is never a question about supporting the Temple with their tithes. While the Temple is in the hands of the Sadducean priesthood, who in turn are in league with Herod, they are nonetheless entitled to their allotment, as spelled out in the people's "Constitution":

> I have given the sons of Levi all the tenth in Israel for an inheritance, for their service which they serve, the service of the tabernacle of the congregation.[8]

"All the tenth" includes one tenth of all agricultural produce, most likely livestock as well. During the First Temple period, these tithes could be brought to any priest, in any part of the land. Now, the Second Temple has become in a real sense the national treasury:

> And the priest, the son of Aaron, shall be with the Levites, when the Levites take tithes, and the Levites shall bring up the tithe of the tithes to the house of our God, to the rooms, into the treasure house.[9]

Moreover, the tithe doesn't support the priests alone, but creates a "food bank" of sorts for the poor.[10] The tithe of every third year is specifically designated to this end:

> At the end of three years you shall bring forth all the tithe of your increase the same year, and shall lay it up inside your gates. And the Levite, because he has no part nor inheritance with you, and the stranger, and the fatherless,

---

8 Numbers 18:21.

9 Nehemiah 10:38.

10 Lester L. Grabbe, *op. cit.*, 1: 235-6.

and the widow, who are inside your gates, shall come, and shall eat and be satisfied...[11]

Aha! say the religious left! Doesn't this amount to a "social safety net," the kind that society ought to provide today? Isn't the Bible is promoting "social justice" as its main concern – code language on the part of some for "socialism"? The answer to that is, of course ... not! For one thing, it's the religious community (rather than a "secular" government), administered by the priests, that is tasked to provide this kind of charity. This is far different from Herod's personal taxes or those mandated by the Romans, which are in a different category entirely.

Secondly, the tithe is by its very nature voluntary. There's no "ITS" ("Internal Tithe Service") auditing the population to determine whether or not they've complied. Nor are there agents of the priesthood sneaking around through the countryside, reporting on "tithe avoidance." The only authority for compliance have been the prophets, who have put the people on a "guilt trip" when required:

> Will a man rob God? Yet you have robbed Me. But you say, In what have we robbed You? In the tithe and the offering! You are cursed with a curse; for you are robbing Me, the nation, all of it. Bring all the tithe into the storehouse, so that there may be food in My house. And test Me now with this, says the LORD of hosts, to see if I will not open the windows of Heaven for you, and pour out a blessing for you, until there is no sufficiency.[12]

Now, if the tithe were in fact a legal tax, rather than a voluntary religious ordinance, why does any prophet need to address is lack of performance? But even if we do acknowledge it as a kind of "tax," establishing at least a precedent for a modern "social safety net" for the poor and needy, we have to ask what kind of "tax" it amounts to. The obvious answer is: a flat tax! Imagine, if, in a modern setting, taxation were limited to ten percent of a person's income. And imagine if business tax – currently a whopping thirty-five percent in the United States – were only ten percent. Does ancient Israelite culture still sound "socialist"?

---

11 Deuteronomy 14:28-29.
12 Malachi 3:8-10.

Let's be clear. It's true that biblical tithing regulations are quite complex, including all manner of categories and sub-categories:

* The first fruits of the harvest (*bikkurim* in Hebrew)
* The produce offering, presented to the priests (*teruman* in Hebrew)
* The tithe on agricultural produce, or "first tithe" (*ma'aser rishon* in Hebrew)
* The "tithe offering" for the Levites (*terumat ma'aser* in Hebrew)
* The "tithe of tithes," requiring the Levites in turn to give one tenth of one tenth (0.01%) to the priests.
* The half-shekel – a final, flat "poll tax" to support the general welfare of the community.

The tithing system is organized into a seven year cycle, followed by a "Sabbatical year" (*Shemittah*), of rest for the whole land. During the first, second, fourth and fifth years of the cycle, a "second tithe" is to be brought directly to the city of Jerusalem. For those living too far from the city, the tithe can be redeemed in coins. We can imagine ancient Judeans, especially the wealthier class, hiring accountants to figure it all out! Nevertheless, compared with modern tax codes, this is the essence of simplicity. Moreover, there's nothing "progressive" about the ten-percent requirement. The rich are not obliged to pay a larger percentage, nor are the less wealthy allowed to pay a lower percentage. It's not redistributionist, and it's not about "spreading the wealth." However the hard left would like to spin it, this isn't Marxism, or socialism, or even an ancient "New Deal." It rather falls into the category of plain, ordinary "charity" (*tzedakah*).

Nonetheless, charity offered to the poor should by no means create a state of dependency, on either individuals as givers, or the state. To this day in Jewish practice, the "grace" said after a meal reflects the attitude, that while compassion and care for the poor is essential, dependency on others or on society at large is to be assiduously avoided:

Do not make us dependent upon the gifts of people, nor on their loans, but only on Your full, bountiful, and capacious hand, that we not be ashamed or humiliated forever.[13]

There's one other point that needs to be stressed. According to Jewish law, even those who are dependent on charity are obligated to give it.[14] None are exempt. Compare this with the modern progressive income tax, which has evolved to the point that fully half the population pays no tax at all, but receives "earned income" tax credits, that basically amount to government handouts. Nowadays, it is fundamentally about the transfer of wealth, from those who have earned it (the productive element of society) to those who have not (a permanent dependent class). Never in history has dependency on big government been so fostered and promoted; never has the spirit of biblical tradition been so utterly distorted.

Make no mistake, the Pharisees are scrupulous about paying their tithes, but they also work outside the formal religious structure to implement a "just" society. Are the Pharisees the forerunners of the modern socialist "utopian" state? Some would like to cast them that way, but in truth they're much more akin to the fraternal, mutual aid societies of the last century. During the Great Depression, there were many such societies, fraternal groups and organizations that continued their commitment to those in need well into the Roosevelt years. After all, it's been demonstrated time and time again that the most effective form of philanthropy is private. These societies addressed all manner of cultural, psychological, and gender needs, while also providing social-welfare services that were otherwise unavailable. Like the ancient Pharisee movement, they organized vast social and mutual aid networks that embraced the poor and working class, offering health and life insurance at affordable prices, establishing hospitals, orphanages, and homes for seniors. It was the extension of the federal government's welfare state, however, that eventually squeezed private fraternal aid societies out of the business of caring for those in need.[15] Even King Herod's megastate never does that, so that the Pharisee movement is able to grow

---

13 http://www.rabbinicalassembly.org/tzedek-justice/tzedakah.

14 *B. Gitin* 7b; *Yad, Matanot Aniyim* 7:5; *Shulchan Arukh Yoreh De`ah* 248:1.

15 David T. Beito, *From Mutual Aid to the Welfare State: Fraternal Societies and Social Services, 1890-1967* (Chapel Hill: University of North Carolina Press, 2000); Amity Shlaes, *The Forgotten Man: A New History of the Great Depression* (New York: HarperCollins, 2007); Brian S. Wesbury, Amity Shlaes, *It's Not as Bad as You Think: Why Capitalism Trumps Fear and the Economy Will Thrive* (Hoboken, NJ: John Wiley & Sons, 2010), xi.

and continue, even beyond the "food bank" created by the tithes, to dispense charity (tzedakah) in their own way.

### Jesus, Socialism, and "Judeo-topia"

In a kindred current with the Pharisees is a popular Galilean teacher-prophet, who comes along in the days of the emperor Tiberias – after Herod has died and been replaced in Judea by a series of Roman governors/ "procurators." His name is Yeshua, though sacred tradition knows him as Jesus of Nazareth. The one thing we know with certainty about Jesus is that we know very little with certainty. As Thomas Jefferson wrote, "Rogueries, absurdities and untruths were perpetrated upon the teachings of Jesus by a large band of dupes..."[16]

Just about everybody wants to lay claim to Jesus as "one of us," so that most of what is thought common knowledge with respect to him amounts to anachronistic stereotype. That, co-mingled with religious doctrine and dogma, leaves us scratching our heads, and scrambling to uncover anything of the "real Jesus." Moreover, when the "religious left" chimes in, justifying everything from massive deficit spending on social welfare programs to outright Marxism ("liberation theology") on the basis of Jesus' teaching, it's clear that somebody needs to set the record straight.

Why is it that those on the left want to turn the man from Galilee into a hardcore socialist, or even a fellow "traveler" on Karl Marx's journey? Perhaps it's because of Jesus' sensitivity to the poor and downtrodden and his unrelenting attacks on the rich:

> It is easier for a camel to go through the eye of a needle than for a rich man to enter into the kingdom of God.[17]

But who, exactly, are the "rich" of Jesus' day? The Galilean fisherman, selling his daily catch for as much hard coinage as he can earn? Or the industrious craftsman, the carpenter, the tool maker, or the tanner, involved in what amounts to a cottage industry? These are the "small businesses" of the day, engaged in by generations of early capitalists – Adam Smith's sort of folks. No, the real "rich"

---

16 Thomas Jefferson, Letter to the Danbury Baptist Association, January 1, 1802.
17 Matthew 19:24.

in this era are the Herodians and their allies, including the Saddu-cees, in their multiple priestly orders, government officials, and the landed gentry, who thrive precisely because of their connection with the ruling authorities. Then we have the horde of Roman rulers who enjoy as lavish a lifestyle as possible in this backwater, desertlike province. The "rich" essentially consist of the "ruling class," who bear not a trifling resemblance to today's ruling class.

Who is more affluent today, small business owners and their employees, struggling under ever-increasing taxes and regulation, or the legion of government lackeys, with their six-figure salaries, lifetime job security and generous perks in the form of health and pension benefits? Is this not the pattern seen in virtually every social-ist state, that the real beneficiaries of "income redistribution" are not the poor whom the ruling class boasts of helping, but the rulers themselves. In such societies, just as in ancient Judea, the only ones to become genuinely "rich" are the bloat-belly bureaucrats of the mega-state.

So, does Jesus still sound like a Marxist/ socialist, filled with righteous indignation against fat-cat "corporate" interests (not that anything similar to corporate enterprise existed in his day)? Or is his castigation of the "rich" code language for a subversive broadside against big-government tyranny? It's not that "proto-Communism" doesn't exist in these days. But if you want to find socialism, or even ancient "Marxism," in the days of Jesus, you'll have to look, not to Jesus himself, but to the Dead Sea Essene sect (referenced above), whom Josephus describes as follows:

> These men are despisers of riches.... Nor is there any one to be found among them who hath more than another; for it is a law among them, that those who come to them must let what they have be common to the whole order, – insomuch, that among them all there is no appearance of poverty or excess of riches... and so there is, as it were, equality among all the brethren.[18]

As noted earlier, their ideal (equality of outcome, not just equality of opportunity), amounts to "Judeo-topia." Jesus, by con-trast, notes the simple economic reality, that "the poor will be with

18 Josephus, *Wars* II, VIII, 3.

you always."[19] He even takes direct aim at the Essenes, who, in the Dead Sea Scrolls, repeatedly mention the "material wealth of wickedness,"[20] admonishing their members not to engage in commerce with the outside world. Jesus declares that people should in fact "make friends" with (using Essene language) "the mammon of unrighteousness," i.e. "capital."[21] So Jesus is really ... a capitalist! Jesus is deeply concerned with the poor – the "people of the land" – not because he's a socialist, but because he is (borrowing a Yiddishism) a mensch. And he's wise enough to know, like his Pharisee counterparts, that charity (*tzedakah*) works best when it's private.

Fortunately, modern scholarship is able to shed even more light on the man from Galilee, so that it's quite possible – with the facts behind us – to take Jesus back from "captivity" to the hard left. Let's take, as a case in point, the remarks of President Barack Obama, who, when speaking at a National Prayer Breakfast, couldn't resist commending his own "redistributionist" policy. He remarked:

> It's hard for me to ask [people]... who can barely pay the bills to shoulder the burden alone. And I think to myself, if I'm willing to give something up as somebody who's been extraordinarily blessed and give up some of the tax breaks that I enjoy... that's going to make some economic sense... For me as a Christian, it also coincides with Jesus's teaching that to whom much is given, much shall be required. It mirrors the Islamic belief that those who've been blessed have an obligation to use those blessings to help others, or the Jewish doctrine of moderation and consideration of others.[22]

That shouldn't surprise us, given the president's long association with leftist spokes-preacher, Jeremiah Wright. As we shall see, when it comes to understanding the overall message of Jesus, Wright is flat wrong. The real question to be asked is: WWJT – "What would Jesus tax?"

---

19 Matthew 26:11; Mark 14:7.

20 *Hon ha-rasha* in Hebrew.

21 Luke 16:9.

22 Quoted by the Family Research Council, "Washington Update": http://www.frc.org/washingtonupdate/cause-god-blessed-taxes-with-his-own-hand.

## What Would Jesus Tax?

Taking up the challenge, let's look at one of the most classi-cally misunderstood and equally misquoted phrases in holy writ, "Render unto Caesar…" It's part an account relating how several "spies" sent by "the chief priests and scribes" approach Jesus with a question designed to entrap him: "Is it lawful for us to give tribute to Caesar or not?"[23] Now, why would anyone ask whether it's "law-ful" to pay taxes? If Rome had made it a law, and if the people are living under Roman rule, then it's lawful, right? Apparently, there's some fundamental problem with the law that's overlooked by mod-ern readers, a problem that only becomes apparent as we read on. "Show me a coin," he commands them. When the coin is produced he behaves in typically Jewish fashion, answering a question with a question:

> Whose image and inscription does it have? They an-swered and said, Caesar's.[24]

Now, the coin in question is identified as a "denarius," with the head of Tiberius, "son of the divine Augustus" on the obverse, and the goddess Livia, depicted as "Pax" ("Peace"), on the flip side. Around her is inscribed an abbreviation for "Pontifus Maximus" – "High Priest." It is a strong declaration that Tiberius Caesar is the son of a god, and the high priest of Roman peace – a stark contrast with the Gospel writers' depiction of Jesus alone as the "Son of God." Jews of course are staunch monotheists, in these days being the only true monotheists on earth. For them, there is no divine power other than Israel's God. Moreover, Israel's God is everyone's God.

On one level, Jews are admonished during eras of foreign domination to be good citizens and to submit to governmental authority, even when oppressive. But the line is drawn at idolatry. "You shall have no other gods before me"[25] is an absolute require-ment, that must be stringently obeyed, even unto death. It's not the

---

23 Luke 20:22. Interestingly, while the Gospels of Matthew and Mark identify the questioners as "Pharisees" and "Herodians," we have seen that the Pharisees are his natural allies. Luke's designation of "chief priests" makes more sense.

24 Luke 20: 24.

25 Exodus 20:3.

failure to worship Israel's God that's forbidden, but the worship of any other deity, including a deified Caesar. The Romans know that their Jewish citizens (comprising some ten percent of the whole Roman Empire) will resist utterly what they deem "idolatry," and have therefore granted official immunity from emperor worship to Jews and Jews alone. Even so, does paying the Roman tax with coins that are clearly idolatrous constitute in infraction of Jewish law? That's the legal question for Jesus.

There is yet another angle to the issue, for had not the psalmist declared: "The earth is the Lord's and the fullness thereof"?[26] As far as the monotheist is concerned, everything in the world belongs to God. That includes all power and all wealth. All human possessions are merely "on loan." Since God owns everything, charity is not only commended, but expected. This is exactly the message of the Pharisees, and of Jesus, all of whom show genuine sensitivity to the poor, the sick and the downtrodden. By the same token, however, only God is the final judge and arbiter of the sufficiency of its level. The coin, by contrast, makes Caesar's claim for him. Everything belongs to Tiberius. The two claims – God's and Caesar's – are in fact mutually exclusive. Either the emperor is entitled to all possessions, or God is. If one is a monotheist, Roman taxation is illegitimate, for it is based on the premise that a person's property actually belongs to Caesar and his government, and it's up to him to determine what his subjects can keep. Jesus' classic response to the quandary is as brilliant as it is misconstrued:

> Therefore render to Caesar the things which are Caesar's, and to God the things which are God's.[27]

It is phrased in such a way as to allow non-Jews to imagine that he is indeed commending the payment of Caesar's tax – good politics at a time when loose talk can get you killed. Any pious Jew, on the other hand, understands immediately that this Galilean is in fact advocating a subtle form of sedition. The Israelite inherently knows that if everything belongs to God, nothing belongs to Caesar.[28]

How odd, that in the Jewish world today, there is considerable support for the "tax and spend" policies of the left, or what Obama

---

26 Psalm 24:1.

27 Luke 20:25.

28 http://www.lewrockwell.com/orig11/barr-j1.1.1.html

calls "the Jewish doctrine of moderation and consideration of others." The one thing clear from our study, however, is that heavy taxation from Caesar's or from Herod's "big government" is hardly a cause supported by Jews in biblical times. True "patriots," then as well as now, understand that if the government owns what its citizens produce, then the citizens are nothing more than "tax serfs." As Samuel Adams opined, "If taxes are laid upon us without our having a legal representation where they are laid, we are reduced from the character of free subjects to the state of tributary slaves."[29] Nor is it surprising that the very notion of a tax on income (with or without "legal representation") was foreign to the Framers of the Constitution. For while governments can rightly tax "consumption," no state authority should be able to lay claim to the monetary wealth and private property that its citizens produce.

### The Great Judean Tax Revolt and the American Patriots

As for Jesus of Nazareth, there will be no end of debates about his meaning, his message, and his sympathies. Some scholars see him as a "pacifistic" Pharisee, aware of the rumbles of anti-Roman sentiment, yet counseling a non-violent approach focused on "social justice." Others see him, not as "Jesus the Jewish socialist," but as "Jesus the Zealot patriot," – an insurrectionist in his own right, in league with the "Galilean Tea Party." Interestingly, there is additional evidence in the Gospel itself for the latter interpretation. After all, when he is tried before the procurator, Pontius Pilate, leading up to his crucifixion, we are told that his opponents:

> ... began to accuse him, saying, "We have found this man subverting our nation. He opposes payment of taxes to Caesar and claims to be Christ/Messiah, a king."[30]

And who are these opponents? Doubtless, the Sadducean priesthood, ever at odds with the Pharisee "patriots" and ready to repeat to the authorities the incriminating rumors that have spread through the land. They know, like the British dealing with their colonies, that tyrannical taxation is the seedbed of revolt.

---

29 John Howard Hinton, Samuel Lorenzo Knave, *The History and Topography of the United States of North America*, Vol. I (Boston: Samuel Walker, 1834), 186.

30 Luke 23:1, NIV.

As in the American experience, revolution is preceded by decades of unrest. Well before Jesus' public teaching, in the year 5 of
the Common Era, a census tax, seen as a sign of Roman enslave-
ment, has provoked riots and mass uprising. In the lead is the "Brutus" of the day, Judah of Galilee (son of Hezekiah), described by
Josephus as having "an inviolable attachment to liberty."[31] Joined
by one of the Pharisee leaders, named Zadok, the revolt is put down
only with great difficulty and over several decades.[32] The worst,
however, is yet to come.

In the year 46 C.E., two of Judah's sons are, like Jesus, crucified as tax insurrectionists. According to Josephus, a third son, Menahem, will live to fight the Romans again, during the Great Jewish
Revolt that breaks out in the year 66 C.E. From the outset it has
much in common with the American Revolution, and it's easy to
harbor great sympathy for it. The thirteen colonies have their Continental Congress; the Judeans have their Sanhedrin, which by now
legislates all aspects of political and religious life. In both cases they
have laid the groundwork for a "republican" government of their
own, independent of foreign rule. The list of grievances against the
British king are not unlike the justifications leading the Judeans
(now ruled by the infamous Nero) to throw off the Roman yoke.
We read in the Declaration of Independence:

...When a long train of abuses and usurpations, pursuing invariably the same Object evinces a design to reduce
them under absolute Despotism, it is their right, it is their
duty, to throw off such Government, and to provide new
Guards for their future security....
[King George] has made Judges dependent on his Will
alone....
(Herod and the Roman governors repeatedly tamper with
the Sanhedrin, and capital cases are removed from its jurisdiction entirely.)
He has erected a multitude of New Offices, and sent hith-
er swarms of Officers to harass our people and eat out
their substance.
(Roman administrators fill the length and breadth of the

31 Josephus, *Antiquities*, XVIII, 1.6.
32 See Acts 5:37.

land of Israel.)
He has kept among us, in times of peace, Standing Armies without the Consent of our legislatures....
(Roman legionaries and centurions are ever-present in Israel.)
For imposing Taxes on us without our Consent....
(The census tax being "Exhibit A.")
For depriving us in many cases, of the benefit of Trial by Jury....
(Jesus being one of innumerable such cases.)
He has plundered our seas, ravaged our coasts, burnt our towns, and destroyed the lives of our people....
(The Romans will do even worse as the Great Revolt plays out.)
He has excited domestic insurrections amongst us....
(From Judah the Galilean's tax revolt to the Great Revolt of 66 C.E.)

Who can blame ancient Israel's "patriots" or their quasi-democratic Sanhedrin for wanting simply to be free from their version of the "mad" King George, the despotic Nero Caesar? What they lack, however, is a "George Washington," without whom the colonial cause would have gone down to the same ignominious defeat as the Judean rebels. Instead, the commander-in-chief of the "heartland" and seedbed of the resistance movement, Galilee, turns out to be Israel's version of Benedict Arnold, Josephus Flavius.

### Josephus Flavius

He is a priest from Jerusalem, the son of an aristocratic woman of Hasmonean stock. On his father's side, he is a descendant of the first Hasmonean high priest, Jonathan (who, as we recall, had "usurped" the office). Drafted into service by an "assembly in the Temple" (likely, the Sanhedrin), Josephus has misgivings about the "hopeless" cause of the rebels from the outset. Had Washington come to the same easy conclusion about the situation of the Continental Army, all would certainly have been lost. Patriots, however, are marked by their ability to redirect hopeless situations to their advantage, playing on the weakness of the enemy while relying on their personal resolve and the rectitude of their cause. The examples are multiple: Valley Forge, Trenton, the crossing of the Delaware, and ultimately Yorktown.

Josephus, as we know, is no George Washington. After the outbreak of revolt, when the Roman garrisons are expelled from Caesarea, Jerusalem, and the rocky fortress in the Judean Desert, Masada, Nero's counter-offensive is only a matter of time. He dispatches his best generals, Vespasian and his son Titus, who descend on Galilee from the north, to face Josephus' ragtag army. Wise and prudent leadership would by now have recognized that the way to defeat Nero is not on Israel's home turf, but on Rome's, by enlisting the tenth part of the empire's population, scattered across its western lands, and in the capital city itself, in support of their brethren in Jerusalem and Galilee. But the revolt's leaders are too busy quarreling with each other; nor is there a Benjamin Franklin who can represent their cause across the sea.

As the Roman legions pour into the land of Israel, Josephus and a band of compatriots hole up in a cave in the Galilean city of Jotapata. All of them enter into a suicide pact, deciding one to slit the throat of the next in line, as determined by drawing lots, until the last one left standing falls on his own sword. As "fate" would have it, that last man is Josephus, who instead surrenders to the Romans, predicting that Vespasian will soon become emperor himself. Vespasian, clearly pleased by this prognostication, spares Josephus and employs him as his assistant during the remainder of the bloody conflict. From that day to the present, Josephus Flavius, who spends the rest of his life as a lackey for the Romans, writing histories of his people and of the war, is remembered as a notorious traitor to the Jewish people.[33]

In the American experience, Benedict Arnold became known, early in the Revolution, for acts of heroism and intelligence, distinguishing himself in the capture of Fort Ticonderoga. But his bitterness at being passed over for promotion by the Continental Congress, which ruled that he was indebted to it as well, led to his "treason" – his plot to surrender West Point to the enemy. The plot being uncovered, Arnold fled to a British warship, and was subsequently offered a commission as brigadier general in the British army.[34] Arnold ends up living in the enemy capital, London, while Jo-

---

33 See Hadas Lebel, Richard Miller, *Flavius Josephus: Eyewitness to Rome's First-Century Conquest of Judea* (New York: Simon & Schuster, 1993).

34 See Barry Wilson, *Benedict Arnold: A Traitor in our Midst* (Quebec City, Canada:

sephus finds himself living in Rome. In his writings he bad-mouths the rebel cause and ascribes the Roman victory to the hand of fate, so that to this day, the entire revolt is viewed through a jaded lens.

Back in Jerusalem, lacking a dynamic leader and mired in internecine strife, the rebel cause goes down in flames. The city is surrounded by Roman forces, who hermetically seal it and starve its captive population. On the ninth day of the Hebrew month of Av, in the year 70 C.E., the Temple – Herod's magnificent monument – is set fire and burned to the ground. It will take even more relentless combat before all the rebels are slaughtered, and another two years before the last Zealot stronghold, Masada (commanded by the cousin of Menahem, Eleazar ben Ya'ir), finally falls. It is the greatest tragedy in all of Jewish history, and will remain so up until the Nazi era and the Holocaust. But this will not spell the end of the story, either for Jews as the "people of the Book," or the libertarian spirit.

Everybody wants to be free, and, Josephus' propaganda notwithstanding, we should probably commend these ancient rebels for their patriotic resolve. They would accept nothing less than complete freedom from tyranny, and, arguably, we need more of that in today's world. Were they wrong because they failed? Not any more than William Wallace and his own ragtag army of rebels, who, in the Middle Ages, fell before the rampaging British in their fight to free Scotland from an oppressive foreign yoke. But the cry of freedom is not easily silenced, and the principles of self-determination in the face of "big government" tyranny are destined to find expression from generation to generation. One day, in the far-distant future, a new Jewish state will arise in Palestine. It will embody the myriad lessons, political and social, learned from the biblical saga, just as its new citizens will be born speaking the biblical tongue – Hebrew. The State of Israel, established by a U.N. Vote in 1947 and yet another War of Independence in 1948, is born as a parliamentary democracy, indeed "a republic, if you can keep it."

### Epilogue: The Lessons

What have we learned in our whirlwind tour of the Bible, and American history? Among other things, we've learned how far we've strayed from America's Founders, and equally, from the unique political lessons of the Bible. Even those who today proudly

McGill-Queen's University Press, 2001).

carry a banner of "limited government" use expressions such as "... the government ought to let us keep more of our money." But even in this, there is an implicit idea that it's not really "our money," but that it somehow belongs to the government, which gets to decide how much of it we can have. Oh really? It's all "our money," and, if we understand biblical teaching, God's. Nothing "belongs" to the government, any more than it "belonged" to Caesar.

In these pages I have for the most part avoided the terms "conservative" and "liberal," and only with great reluctance employed the words "left" and "right." After all, these terms hardly apply to antiquity and even in the present are as misleading as they are instructive. Looking back through history and all the way back to biblical times, it's what we would have to call "conservative" elements that were without exception linked to "big government" – the monarchy, the emperor, the pharaoh, or whatever potentate happened to have absolute power in his hands. By contrast, the marginalized, disenfranchised elements, the urban poor, the agrarian folk of the countryside, as well as anyone, anywhere, who opposed tyranny and monarchical rule, would have to be called "liberal." That includes the American revolutionaries (and not a few biblical heroes), whom we might define as "classical liberals." The tenets of "classical liberalism" include values we have seen ensconced (either overtly or covertly) in holy writ:

* Liberty – as the primary political value
* Individualism – as more important than the collective
* Skepticism about power – especially the claim that obedience to central authority is in one's own interest
* Rule of law – higher principles by which government itself is judged
* Civil society – private institutions (including charities) standing between the individual and the state
* Spontaneous order – as opposed to dictatorial rules imposed from above
* Free markets – voluntary economic activity between individuals (as opposed to "mercantilism")
* Tolerance – including free speech; not imposing one's ideas and values on others
* Peace – including a non-interventionist approach to the world

\* Limited government – the legitimate goals of government being the protection of life, liberty and property.[35]

Especially in Europe, both east and west, there was basically a conservative cabal, consisting of the monarchy, the military and the church, to oppress marginalized peoples, including the "people of the Book," the Jews. The conservative government of Russia's czars was notoriously antisemitic, as were not a few monarchs in western Europe. In the French Legislative Assembly of 1791, the moderate royalist delegates sat on the right side of the chamber, hence the term "right wing," while the "radicals" of the day, the Montagnards, sat on the left. Historically, it was the conservatives who favored "statist" regimes, while the liberals favored limited government. But something happened during the intervening centuries, down to the present. The conservative-liberal, left-right divide largely flip-flopped, so that today, it's the left that is the bastion of big government, whereas those who oppose it – who favor what the Founders would have called "individual liberty" and what we may understand as "classical liberalism" – are today's "conservative" voices on the right.

The irony is that the left still claims that it champions the poor, the underprivileged, the marginalized; but its aims are today wedded to the very "big government" that in times past it used to oppose. The end of monarchy in Europe, coupled with the ideologies of socialism and Marxism that exploded in the nineteenth century, may certainly have something to do with that, since according to the Marxist mindset, the oppressed can only be liberated via a temporary dictatorship of the proletariat. But of course, all through history, big government regimes have never been able to lift the poor out of their poverty, and today's big government bureaucrats only pay lip service to that end, while keeping the poor in a perpetual state of dependency upon them and them alone.

In any case, notwithstanding the natural tendency of the multitudes to relinquish power to a central Leviathan, the flame of liberty still burns brightly. The Brutus current, evident throughout the pages of the Bible, is certainly with us today. It's the spirit of rug-

---

35 Nigel Ashford (George Mason University), "What is Classical Liberalism," LearnLiberty,org; Edward Ashbee, Nigel Ashford, *U.S. Politics Today* (New York: St. Martin's Press, 1999), 25ff.; see also David Conway, *Classical Liberalism: The Unvanquished Ideal* (New York: St. Martin's Press, 1995).

ged individualism, of the Bible's patriarchs and matriarchs, and the spirit of America's first Pilgrims. It's the spirit of the biblical Judges, and the spirit of America's revolutionary-era patriots. It's the spirit of the biblical prophets, and of modern American libertarians. It's the spirit of Jesus, and of the ancient Judean rebels, in their struggle against Roman hegemony. And it's the spirit of today's Tea Party patriots. The question posed to Jesus still looms before us. What belongs to Caesar? Nothing. Brutus would be very proud indeed.

# BIBLIOGRAPHY

Abbot, Phillip, *Strong Presidents: A Theory of Leadership* (Knoxville: Univ. of Tennessee Press, 1996).

Anderson, Jon Lee, *Che Guevara: A Revolutionary Life* (New York: Grove Press, 1997).

Angle, Sharon, *Right Angle: One Woman's Journey to Reclaim the Constitution* (Bloomington, IN: Author House).

Armstrong, Karen, *A History of God: The 4,000 Year Quest of Judaism, Christianity and Islam* (New York: Ballantine, 1993).

Ashbee, Edward, and Ashford, Nigel, *U.S. Politics Today* (New York: St. Martin's Press, 1999).

Aron, Paul, *We Hold These Truths...: And Other Words That Made America* (Latham, MD: Rowman & Littlefield, 2008).

Aschkenasy, Nahama, *Woman at the Window: Biblical Tales of Oppression and Escape* (Detroit, MI: Wayne State Univ. Press, 1998).

Avian, Mordecai, and Green, William Scott, "The Ancient Synagogue: Public Space in Judaism," in Jacob Neusner, William Scott Green, Alan Jeffery Avery-Peck, eds., *Judaism from Moses to Muhammed: an Interpretation* (Leiden: Brill, 2005).

Baker, Randall, ed., *Transitions from Authoritarianism: The Role of Bureaucracy* (Westport, CT, Praeger Publishers, 2002).

Bandstra, Barry, *Reading the Old Testament: An Introduction to the Hebrew Bible* (Belmont, CA: Wadsworth Publishing, 2008).

Basler, Roy P., ed., *The Collected Works of Abraham Lincoln*, 9 vols. (New Brunswick: Rutgers University Press, 1953–1955).

Bauer, K. Jack, *Zachary Taylor: Soldier, Planter, Statesman of the Old Southwest* (Baton Rouge: Louisiana State Univ. Press, 1985).

Beck, Glenn, and Bale, Kevin, *Broke: The Plan to Restore Our Trust, Truth and Treasure* (New York: Threshold Editions, 2010).

Beschloss, Michael R., *Presidential Courage: Brave Leaders and How They Changed America 1789-1989* (New York: Simon & Schuster, 2007).

Beer, Samuel H., "The Idea of the Nation" in *How Federal is the Constitution?,* Goldwin and Schambra, eds. (Washington, D.C.: American Enterprise Institute, 1986).

Beito, David T., *From Mutual Aid to the Welfare State: Fraternal Societies and Social Services, 1890-1967* (Chapel Hill: University of North Carolina Press, 2000).

Benedict, Michael Les, "Abraham Lincoln and Federalism," *Journal of the Abraham Lincoln Association*, 10:1, 1988.

Ben-Sasson, Haim Hillen, and Ettinger, Samuel, *Jewish Society Through the Ages* (New York: Schocken, 1973).

Ben-Tor, Amon, and Greenberg, R., *The Archaeology of Ancient Israel* (New Haven, CT: Yale Univ. Press, 1994).

Berman, Joshua, *Created Equal: How the Bible Broke with Ancient Political Thought* (New York: Oxford Univ. Press, 2008).

Binkley, Wilfred E., *American Political Parties* (New York: Alfred A.

Knopf, 1943).

Block, Clint, *Grassroots Tyranny: The Limits of Federalism* (Washington, D.C.: Cato Institute, 1993).

Boller, Paul F., Jr., *Presidential Anecdotes* (New York: Oxford University Press, 1981).

Borgman, Paul, *David, Saul, and God, Rediscovering an Ancient Story* (New York: Oxford University Press, 2008).

Boswell, John. *Same-sex Unions in Premodern Europe* (New York: Vintage, 1994).

Bradford, William, Winslow, Edward, Cushman, Robert, Robinson, John, and Cheever, George Barrell, *The Journal of the Pilgrims at Plymouth: in New England in 1620*: reprint from the original volume, New York, J. Wiley, 1848.

Britt, Brian M., *Rewriting Moses: The Narrative Eclipse of the Text* (London: T&T Clark, 2004).

Brooks, Noah, *Washington, D.C., in Lincoln's Time: A Memoir of the Civil War Era by the Newspaperman Who Knew Lincoln Best* (Athens, GA: Univ. Of Georgia Press).

Brooks, Simcha Shalom, *Saul and the Monarchy: A New Look* (Hampshire, England: Ashgate Publishing, 2005).

Bronner, Stephen Eric, *Twentieth Century Political Theory: A Reader* (New York: Routledge, 1996).

Brueggemann, Walter, *Theology of the Old Testament: Testimony, Dispute, Advocacy* (Minneapolis, MN: Augsburg Fortress, 2005).

Butler, Trent C., "An Anti-Moses Tradition," *Journal for the Study of the Old Testament* 12 12 (May 1979): 9, 11.

Chace, James, *1912: Wilson, Roosevelt, Taft & Debs – The Election that Changed the Country* (New York: Simon & Schuster). See Chap. 3,

"The Heirs of Hamilton and Jefferson."

Codevilla, Angelo M., "America's Ruling Class – And the Perils of Revolution" in *The American Spectator*, July-August, 2010 issue.

Conway, David, *Classical Liberalism: The Unvanquished Ideal* (New York: St. Martin's Press, 1995).

Craig, Peter C., *The Book of Deuteronomy* (Grand Rapids, MI: Eerdmans, 1976).

*Debates and Proceedings in the Convention of the Commonwealth of Massachusetts, Held in the year 1788, and Which Finally Ratified the Constitution of the United States* (Boston: W. White, 1856).

D'Souza, Dinesh, *What's So Great About America* (Washington, D.C.: Regnery).

De Vaux, Roland, *Ancient Israel: Its Life and Institutions* (Grand Rapids: Eerdmans, 1997).

Dever, William G., *Who Were the Early Israelites and Where Did They Come From?* (Grand Rapids: Eerdmans, 2003).

Diggins, John P., *Ronald Reagan: Fate, Freedom, and the Making of History* (New York: W.W. Norton & Co., 2007).

DiLorenzo, Thomas, *The Real Lincoln: A New Look at Abraham Lincoln, His Agenda, and an Unnecessary War* (New York: Three Rivers Press, 2003).

Donin, Hayim, *To Be a Jew: A Guide to Jewish Observance in Contemporary Life* (New York: Basic Books, 1972).

Dorrien, Gary, *Imperial Designs: Neoconservatism and the New Pax Americana* (New York: Routledge, 2004).

Dozeman, Thomas B., *God on the Mountain: A Study of Redaction, Theology, and Canon in Exodus 19-24* (Atlanta: Scholars Press, 1989).

Eliken, Robert S., *Why Nicaragua Vanished: A Story of Reporters and Revolutionaries* (Latham, MD: Rowman & Littlefield, 2003).

Ellis, Richard E., *The Union at Risk: Jacksonian Democracy, States' Rights and the Nullification Crisis* (New York: Oxford Univ. Press, 1987).

Federer, William, *America's God and Country* (St. Louis: Amerisearch, 2000).

Feiler, Bruce, *America's Prophet: Moses and the American Story* (San Francisco, Harper Collins, 2009).

Felzenberg, Alvin S., *The Leaders We Deserved (and a Few We Didn't): Rethinking the Presidential Rating Game* (New York: Basic Books, 2008).

Finkelstein, Israel, and Mazar, Amihay, *The Quest for the Historical Israel: Debating Archaeology and the History of Early Israel* (Atlanta: Society of Biblical Literature, 2007).

Franklin, Benjamin, and Franklin, William Temple, *Memoirs of the Life and writings of Benjamin Franklin*, Vol. 1, (London: A.J. Valpy, 1818).

Gabriel, Richard, *The Military History of Ancient Israel* (Westport, CT: Praeger Publishers, 2003).

Gonen, Rivka, *Contested Holiness: Jewish, Muslim, and Christian Perspectives on the Temple* (Jersey City: NJ: KTAV Publishing House, 2003).

Gooch, G.P., *History and Historians in the Nineteenth Century* (London: Longmans, Green, and Co., 1913).

Goodblatt, David M., *The Monarchic Principle: Studies in Jewish Self-Government in Antiquity* (Tubingen: J.C.B. Mohr, 1994).

Grabbe, Lester L., *Israel in Transition: From Late Bronze II to Iron IIA* (New York: T & T Clark, 2010).

Haggerty, George E., *Gay Histories and Cultures: An Encyclopedia* (New York: Taylor & Francis, 2007).

Halpern, Baruch, *David's Secret Demons: Messiah, Murderer, Traitor, King* (Grand Rapids: Eerdmans, 2001).

Halperin, David M. *One Hundred Years of Homosexuality* (New York: Routledge, 1990).

Hamilton, Neil A., and Friedman, Ian C., *Presidents: A Biographical Dictionary* (New York: Facts on File, 2010).

Harris, Mark, *City of Discontent* (Sag Harbor, NY: Second Chance Press, 1992).

Harris, Richard A., and Tichenor, Daniel J., eds., *History of the United States Political System: Ideas, Interests, and Institutions* (Santa Barbara, CA: ABC-CLIO, LLC, 2010).

Hayward, Steven F., *The Age of Reagan: The Conservative Counterrevolution: 1980-1989* (New York: Random House, 2009).

Heschel, Abraham Joshua, *The Prophets* (New York: Harper & Row, 1962).

Highland, William G., *In Defense of Thomas Jefferson: The Sally Hemings Sex Scandal* (New York: Thomas Dunne Books, 2009).

Hinton, John Howard, and Knave. Samuel Lorenzo, *The History and Topography of the United States of North America*, Vol. I (Boston: Samuel Walker, 1834).

Hoeing, Sidney Benjamin, *The Great Sanhedrin: A Study of the Origin, Development, Composition, and Functions of the Bet Din ha-Gadol during the Second Jewish Commonwealth* (New York: Boch Publishing Co., 1953).

Hogeland, William, *The Whiskey Rebellion: George Washington, Alexander Hamilton, and the Frontier Rebels Who Challenged America's Newfound Sovereignty* (New York: Simon & Schuster: 2006).

Houston, Walter, *Contending for Justice: Ideologies and Theologies of Social Justice in the Old Testament* (London: T&T Clark, 2006).

Ireland, John Robert, *The Republic, or, A History of the United States of America in the Administrations*, Vol. 4 (Chicago, Fairbanks and Palmer, 1886).

Ishay, Micheline, ed., *The Human Rights Reader: Major Political Essays, Speeches, and Documents from Ancient Times to the Present* (New York: Routledge, 2007).

Jones, Gwilym Henry, *The Nathan Narratives* (Sheffield, England: Sheffield Academic Press, 1990).

Karabell, Zachary, *Chester Alan Arthur* (New York: Times Books, 2004).

Kelley, Alison, *Theodore Roosevelt* (New York: Chelsea House Publishers, 2004).

Kennedy, David M., Cohen, and Piehl, Elizabeth, Mel, *The Brief America Pageant: A History of the Republic* (Boston: Wadsworth Engage, 2008).

Kettle, Thomas Prentice, ed., *United States Magazine and Democratic Review*, Vol. XXI (New York: Publication Office, 1847).

Kibritçioglu, Aykut (1994): *On Adam Smith's Contributions to the International Trade Theory*. Published in: *Uluslararası (Makro)Iktisat* (1996): 31-38.

Kirsch, Jonathan, *The Harlot by the Side of the Road* (New York: Random House, 1998).
_____, *Moses: A Life* (New York: Ballantine, 1999).
_____, *King David: The Real Life of the Man Who Ruled Israel* (New York: Ballantine, 2000).

Lau, Peter H.W., *Identity and Ethics in the Book of Ruth: A Social Identity Approach* (Berlin, New York: Walter de Gruyter GmbH & Co., 2011).

Lebel, Hadas, and Miller, Richard, *Flavius Josephus: Eyewitness to Rome's First-Century Conquest of Judea* (New York: Simon & Schuster, 1993).

Leonard, Thomas M., *Fidel Castro: A Biography* (Westport, CT: Greenwood Press, 2004).

Levin, Mark R., *Ameritopia: The Unmaking of America* (New York: Simon & Schuster, 2012).

Levine, Lee I., *The Ancient Synagogue* (New Haven, CT: Yale University Press, 1999).

Lewis, C.S., *God in the Dock* (Grand Rapids: Eerdmans, 1994).

Locke, John, *Of Civil Government and Toleration*, Chap. VII, "Of Political or Civil Society," 1688 (London, Cassell & Co., 1905).

Olh, Christine, *Underground Front: The Chinese Communist Party in Hong Kong* (Hong Kong: Hong Kong Univ. Press, 2010).

Malamat, Abraham, and Ben-Sasson, Haim Hillel, eds., *A History of the Jewish People* (Tel Aviv, Dvir, 1976).

Magnusson, Lars, *Mercantilism: The Shaping of an Economic Language* (London: Routledge, 1994).

Marx, Karl, and O'Malley, Joseph, ed., *Critique of Hegel's Philosophy of Right* (New York: Press Syndicate of the Univ. of Cambridge, 1982).

Massie, Robert K., *Nicholas and Alexandra* (New York: Random House, 2011).

Maurois, André, *The Art of Living* (San Francisco: Harper, 1960).

McClanahan, Brion T., *The Politically Incorrect Guide to the Founding Fathers* (Washington, D.C.: Regency, 2009).

McFerran, Warren L., *Political Sovereignty: The Supreme Authority in the United States* (Sanford, FL: Southern Liberty Press, 2005).

McHenry, James, *American Historical Review*, vol. 11 (1906).

McKenzie, Steven L., *King David: A Biography* (New York: Oxford Univ. Press, 2000).

Meckler, Mark, and Martin, Jenny Beth, *Tea Party Patriots: The Second American Revolution* (New York: Henry Holt, 2012).

Mendelssohn, Isaac, "State Slavery in Ancient Palestine," *Bulletin of the American Schools of Oriental Research*, 85 (1942).

Michaelson, Gerald A., Michaelson, Steven, *Sun Tzu - The Art of War for Managers: 50 Strategic Rules Updated for Today's Business* (Avon, MA: Adams Media, 2010).

Miller, Bill, *The Tea Party Papers: The American Spiritual Evolution Versus the French Revolution* (Bloomington, IN: Xlibris, 2011).

Miller, Geoffrey P., *The Ways of a King: Legal and Political Ideas in the Bible* (Gottingen: Vandenhoeck & Ruprecht, 2011).

Mills, Mar E., *Joshua to Kings: History, Story, Theology* (London: T&T Clark, 2006).

Miitterand, Francois, and Wiesel, Elie, *Memoir in Two Voices* (New York: Arcade Publishing, 1995).

Mooney, Edward F., *Knights of Faith and Resignation: Reading Kierkegaard's Fear and Trembling* (Albany, NY: State Univ. of New York Press, 1991).

Morton, Nathaniel, William Bradford, Thomas Prince, Edward Winslow, *New-England's Memorial* (Boston, Congregational Board of Publication, 1855).

Neal, Richard McKenzie, *The Compromising of America: An American Tragedy* (Bloomington, IN: AuthorHouse).

Nelstrop, Louise, Magill, Kevin, and Knish, Bradley B., *Christian Mysticism: an Introduction to Contemporary Theoretical Approaches* (Surrey, England: Ashgate Publishing, 2009).

Newey, Vincent, *The Pilgrim's Progress: Critical and Historical Views* (Liverpool, England: Liverpool Univ. Press, 1980).

Nicolay, J.G. and Hay, J. *Abraham Lincoln*, I (New York: Cosimo Classics, 2009).

O'Connell, Robert H., *The Rhetoric of the Book of Judges* (Leiden: E.J. Brill, 1996).

Osborn, Andrew, "As if Things Weren't Bad Enough, Russian Professor Predicts End of U.S." in *The Wall Street Journal*, Dec. 29, 2008.

Paine, Thomas, *Common Sense* (Alexandria, VA: TheCapitol.Net, 2009).

Pangle, Thomas L., *The Theological Basis of Liberal Modernity in Montesquieu's "Spirit of the Laws"* (Chicago: Univ. of Chicago Press, 2010).

*People Shall Judge, The*, Vol. 1, Part 1 (Chicago: Univ. of Chicago Press, 1976).

Podhoretz, Norman, *The Prophets: Who They Were and What They Are* (New York: Free Press, 2010).

Potok, Chaim, and Walden, Daniel, ed., *Conversations with Chaim Potok* (Jackson, MS: University Press of Mississippi, 2001).

Pressler, Carolyn, *Joshua, Judges, and Ruth* (Louisville, KY: Westminster John Knox Press, 2002).

Provan, Lain William, Long, V. Phillips, and Longman, Tremper III, *A Biblical History of Israel* (Louisville, KY: Westminster John Knox Press, 2003).

Purdy, Jedediah, "Languages of Politics in America," in James

Boyd White, Jefferson Powell, eds., *Law and Democracy in the Empire of Force* (Univ. of Michigan Press, 2009).

Renan, E., *History of the People of Israel*, II (Boston: Roberts Brothers, 1896).

Rice, Enamuel, *Freud and Moses: The Long Journey Home* (Albany, NY: State Univ. Of New York Press, 1990).

Richards, Jay W., *Money, Greed, and God: Why Capitalism Is the Solution and Not the Problem* (New York: Harper Collins, 2009).

Roberts, Jeremy, *Zachary Taylor* (Minneapolis: Lerner Publications, 2005).

Robinson, George, *Essential Torah: A Complete Guide to the Five Books of Moses* (New York: Random House, 2006).

Rossiter, Clinton, *Constitutional Dictatorship: Crisis Government in the Modern Democracies* (Piscataway, NJ: Transaction Publishers).

Rubenfeld, Jed, *Freedom and Time: A Theory of Constitutional Self-Government* (New Haven, CT: Yale Univ. Press, 2001).

Sachar, Howard Morley, *The Course of Modern Jewish History* (New York: Vintage Books, 1990).

Schaeffer, Francis A., *How Should We Then Live?: The Rise and Decline of Western Thought and Culture* (New York: Fleming H. Revell, 1979).

Schafer, Peter, *The History of the Jews in the Greco-Roman World* (New York: Routledge, 2003).

Sharansky, Natan, and Dermer, Ron, *The Case for Democracy: the Power of Freedom to Overcome Tyranny and Terror* (New York: Public Affairs, 2004).

Scherman, Nissan, and Zlotowitz, Meir, eds., *History of the Jewish People: The Second Temple Era* (New York: Menorah Publications, 1982).

Schultz, Joseph P., *Judaism and the Gentile Faiths: Comparative Studies in Religion* (East Brunswick, NJ: Associated University Presses, 1981).

Seigenthaler, John, *James K. Polk* (New York: Times Books, 2004).

Service, Robert, Lenin: *A Biography* (New York: Macmillan, 2000).

Shlaes, Amity, *The Forgotten Man: A New History of the Great Depression* (New York: HarperCollins, 2007).

Slater, Dan, *Ordering Power: Contentious Politics and Authoritarian Leviathans* (Cambridge University Press, 2010).

Sperling, S. David, *The Original Torah: The Political Intent of the Bible's Writers* (New York: New York Univ. Press, 1998).

Sprague, Dean, *Freedom Under Lincoln: Federal Power and Personal Liberty Under the Strain of Civil War* (New York: Houghton Mifflin, 1965).

Steyn, Mark, *After America: Get Ready for Armageddon* (Washington, D.C., Regnery, 2011).

Sun Tzu, *The Art of War* (eBookEden.com, 2009).

Tandy, David W., *Warriors Into Traders: The Power of the Market in Early Greece* (Berkeley: Univ. of California Press, 1997).

Taylor, Frank Hamilton, *Valley Forge: A Chronicle of American Heroism* (Philadelphia: Valley Forge Park Commission, 1920).

Taylor, William Mackergo, *David, King of Israel: His Life and its Lessons* (New York: Harper & Brothers, 1874).

*Tear Down this Wall: the Reagan Revolution - a National Review History* (New York: Continuum International, 2004).

Urman, Dan, Virgil, Paul, and Fleshe, McCracken, *Ancient Synagogues: Historical Analysis and Archaeological Discovery* (Leiden: Brill,

1995).

VanderKam, James, *The Dead Sea Scrolls Today* (Grand Rapids: Eerdmans, 1994).

Warren, Charles, *The Supreme Court in United States History: Volume Two, 1821-1855* (Washington, D.C.: Beard Books, 1999).

Watson, Harry L., *Liberty and Power: The Politics of Jacksonian America* (New York: Hill and Wang, 2006).

Wein, Berle, *Triumph of Survival: The Story of the Jews in the Modern Era, 1650-1900* (New York: Mesorah Publications, 1990).

Wesbury, Brian S., and Shlaes, Amity, *It's Not as Bad as You Think: Why Capitalism Trumps Fear and the Economy Will Thrive* (Hoboken, NJ: John Wiley & Sons, 2010).

Whiston, William, and Maier, Paul L., *The New Complete Works of Josephus* (Grand Rapids: Kregel, 1999).

Williams, David Rhys, *World Religions and the Hope for Peace* (Boston: Beacon Press, 1951).

Wills, Gary, *Cincinnatus: George Washington and the Enlightenment* (Garden City, NY: Doubleday, 1984).

Wilson Barry, *Benedict Arnold: A Traitor in our Midst* (Quebec City, Canada: McGill-Queen's University Press, 2001).

Wilson, Clyde N., ed., *The Essential Calhoun: Selections from Writings, Speeches, and Letters* (New Brunswick, N.J.: Transaction Publishers, 2000).

Winterbotham, Rayner, and Whitewall, Thomas, *Numbers: The Pulpit Commentary* (London: C Kegan Paul & Co., 1881).

Wolfe, Robert, *From Habra to Hebrews and Other Essays* (Minneapolis: Mill City Press, 2011).

Wood, John A., *Perspectives on War in the Bible* (Macon, GA: Mercer Univ. Press, 1998).

Wootton, David, *The Essential Federalist and Anti-Federalist Papers* (Indianapolis, IN: Hackett Publishing, 2003).

Yates, Robert, Lansing, John, and Martin, Luther, *Secret Proceedings and Debates of the Convention Assembled at Philadelphia, in the Year 1787* (Ithaca, NY: Cornell Univ. Library, 2009).

www.ingramcontent.com/pod-product-compliance
Lightning Source LLC
Chambersburg PA
CBHW031246090426
42742CB00007B/333